THE MEN
WHO KILLED
QANTAS

Also by Matthew Benns

When the Bough Breaks
100 Years: A Celebration of Surf-Lifesaving at North Steyne

THE MEN
WHO KILLED
QANTAS

*Greed, lies and crashes
and how they destroyed the reputation of
the world's safest airline*

Matthew Benns

WILLIAM HEINEMANN: AUSTRALIA

A William Heinemann book
Published by Random House Australia Pty Ltd
Level 3, 100 Pacific Highway, North Sydney NSW 2060
www.randomhouse.com.au

First published by William Heinemann in 2009

Addresses for companies within the Random House Group can be found at
www.randomhouse.com.au/offices.

National Library of Australia
Cataloguing-in-Publication Entry

Benns, Matthew.
The men who killed Qantas.

ISBN 978 1 74166 891 9 (pbk).

Qantas Airways – History.
Aircraft accidents – Australia.
Airlines – Management.
Aeronautics – Safety measures.

387.706594

Cover photograph courtesy of Getty Images
Cover design by Natalie Winter
Typeset in 12.5/17 pt Minion by Post Pre-press, Brisbane, Queensland
Printed and bound by Griffin Press, South Australia

Random House Australia uses papers that are natural, renewable and recyclable products
and made from wood grown in sustainable forests. The logging and manufacturing processes are expected to conform to the environmental regulations of the country of origin.

10 9 8 7 6 5 4 3 2 1

CONTENTS

*This book is dedicated to the tireless Qantas staff
and crew, who work so professionally to keep
passengers and planes safe.*

'Qantas never crashes'
Rain Man

'He was wrong'
Macarthur Job, air-crash investigator

QF1

CUT-PRICE TOUCHDOWN

The Qantas Boeing 747-438 aircraft had begun its descent from 35,000 feet and was still 70 kilometres from Bangkok's Don Muang airport when the captain pointed out the build-up of cumulonimbus cloud ahead. His comment would later be one of many picked up on the cockpit voice recorder and examined by investigators as they pieced together what went wrong on Qantas Flight 1 on 23 September 1999.

The flight crew of QF1, with 391 passengers on board, had transferred to the Bangkok Approach frequency and had been told there was heavy rain at the airport. At the plane's controls, the first officer suggested to the captain they could hold off to the south if the rain looked bad during the approach. Well-respected Qantas training officer Captain Jack Fried reassured him that four kilometres of visibility was fine and that it was 'just a shower'.[1]

But it wasn't. At Bangkok a torrential thunderstorm had reduced visibility to 1,500 metres and sluiced the ungrooved runway with a potentially fatal sheen of water. This, combined with cost-cutting measures and a number of poor management decisions within Qantas over previous years, had set the scene for disaster for the airline's signature Sydney to London flight.

In the cockpit the three flight crew had completed the approach checklist. Sitting behind the captain in the second observer's seat and watching the drama unfold was the second officer's wife. In keeping with standard procedure, the crew changed radio frequency to Bangkok Arrivals as they descended to 2,500 feet. Three minutes ahead of them the crew on board the Rome-bound Qantas Flight 15 noted a cluster of well-defined storm cells over the airport as they too prepared to land. Three minutes and 20 seconds ahead of the Rome flight, a Thai Airbus 330 was on the final approach to the rain-slicked runway. It touched down without incident, but as it howled to a standstill, a special weather observation at the airport noted the visual range on the runway – the distance the pilot can still see the runway markings – was down to 750 metres. The arrivals controller did not pass on this information to the crew of QF1.

On the flight deck of QF1 things were getting busy. The Royal Australian Air Force-trained second officer tuned in to the Qantas frequency and listened to a conversation between the Qantas ground engineer and the company agent. The engineer said it was 'raining quite heavily'. The second officer, secure in the knowledge that the other pilots knew it was raining heavily, did not pass on the information. Ahead of them QF15 was on its final approach. At 700 feet above the ground it started raining. At 500 feet the rain became so heavy the Rome-bound crew could no longer see the runway lights. At 250 feet the pilot pulled out, powering up the engines and taking the plane around for another attempt.

QF1 had not reached its final approach point and was not tuned in to the tower radio frequency, so heard none of the conversations between QF15 and the tower. The crew had no idea that just ahead of them their fellow Australians had decided conditions were too difficult to risk a landing. Instead, they extended the landing gear and the 36-year-old first officer disengaged the autopilot. The control tower informed them: 'Caution runway wet and braking action reported by Airbus three three is good'. The crew assumed the Thai Airbus had been immediately in front of them and that this was the most up-to-date information available. They completed their landing checklist, confirming the speedbrakes were armed and selecting flaps 25 for landing.

At this point no one on the plane had any idea that they were just minutes from disaster. The 16 cabin crew and 391 passengers were strapped into their seats and preparing for a routine night landing at just before 11 pm local time. But in the cockpit the first signs that all was not well were beginning to appear. Flying in the plane manually, the first officer commented to his colleagues that the jet 'doesn't want to slow down'. Sitting next to him, 49-year-old Captain Fried noted that, at 307 kilometres per hour, the approach was above the 285 kph target speed but was decreasing and was within the company limits. They could see the runway lights ahead of them. He felt the situation was under control. The jet descended into light rain and at 350 feet the first officer called for the windscreen wipers to be turned on. But as the plane dropped to 200 feet the rain got heavier. The runway lights appeared only briefly as the wipers passed over the windscreen before the torrential downpour obscured them again. Anxious, the first and second officers exclaimed that it was the heaviest rain they had ever experienced on approach to landing. The aircraft had also drifted above the Independent Landing System glideslope that guides an aircraft onto the tarmac. 'You're getting high now,' Captain Fried warned the first officer.

The automatic altitude advisory called 100 feet as the plane hurtled towards the runway at 315 kph. 'You happy?' demanded Captain Fried. Beside him the first officer felt the visibility was getting near his personal limits but replied: 'Ah, yes.' The plane crossed the threshold of the runway almost 40 kph too fast and – at 76 feet – almost double the ideal height for landing.

To provide a soft landing for the passengers, pilots flare the aeroplane – slowing the descent by lifting the aircraft's nose. The Qantas training manual states that the landing flare should begin when the wheels are 30 feet above the runway. On the flight deck of QF1 the automatic altitude advisory called 50 feet as the first officer began the flare. 'Get it down, get it down, come on, you're starting your flare,' barked Captain Fried. The first officer began retarding the engines' thrust but decided there was enough runway to continue the flare and let the aircraft down gently onto the ground. In normal circumstances he would have been right. But these were not normal circumstances. Rain was hammering on the windshield, rattling against the plane's hull like frozen peas.

The long interval before the next altitude advisory call at 30 feet made the crew aware the plane was coming down more slowly than normal. Captain Fried quietly increased the automatic braking capacity. At ten feet the jet was still hurtling along at 290 kph and had already covered almost three-quarters of a kilometre of the 3250-metre-long runway. Visibility was down, the speed was high and the aircraft was floating. 'Go around!' commanded Captain Fried, and within a second the first officer had advanced the thrust levers, adding power to the four Rolls-Royce Turbofan engines. He did not press either of the two switches near the thrust levers that would have automatically provided enough thrust to power the plane into the air at the rate of 2,000 feet a minute, believing his own reactions were quicker.

Things then happened very swiftly. The wheels touched down smoothly. Suddenly the rain eased enough to see the end of the runway. Captain Fried silently reached out, put his right hand over the left hand of the first officer and cut the power to three of the engines. Engine one remained powered up because it was just out of the first officer's reach. Captain Fried had decided the engines were not spooled up enough to successfully go around and there was enough runway left to land safely. His decision was based on inadequate training and company procedures, but on a dry runway he would have been right. His actions confused the first and second officers, who were unsure whether to go around or continue the landing. The first officer was also unsure if Captain Fried had taken over control of the plane. 'Okay, we're on,' he said.

'Got it?' said Captain Fried.

'Yeah, I've got it,' said the first officer.

The rapid sequence of commands to the engines meant they had been cut back, revved up and cut back in quick succession. Meanwhile, engine one was continuing to race up to full power, until the first officer noticed the thrust lever and pulled it back. It was only at this point, with all engines retarded, that the automatic spoiler system could be deployed. However, the fact that engine one had been advanced for more than three seconds while the plane was on the ground disarmed the automatic braking system. Take-off warnings began to sound in the cockpit and the crew manually applied the brakes as they stared at the end of the runway and wondered why they were not stopping. Halfway down the soaking runway and still hurtling along at over 285 kph, the giant jet began to fishtail wildly. The second officer's wife screamed. Three flight crew emergency escape reels fell from the overhead stowage, at least one of them striking the second officer on the shoulder.

Behind the pilots in the main cabin the customer service manager had just said, 'Welcome to Bangkok,' when the plane started to skid. The cabin juddered and began to shake. The violent vibration jerked open overhead lockers, their contents flying onto the floor, littering it with handbags, jackets and duty-free purchases. 'Heads down! Stay down! Brace, brace, brace!' shouted some of the flight attendants. Pillows, blankets and magazines flew into the aisles as seat panels were torn free. Galley doors banged open and shut, spewing food scraps and rubbish onto the floor. Water and ice slicked the linoleum. Pieces of trim started to break free, exposing wires underneath. As the fuselage flexed and twisted, oxygen masks, air-vent outlets, reading lights and ceiling panels all came tumbling down. One passenger rolled onto the floor because her seatbelt was undone. Passenger service units, which contain lights and air vents, above the heads of the passengers near the windows in the middle of the plane broke free from their fittings, striking four passengers and narrowly missing a nursing baby.

All 18 wheels were on the tarmac and the 250-tonne Boeing with 410 people on board was aquaplaning down the sodden runway at almost 300 kph.

The flight crew were applying maximum braking power as the jet crossed the end of the runway and flashed through the 100-metre stopway at 178 kph. Another 117 metres on, the plane crashed into the antennae of the airport's Independent Landing System, damaging the nose and right-wing landing gear, and shredding the tyres under the right wing. Still the plane ploughed on through trees and 103 metres of wet, boggy soil before coming to a standstill with its nose resting on the airport perimeter road right next to the third hole of the Royal Thai Air Force Golf Course.

It had taken just 41 horrifying seconds from the moment the wheels touched down until the nose gear collapsed and the jet came to a standstill.

But it was the long delays that occurred next that terrified the passengers. As the shaken first officer began the checklist and shut down the engines by selecting the fuel cut-off, the passengers could smell oil. Unbeknown to the people on board, the fuel tanks had survived the crash intact but hydraulic fluid was leaking from the shattered landing gear, and the passengers were afraid of fire. The emergency lights came on. Things were not helped by the lack of communication from the crew. The collapse of the nose gear meant it had been pushed up into the fuselage, forcing the cargo bay floor up by half a metre. This in turn had damaged the electronic rack support and cut off the cabin passenger address and interphone systems. The cockpit was operating in silence.

In the first-class cabin, senior International Olympic Committee member Kevan Gosper was on his way to Switzerland for an ethics and reform conference via London when the seasoned traveller found himself in the middle of a real-life drama. 'It took some time to get down on to the tarmac and it seemed to float for a while. Then the brakes grabbed very hard. And then suddenly we shot off the end of the strip,' he told Fairfax journalists.[2]

'Quite a big section of the ceiling in our cabin flew out and the oxygen masks came down but the cabin compartments stayed intact. We were thrown forward in our seats as the plane was coming to a sudden stop,' he said.[3] 'All the lights went out . . . inside panelling and internal arrangement were thrown about and there was a lot of disorder. We heard the nose wheel go and the plane dipped to one side. It was raining at the time. It was quite frightening. We didn't know whether we were going to break up and catch fire.'[4]

At the rear of the plane, Dr James O'Brien remained in his seat for five nail-biting minutes as the air became hot, humid and smoky. He too was worried about fire and just how he would get out. The cabin was already lit only by the emergency lighting. 'There were orders being shouted, apparently, but you couldn't hear them . . . because the radio control system had broken down,' he told reporters.[5]

Once the plane had come to a standstill, the tower controller radioed the pilots asking if it had cleared the runway. Visibility was so bad that the Thai authorities had no idea the plane had overshot and crashed through the perimeter of the airport. The first officer replied twice that the plane was in need of assistance, but the transmissions were weak and not understood by the controller.

Meanwhile, the second officer headed back into the main cabin to find the cabin services manager. They returned to the cockpit together and told Captain Fried there was no sign of fire and there appeared to be no injuries to the passengers or crew. The captain now had to make a choice between an emergency evacuation of the aircraft or an orderly disembarkation. With no immediate danger inside the plane, he decided to 'hasten slowly'. He was aware it was still raining heavily and there was no lighting outside the aircraft. He had no idea what other hazards awaited. The emergency response teams from the airport had still not arrived. He wanted to wait for steps to give the passengers the feeling of a 'more regular' exit and also decrease the risk of injury for the elderly or young passengers on board. Also on his mind was the thought that an emergency evacuation might spark panic among the passengers and could lead to injury. Once the passengers were out of the plane their first instinct might be to walk towards the terminal lights, which would take them across an active runway.

For the passengers it was an agony of uncertainty. With no PA system they had no idea what was happening. Some got angry that the crew were standing by the emergency exit doors apparently 'doing nothing'. They had no idea that the crew had changed from service providers to trained safety personnel standing on station ready to begin emergency evacuation procedures should a fire suddenly break out. One of the passengers was an off-duty Qantas pilot travelling as a passenger. He suggested the crew inform the flight deck about the fumes. As time went on passengers began to suffer irritated eyes and struggled to breathe. The captain ordered the over-wing doors to be opened for ventilation.

The delay in evacuation also puzzled the Thai authorities. 'Fire fighters banged on the door, shouting: "Open, open, open",' Vichai Prateepprecha, the director of the Department of Air Safety, told the *Australian Financial Review*. 'Our rescue teams were on the spot as soon as the plane came to a halt. Our crash investigators want to know why the doors were not open.'[6] The final Australian Transport Safety Bureau (ATSB) investigation report confirmed that some airport personnel got to the aircraft and conducted an initial inspection before the fire vehicles arrived. They attempted to contact the crew by tapping on the fuselage of the plane but the crew did not hear them. The chief of the emergency services also asked the control tower to tell the pilot to open the doors but the message did not get through. Around ten minutes after the plane had come to a halt, the pilot and crew watched a procession of fire vehicles with lights flashing reach the plane and, because of the earlier failed communication attempts, wait for the evacuation to begin, with floodlights illuminating the nose-down jet.

Back in the first-class cabin Mr Gosper said: 'I was a bit surprised they kept us in the plane so long. I worked out that [it was] twelve to thirteen minutes before emergency crews turned up . . . twenty to twenty-four minutes before we left the aircraft.

'We didn't know whether the plane would break into fire . . . there were some very anxious moments. I would have thought, given these circumstances, [we would have] been evacuated from the plane immediately. But one or two of us asked that question twice, particularly when we smelt some burning, and we were reassured by the crew that the smell was from the sudden cutback of the engines and there was no dangerous fire,' he said.[7]

Heather Rollo was flying to Casablanca via London for a holiday with her husband, Michael, and son Christopher, eight, and seven-year-old twins, James and Gregory. They were sitting near the damaged wing and were convinced after the plane came to a standstill they were going to die in a fireball. 'We were just in the dark. We could see we were on grass and the wing was damaged,' she told the *Australian* newspaper. 'The emergency lights came back on after a few minutes and it was very quiet, almost like a death quiet.

'Nobody was moving or saying anything. I thought the plane was going to catch fire.' A steward came through the cabin 'sniffing around' and asking: 'Can anyone smell fuel?', she said. 'Nobody gave us any information, no reassurance of crash evacuation procedure. They didn't open any doors or anything. We thought we were entombed.'[8]

The subsequent ATSB report into the accident observed that, although the crew acted with the passengers' safety as their 'primary consideration', an immediate evacuation would have been the 'most appropriate option'. It said the crew had gaps in their knowledge about hazards outside the aircraft, particularly underneath, because they had not been able to receive information from anyone outside. Their information was based on what they could tell from inside the cabin. 'However, any aircraft which overruns a stopway at over 80 knots is likely to sustain substantial damage. Although the crew had information that no signs of fire had been detected within the cabin, they had no clear understanding of the potential for a fire outside the cabin, particularly during the period before the emergency services arrived,' said the report.[9]

The crew were, of course, hampered by the lack of a PA system to communicate with passengers. An immediate evacuation would have overcome this problem by the crew initiating evacuation procedures at their individual doors or issuing the general evacuation alarm. It also pointed out that the crew had not considered the battery life of the emergency lighting – normally 20 minutes. According to the ATSB report, 'Had this power source failed it could have led to difficulties with passenger control and the disembarkation.'[10] As Mr Gosper noted, it was at least 20 minutes before the emergency doors were opened and the evacuation begun.

Final criticism was reserved for Qantas, which had not provided adequate guidance in its company procedures or crew training for making the right decision when the appropriate choice in an emergency response situation is not clear. 'Many airlines do not include the "precautionary dis-embarkation" in their procedures, having the "emergency evacuation" as the only option available for crews. However, if an airline chooses to include the precautionary disembarkation in its procedures, then it should ensure that its crews are appropriately prepared for deciding when a precaution-ary disembarkation is appropriate,' said the report.[11]

On this occasion there were no hazards outside the plane that would endanger the lives of the passengers. The ATSB report was simply hammering home the point that the crew could not be sure of that. The report added: 'By initiating a precautionary disembarkation when they did, the crew was able to ensure an orderly process. The absence of any serious injuries during the disembarkation indicated that the result was consistent with the intention.'[12] Not all the passengers agreed.

It had seemed like an eternity sitting in silence in the dim emergency light. Finally, at seven minutes past 11 pm – 20 minutes after the plane came to a standstill near the golf course – the crew began the evacuation procedure. Captain Fried had been told by the Qantas representative that buses were on their way to the plane. He instructed the cabin ser-vices manager to use inflatable slides on the right front and middle, R2 and R4, doors for the 'precautionary disembar-kation' of the passengers. He opted against using slides on the left side of the plane because it was higher, there were trees in the way and no lights to guide the passengers. The crew began to brief the passengers on the exit procedures. An Italian tour group leader translated the instructions. But, as the individual crew members relayed directions, some of the

anxious passengers were on the move, well before the brief-
ings were complete.

The crew told passengers to remove high-heeled shoes and
leave their cabin baggage behind. Many of the passengers
chose to ignore this. When the crew again told them to leave
their bags behind, arguments started. Some crew allowed
passengers to take their bags because it was not a 'full emergency' situation. One passenger was allowed to send his cabin
bag down the chute ahead of him, putting passengers below
at risk. A mother with her baby and a passenger with special
medication were also allowed to take their bags. As passengers came down from the upper deck, a bottleneck built up
in the cabin and the slide at the very front of the plane was
deployed. Because the jet was tipped on its nose, the slope of
the emergency chute at the front of the plane was so shallow
that people could walk down it. At the tail it was a different
story when, to alleviate the crush in the middle of the plane,
the rear door, R5, was opened. The angle of the plane meant
the tail was up in the air. The slope of the emergency chute
was so steep that thirteen passengers refused to go down it. It
was 'more like a rubber cliff,' one passenger told reporters.[13]

Many of the 38 injuries arising from the crash of QF1 in
Bangkok came from the evacuation. None of the injuries
were serious – 17 people sustained whiplash or bruising,
three were struck by dislodged panels and 13 were injured
during the evacuation. More than half of those occurred on
the near vertical incline of the emergency chute at the tail
of the plane. One passenger literally somersaulted down the
slide. 'We were instructed to use slide five, however this was
a particularly steep slide,' another passenger told the Fairfax

journalists. 'With unwilling small children, my wife argued with the steward until a passenger or another steward suggested to use the forward exits as they were closer to the ground.'[14] A total of 37 people used the rear slide and seven of those were injured.

As the passengers slid down the emergency chutes, the relief Qantas crew, who had been waiting for the plane in Bangkok, clambered into the cabin and were summarily told by the captain to leave. Their lack of knowledge of the 'terrain, wreckage and cargo' exposed them to 'potential injury', said the ATSB report.[15] The first officer secured the flight deck. Meanwhile, the off-duty pilot travelling as a passenger relieved a cabin crew member at one of the two front doors to assist the final passengers out of the plane, while the crew conducted a final check to ensure all the passengers had left.

On the ground, things were not much clearer. Seemingly oblivious to the possible risks of leaking fuel, Thai ground staff stood and watched the evacuation while calmly smoking cigarettes. Only just over half the passengers were told what to do when they got to the bottom of the chutes. Around three-quarters of them were given a hand at the bottom of the emergency chutes but only 52 per cent were told where to go next. Those who did receive instructions were told to go round the front of the aircraft and wait on the other side for buses. Most of the remaining passengers simply followed them. The Airport Authority of Thailand later noted that there were 'some deficiencies in the coordination between appropriate parties at the accident site'.[16]

With the plane on the ground and the passengers safe, the fallout began. Fifteen passengers reported suffering psychological distress as a result of the accident. One of those was Heather Rollo. She received psychiatric and psychological treatment for her terror of flying. 'I'm petrified. Even a little air pocket now and I'm convinced I am going to die,' she told the *Australian*. It is so bad that she has to take a Valium to calm her and insists on being inside the cockpit during landing. 'For me that's part of the closure.' She lodged a complaint with Qantas when the family returned from its trip two weeks later and received a reply from Qantas Chief Executive James Strong after a month and a half, which 'waffled on' about the accident's 'general inconvenience' and 'disruption' to their travel plans. The newspaper reported that each passenger received $1,000 compensation from the airline in return for signing confidentiality clauses.[17]

Photographs of the jet nose-down on the grass flashed around the world. Qantas went into damage limitation mode. The chief executive was anxious to show that the airline's impeccable safety record had not been harmed by the accident. 'I think it's possible to say that this maintains our reputation because while there was a serious incident, the net effect was that nobody was seriously injured. It does not harm our reputation at all,' said Mr Strong. 'On a Qantas scale, this is a serious incident but there is no point rating them.'[18]

He was also reported to be anxious that the airline did not suffer its first ever jet hull loss, which occurs when it is cheaper to write the hull off and buy a new plane than foot the damage and insurance bills. Reports in the *Australian Financial Review* at the time suggest it was the 'biggest repair job in Australian aviation history, conservatively estimated to cost $100 million.'[19] Fixing the crashed plane, christened *City of Darwin*, would maintain Qantas's claim to have never lost a jet.

But the airline's reputation was about to take an incredible battering as it emerged that cost-cutting and poor management procedures had led directly to the accident that put passengers' lives at risk.

When the pilots were landing QF1 it never occurred to them at any stage to put the engines into full reverse thrust. Had they landed with the flaps fully open – at flaps 30 instead of flaps 25 – and thrown the four powerful Rolls-Royce engines into full reverse thrust then, according to the subsequent ATSB report, 'the overrun would most probably have been avoided'. That they didn't was because it had been trained out of them to save money.[20]

Up until 6 December 1996, Qantas instructed all pilots flying the B747-400 to land with flaps 30 and maximum reverse thrust. At flaps 30, one senior pilot noted that the plane 'wants to land'. But as from 6 December 1996, Qantas had instructed all pilots to land at flaps 25 at which, the same pilot noted, the plane 'wants to fly'. Boeing wrote to Qantas in 2000 reiterating that it recommended flaps 30 to 'minimise landing distance'. Landing at flaps 25 meant the plane came in five to six knots faster and had a slightly longer touchdown. Boeing also warned against the policy of using only idle thrust on landing. The aircraft manufacturer said that not using full reverse thrust could be habit-forming in pilots. 'The pilot may then fail to respond quickly when such reverse thrust is needed during a . . . landing in some type of performance critical situation.'[21]

Qantas pilots had been trained not to land with the flaps full out or use full reverse thrust on landing. A survey of Qantas 747-400 pilots after the QF1 crash found that more than half said their training did not include a variety of situations where flaps 30 and full reverse were required, and over a third said they had received adverse comments from captains and trainers for selecting flaps 30 and full reverse on landing. Around half the pilots said they had only rarely used flaps 30 or full reverse in the 12 months before the accident in Bangkok. The crew on the flight deck of QF1 had barely used flaps 30 or full reverse since the company brought out the edict instructing pilots to use flaps 25 and idle reverse, almost three years earlier.

This was coupled with the fact that most Qantas pilots, including the pilots of QF1, had not received any simulator training for landing on contaminated runways such as the rain-soaked one they encountered at Bangkok. Crucially, they were not aware of how reverse thrust was a 'critical stopping force on water-affected runways', said the ATSB report. 'The QF1 flight crew were not atypical of most other company B747-400 pilots. There was therefore an unquestionable link between the performance of the crew and the company flight operations system in which they trained and operated.'[22]

Qantas brought in the flaps 25 and idle reverse thrust edict to save money. Prior to December 1996 the Qantas philosophy had been to provide aircraft with the shortest possible landing distance. The change began in June 1996, when a representative from the wheel brake manufacturer for the 747-400s met with staff from the Qantas Flight Operations

Branch and the Engineering and Maintenance Branch. It was explained that, unlike the traditional steel brakes, the new carbon brakes used on the jets had low wear and tear at high temperatures. This was new. It meant that wear and tear on the brakes would be reduced if they were put on hard just once or twice. Landing at flaps 25 and with idle thrust would do the trick.

The airline staff went into a research and development phase during which no formal risk assessment was undertaken. The Operations Procedures Committee then got involved and noted that using idle reverse thrust and fewer, harder and longer applications of the carbon fibre brakes would have financial benefits. It estimated the airline would make a number of savings, including $700,000 a year on overhauling brakes and $1,640,000 on fuel. The ATSB report critically observed: 'The cost-benefit analysis for the introduction of flaps 25/idle reverse procedures listed all the benefits of the new procedures in financial terms. It did not consider cost items such as tyre wear and the fact that flaps 25 may not be used on all approaches. It was also not updated after maintenance of the brakes was outsourced.'[23]

The ATSB report was critical of the organisational structure within Qantas that brought in the cost-cutting measure without 'a proper risk assessment'. It said: 'There were also significant deficiencies in the manner in which the company implemented and evaluated the new procedures.' More specifically it found that Qantas had not sought Boeing's opinion on the safety impact of the new landing procedure and that its examination of the flaps 25 and idle reverse procedure used by two other airlines was incomplete. Neither did Qantas allow for the fact that the procedures used by the other airlines were more conservative than the ones Qantas was bringing in and had additional safeguards for water-affected runways. Similarly, the performance differences between the two types of landing were not fully examined. 'Such an examination would probably have highlighted the significant differences in landing distance on wet or contaminated runways using these various configurations,' said the report.[24]

Investigators found that the documentation for the project and its history was 'disorganised and incomplete'. According to the report, there were scant records of conversations or meetings held about the project, or of the timing and reasons for important decisions. It said that the decision to bring in the new landing procedure was based on test flights by a small number of experienced pilots in a flight simulator. This was informal and undocumented. No records were kept of what they thought and there was no evidence that active line pilots flying for Qantas were consulted.

Once the system had been brought in, flight crews were asked in newsletters what they thought. The few pilots who did respond, most critically, either in writing or verbally, were disregarded because they were considered 'resistant to change'. It noted that many management jobs had been taken by senior pilots with no management training. 'The management culture was over-reliant on personal experience and did not place adequate emphasis on structured processes, available expertise, management training, and research and development when making strategic decisions.'[25]

It was this combination of management factors that

directly led to QF1 finishing nose-down next to a golf course in Thailand. But why hadn't the air safety watchdog, the Civil Aviation Safety Authority (CASA), picked up the problem sooner? The ATSB report was damning: 'The surveillance of airline flight operations was deficient.'[26] CASA was actually letting Qantas check on itself. Before the 1990s one per cent of all Qantas operations were monitored. This figure was cut three times by CASA in the decade before the crash in Thailand. In 1993 CASA cut its surveillance by half after Qantas, in consultation with the Civil Aviation Authority, set up its own Flight Standards Department to do half the required checks. More cuts in surveillance were brought in over the years.

More damning was the December 1999 review of the relationship between Qantas and CASA that found in the financial year before the QF1 crash only 22 per cent of the planned surveillance tasks had been achieved. Training of cabin crew had not been checked by CASA for ten years. CASA had also failed to put in place and monitor safety regulations. There was a regulatory requirement for airlines to provide landing distances for conditions worse than wet but, not only was this not clearly spelled out, neither Qantas nor CASA really understood what it meant.

Nor were there enough regulations for emergency procedures or training for emergencies. The ATSB report said: 'In the two years before the accident, CASA conducted minimal product-based surveillance of Qantas flight operations.' Even if CASA had carried out more surveillance it was unlikely the problems would have been picked up. 'Most of these deficiencies had probably existed in Qantas flight operations for many years,' said the report.[27]

The incident was a wake-up call for Qantas, which put in place 'substantial changes' to its management policies and procedures in all the areas highlighted by the ATSB. CASA also made substantial changes to its surveillance processes and regulations. But the relationship between Qantas and CASA would come up again when another Qantas jet got into trouble.

The final ATSB report into the QF1 accident left traumatised passenger Mrs Rollo feeling 'sick to the stomach'. She told the *Australian* on the day the report came out: 'When you are flying a national airline and putting your life in their hands, you don't expect to get a lot of cost-cutting that puts lives at risk. It was only a matter of time [before a major accident]. Thankfully, we weren't killed.'[28]

QF2

EARLY EMERGENCY

QANTAS HAS HAD its fair share of airborne drama. During the airline's first hour of flight a mid-air emergency almost claimed the life of one of its founding fathers, Hudson Fysh. It was 21 January 1921 and Fysh, with just 36 operational hours' flying time under his belt, was delivering one of Qantas's first two planes from Mascot aerodrome in Sydney to Central Queensland. Fysh, with chief engineer Arthur Baird as his passenger, was flying an army surplus BE2E string and canvas biplane. At 6,500 feet the plane's 90 horsepower motor would push it to a top speed of 82 mph. Fysh was following Qantas co-founder and former Australian Flying Corps pilot Paul J. McGinness in the other plane, an Avro Dyak. McGinness was by far the more experienced pilot, with over 500 hours' flying time, and so took the lead. It was a flight that almost ended in disaster, as Fysh later recalled in his 1965 autobiography, *Qantas Rising*:

> We taxied to the far end of the aerodrome, opened the throttles and were at last off on our great adventure, an adventure which almost right away provided us with our first little bit of drama. We sailed away happily over Sydney, towards Manly and up the coast, but the weather was steadily getting worst, with ominous dark clouds gathering ahead. Dodging in and out through clear patches, McGinness and I soon lost contact. I continued my dodging with growing apprehension, for I realised that with my limited experience I was not up to blind flying in cloud: indeed I would have defied anyone to do it in the old machine only fitted with a compass, airspeed indicator, rev counter and inclinometer, plus the fact that fore and aft trim was not possible and as steady pressure was needed on the left rudder bar to keep her straight. This was real flying: one flew the aeroplane by one's senses.[1]

Despite his roiling stomach and heightened nerves, Fysh decided to tackle the cloud head-on, hoping that it would not be as dense as it looked. It was. He had his work cut out keeping control of the aircraft, which he prayed was not positioned above hilltops. With the compass swinging wildly the plane began the first stages of what would be a dangerous spin, before bursting into a small clearing near Red Head coalmine in a valley with cloud on the ground all around.

Fysh quickly stabilised the plane and looked around to get his bearings:

> On my right were the buildings and pithead structure of a coal mine, with a sloping bushy hillside alongside. I promptly put the BE2E down on the hillside, careered uphill through the bushes, and came to a halt alongside a miner's cottage. As Baird and I climbed out after our ordeal we were met by a miner's wife who asked us in for a cup of tea while we waited for the clouds to clear, and to make a decision as to whether we could get off. The clouds broke, a few bushes were cleared, and starting off downhill we careered ahead and then into the air, skimming by inches a group of telephone wires – which still loom up in my memory.[2]

In his book *Air Crash*, respected air-safety expert Macarthur Job said: 'The situation in which Hudson Fysh found himself on that first flight was a classic setting for a fatal accident. It is not exaggerating to say that essentially the same circumstances have since claimed the lives of countless inexperienced light aircraft pilots – and still do so even today. Had that small valley not been directly below where Fysh lost control of the BE2E in cloud – or indeed, had the aircraft failed to clear those telephone wires on his subsequent takeoff – the history of Australia's airlines could have been very different!'[3]

At the end of World War One, two young airmen had come back to Australia with big ideas. They were inspired by the Commonwealth government's offer of a £10,000 prize 'for the first successful flight to Australia from Great Britain of a machine manned by Australians'. Aviation was in the air. The pair's dreams of competing for the money died along with their sponsor, the wealthy New South Wales grazier Sir Samuel McCaughey. Instead, they were hired by the Defence Department to survey a possible route and landing grounds for the race contestants between Longreach in western Queensland and Darwin in the Northern Territory. Back in their Australian Flying Corps uniforms, Fysh said he and McGinness generated the same amount of comment on the street as spacemen in 'full space rig-out'. Together with driver and handyman George Gorham, they set out on a 1,354 mile cross-country odyssey in a Model T Ford. McGinness was inspired by the huge spaces between the unconnected railheads of Charleville, Longreach, Winton and Cloncurry. Cut off for parts of the year by heavy rains, the route seemed a problem tailor-made for solving by airplane. In fact the route was so tough that they advised the Defence Department to send competitors inland across the Barkly Tableland. Afterwards they were ordered to prepare landing grounds – Fysh in Darwin and McGinness in Cloncurry.

It was in Cloncurry that McGinness met another man who would be crucial to the establishment of Qantas – Fergus McMaster. The youthful aviator was about to drive a young lady out for a picnic on a Sunday afternoon when he saw McMaster, chairman of the Anti Cattle Duffing Organisation, wearily walking up the sunbaked street. McGinness knew exactly who he was. He stopped to find out that McMaster had snapped the front stub-axle of his car attempting to cross the Cloncurry River. In his personal papers, uncovered by the author John Gunn for the book *The Defeat of Distance*, McMaster described how the young airmen impressed him: 'I did not know McGinness very well and was surprised when he said he would make arrangements for his friend to attend the picnic with someone else, and that he would give me a hand to fix up my car.' The garages were all closed. 'If there was a door that it was possible to open, or a sheet of iron that could be removed to give access to a garage well, he was in. I was so impressed with the help and alertness of McGinness – and so grateful for his assistance – that the ground was prepared for my ready help when he and Hudson Fysh later submitted their ideas to me in Brisbane.'[4]

On the other side of the world, KLM Royal Dutch Airlines had been registered with backing from Her Majesty Queen Wilhelmina, the Dutch government, banks and the business community. The second oldest airline remaining from those pioneering days had its true beginnings in slightly less august company – Qantas took its first tentative footsteps in the lounge bar of the Gresham Hotel in Brisbane. It was there in June 1920 that McGinness and Fysh met again with McMaster, to present their proposal for an air taxi-service that would be supplemented by joy rides in western Queensland and the Northern Territory. At a time when the average weekly wage was £4, McGinness was backing the dream to the tune of £1,000 and Fysh with £500. McMaster was impressed by their enthusiasm and jumped on board.

After McGinness and Fysh left him in the Gresham Hotel,

he immediately fronted Longreach sheep-station owner and grazier Ainslie Templeton with the idea. Templeton agreed to match him pound for pound. That afternoon McMaster set off around the town to raise capital for what would become one of the world's major airlines.

In Queen Street, bookshop owner John Thompson coughed up £100; in Eagle Street, Queensland Primary Producers Association managing director Alan Campbell provided cash and volunteered to act as company secretary; back in Queen Street, McMaster bumped into Winton shopkeeper T. J. O'Rourke, who took him back to his hotel and immediately signed a cheque for £250 with the promise of another £250 when it was needed. The money was put in McMaster's personal bank account. 'Qantas was founded on trust and co-operation, and that is what stuck to it through its first severe years of pioneering life,' wrote McMaster in his personal papers.[5]

McGinness and Fysh rushed to Sydney to start the process of acquiring their first aircraft. On 16 November 1920 the certificate of incorporation was given in Brisbane for Queensland and Northern Territory Aerial Services Ltd. It was written as Q.A.N.T.A.S. – drawing on the Anzac legend for its inspiration.

McGinness and Fysh got hold of two planes and two months later undertook that first flight from Sydney that so nearly ended in disaster. They had bought the Avro, but were simply delivering the BE2E to its owner, Longreach stock and station agent Charlie Knight. On the second leg of the flight Knight joined the BE2E, still piloted by Fysh, as a passenger. Fysh again missed his track and this was altogether too much for Knight, who was airsick and swore he would never fly again. He agreed to sell the BE2E to Qantas for 450 pounds.

The two aviators were due to meet their key financial backer, McMaster, at Barcaldine. They picked him up and beat the mail train to Longreach by 20 minutes, despite giving it a two-hour head start. The final leg was to Winton, where the press and public had been primed for the arrival of the two planes. The flight should have taken only one and a half hours, but up in the air McMaster had difficulty telling roads from ploughed fire tracks. 'We went wrong,' he said.[6]

He was a passenger in the Avro, together with company shareholder Templeton. Slowly he realised they were off course and, in the windy open cockpit of the plane, wrote a series of pencil notes to the unflappable McGinness to the effect that they were heading in the wrong direction. 'One hour from Longreach. Too many mountains on our right,' he wrote. McGinness was unmoved. 'He was cool; too cool for Templeton and myself. He kept pointing to his compass, which showed west.'[7] Eventually he wrote that Winton is north north-west of Longreach. McGinness finally reacted, adjusted course and they landed in Winton in front of a large crowd after three hours in the air and with just 15 minutes of fuel left in their tanks. 'Much relieved,' wrote McMaster in the papers researched by John Gunn. 'We had a drink.'[8]

Despite some debate and Longreach taking a larger role in the life of the business, Winton was the official birthplace of Qantas. Harriet Rylie did the secretarial chores free of charge from her stock and station agent father's offices in Winton; Miss K. Tighe did the bookkeeping for free in the town and the first 'special meeting' of directors was held at the Winton Club on 10 February 1921.

The company now had a pressing financial problem. Half its capital was tied up in a new Avro triplane that McGinness and Baird travelled to Sydney to collect. The hope was that the five-seater triplane would help open up the passenger service between Winton and Longreach. Unfortunately McGinness sent a telegram that the plane's undercarriage had been damaged during trials. He did not let on just how massively damaged the plane really was. It never saw service, ending up as a hen house in Sydney.

Meanwhile, Fysh was steadily recouping the cost of the BE2E with joyrides that even included one passenger shooting two turkeys from the observer's seat at the front. Times were hard and they became even harder when McGinness, flying joyriding passengers in the Avro Dyak, was forced to land in sugar cane near Ingham. No one was injured in what was the airline's first operational accident, but the aircraft was badly damaged and had to be taken to Sydney for repairs. That left the company with one operational plane and the ability to carry just one passenger at a time.

It became a battle to secure more private funding – there was none forthcoming from the government. Finally, in February 1922, the airline won the tender for the Charleville to Cloncurry mail service against strong opposition. The tender was based on the service being provided by two expensive giant Vickers Vulcan biplanes that could carry eight passengers. They were bigger than the Qantas team thought was necessary, but were favoured by the controller of civil aviation and thus the only real plane of choice. They were expensive, delayed by strikes and unsuited to hot Australian conditions. Plus, it was difficult to find a pilot to fly one of the planes because McMaster insisted they sign a pledge to abstain from drinking.

The delay in the supply of the Vickers aircraft was resolved with a loan from the government for an Armstrong Whit-worth DH4. After a string of delays McGinness finally flew the inaugural Qantas service – carrying 108 letters from Charleville to Cloncurry. McGinness flew two more trips before leaving the company, finding the reality of timetables and alcoholic abstinence too constricting for his romantic nature.

He left the company in dire straits. The Vulcans were unsuitable and could not climb in the heat. Qantas found itself short of pilots willing to stay in the outback, and sad-dled with second-rate equipment. Crashes followed but the pilots and passengers walked away and the planes were repaired. Despite the hardship, only one of the 205 scheduled flights was missed in the first year of operation.

Qantas moved on, finally making a profit and looking at Brisbane as a key part of its plans to expand. Its Queensland route was a vital part of the air highway between England and the eastern states. But as the company expanded so did the chance for things to go wrong. On 24 March 1927 a DH9 flown by relatively new and inexperienced pilot A. D. Davidson stalled on approach to landing. The pilot and two passengers were killed. It was Qantas's first fatal accident – but not its last.

Qantas briefly dabbled in manufacturing its own planes – DH50s made in its Longreach hangar from mostly imported parts. They were reliable but the saving to the company from building them rather than importing the same finished plane from England was just £50. The company was working commercially and in 1928 it also began one of the most romantic and practical chapters in Australian aviation history – a flying doctor service. The venture began as a one-year trial with the Reverend John Flynn, who pioneered the idea of an air ambulance to help people in the remote regions of the bush. The trial proved a remarkable success and led to the foundation of the Royal Flying Doctor Service.

In the pioneering days airlines were making up the rules as they went along. Qantas put out a set of 'Rules for the Observance of Pilots' in November 1928 following another fatal crash. Pilot Charles Scott, a charming poet and musician, had taken Sir John Salmond, visiting from Britain to advise on aerial defence, on a far-ranging tour that ended in Adelaide. Scott left Adelaide early in the morning with engineer George Nutson and flew the plane into cloud. It went into a spin at 1,800 feet and crashed in hilly country. Scott's jaw was broken and the plane caught fire but the former Royal Air Force heavyweight champion still managed to drag Nutson from the wreckage. The engineer died from his injuries on the way to hospital. Fysh said Scott was 'a brilliant but over-volatile pilot . . . too brilliant to be stable.'[9]

McMaster was perturbed by the 'street talk' of Scott's carousing that was known at the hotel, the club and the golf links, but despite their reservations, the board allowed Scott to keep flying with Qantas. However, the crash delayed the new

Brisbane to Charleville route by six months. Qantas had moved its head office to the Queensland capital as it realised other airlines were competing for government subsidies to provide airmail services and were striving to take control of the market. Norman Brearley's West Australian Airways in Western Australia, Jim Larkin's company Lasco in Victoria and Qantas in Queensland all faced up to a new challenge in 1930 when two of the nation's aviation pioneers, Charles Kingsford Smith and Charles Ulm, launched Australian National Airlines between Sydney and Brisbane and Sydney and Melbourne.

In 1931 the British Post Office announced two experimental trips for an airmail service between London and Sydney as an extension of Imperial Airways' London to Delhi service. Qantas was to fly the mail from Darwin to Sydney. Unfortunately, the Imperial plane ran short of fuel and crashed in Timor. There were no injuries and the mail survived but now Qantas did not have a multi-engined plane to fly over water and collect the mail. Instead Kingsford Smith heroically came to the rescue in the famous Australian National Airways plane *Southern Cross*. Qantas was at risk of being forced off its route altogether.

With KLM also launching an experimental route into Melbourne via Batavia and the Australian government struggling to find funds, the Qantas board decided to establish formal links with Imperial Airways. They were helped by the highly publicised loss of an Australian National Airways plane, *Southern Cloud*, the wreckage of which was not found until 1958, despite a massive search.

In 1932 Fysh reached a 'gentleman's agreement' with Sir Walter Nicholson, the government representative on the board of Imperial Airways. One of the key clauses said: 'It is the intention of both parties that each shall have a "square deal", in the sense that expression is understood by fair and reasonably minded men.'[10] And with that, a link was forged between Australian and British airlines that would carry on for many decades.

The partners brought their combined muscle to bear in the middle of 1932, when Australia established a committee to decide on the best option for an airmail route to London. Imperial Airways and Qantas registered a company in Queensland under the name Qantas Empire Airways Ltd to tender for the Australia to Singapore airmail service. It was a highly public battle for the much-coveted role. The de Havilland Aircraft Company was accused of collusion by withholding its prices and details from at least one tenderer. When Qantas Empire Airways won the tender, Kingsford Smith told the *Sydney Morning Herald*: 'Apparently my tender was not even considered.'[11] He felt the pioneers of aviation in Australia had been 'overlooked'. His airline was finished and he died the following year when his plane went missing on a flight from Kent to Australia.

Just as Qantas was on the verge of entering a new era of aviation, its old business of delivering mail in the bush brought a timely reminder that flying was a dangerous business. Seasoned pilot Norman Chapman, earmarked for a role on the new Singapore airmail service, took off from Longreach for Winton on the regular mail run. He had two passengers on board – R. McKnow from Roma travelling to Winton on business and R. H. Hendrickson from the Shell Oil Company in Sydney, who was flying with his little dog.

The plane dropped a package of papers at Qantas chairman Fergus McMaster's property and then headed on to Winton. It never turned up. A search was launched but nothing was found that first day. At 7.20 am the following morning a plane spotted the burned-out wreckage on the edge of a station 20 miles from Winton. All three had died in the flames that followed the crash. The dog's charred remains lay with them.

What caused the crash remains a mystery. Dust regularly reduced visibility in the bush so a pilot could not see beyond the spinning prop in front of him. When Chapman crashed, it appeared to investigators he had been under full power and had flown at 45 degrees straight into the ground. Fysh himself believed Chapman had not recovered from an earlier bout of influenza and, with the quick turnaround of flights, had been exhausted and simply nodded off at the controls.

COVER-UP

Just before 6 am on the morning of 15 November 1934 two kangaroo shooters were finishing off an early breakfast by their roadside campfire a few miles out of Longreach, Queensland, along the Ilfracombe road. Their blue cattle dog cocked an ear as with a roar a large four-engined aircraft appeared above a line of gidgee trees towards Longreach. The early morning sun glinted off the aluminium painted sides of Captain Prendergast's DH86 as it rose and roared towards them.

The shooters shaded their eyes and stood up to watch. Suddenly they saw the aeroplane start a turn to the right, a flattish turn that increased in speed and developed into a flat spin while forward speed was lost. A rapid flat turning descent now ensued and with a startling suddenness the DH86 hit the ground with a sickening crash. A great cloud of dust drifted off over the dry summer terrain while the two kangaroo shooters sprinted for the wreck only some two hundred yards from their camp.[1]

Qantas founder Hudson Fysh described the crash of the brand new DH86 on the last leg of its delivery run from England on the opening page of his second volume of memoirs, *Qantas at War*. But it was only years after the book was published in 1968 that the true story of the cover-up behind the ill-fated DH86 plane was discovered. Commercial necessity produced a plane that was unsafe. Pride and poor communication kept it flying when it should have been grounded and vital life-saving modifications put in place.

The plane had left Longreach early under the command of Captain Prendergast, with First Officer W. V. Creates and Flight Engineer F. R. Charlton. Also on board was Australian Shell aviation representative E. 'Bunny' Broadfoot. A spare Gypsy Moth engine had been lashed into place inside the fuselage. It was a fine, cloudless day with only a light south-east wind. So what could have gone wrong for a brand new plane to fall out of the sky just ten minutes later? A smashed watch on the arm of one of the crew had stopped at 5.50 am. Teenager Doreen Coleman got out of bed to watch the plane as it flew overhead and saw it descend in a spin before appearing to come out of it in a swoop at just 200 feet and then crashing to earth.

The Accident Investigation Committee Report pieced together what had happened. Captain Prendergast had climbed out of the pilot seat and gone to use the toilet compartment at the rear of the plane. Control was left in the hands of the first officer, but he was busy attempting to send a test radio message. Therefore the experienced flight engineer, whilst not a pilot, was in fact in control of the plane. The DH86 became notorious for its lack of directional stability. Once it started to yaw it took a great deal of skill to prevent it going into a spin. The report suggested that the captain's weight in the toilet at the back of the cabin, combined with the weight of the engine, had moved the aircraft's centre of gravity too far back. The position of the bodies in the wreckage indicated that Captain Prendergast had realised what was happening while in the toilet and had been rushing forward to retake the controls as the plane slammed into the ground.

The DH86 was the plane Qantas had to have. To pull off the airmail tender Qantas Empire Airlines needed a reasonably quick, economical, four-engined plane to cover the route. The multiple engines were needed to safely cover the 825 kilometres of ocean that comprised the feared Timor Crossing. The result was the DH86, which, Fysh himself wrote in his book *Qantas at War*, was 'built expressly to the order of Imperial Airways and Qantas and very much to their basic design'.[2] And it was a rush job. As Fysh explained, their opponents said it could not be done in the time. But the manufacturers,

de Havilland, were brilliant in their planning and produc-
tion, and in only four months the DH86 was ready, obtaining
its certificate of airworthiness at Martlesham Heath just one
day before tenders for the operation of the new service closed.
The fabric-covered, wooden biplane could carry 10 to 12 passengers and cruise at 225 kph. It became synonymous in the
public's mind with Qantas . . . and disaster.

Qantas Empire Airways had also agreed to let de Havilland
sell its specially designed DH86 planes to Holyman Airways,
the winner of the tender for the Hobart–Launceston–
Melbourne airmail route. The first DH86, *Miss Hobart*, began
flying the route on 1 October 1934 and just 18 days later the
aircraft, with its two pilots and nine passengers, vanished
without trace. Among those on board were a young dentist
with his wife and baby, a vicar and a well-known Tasmanian
horsewoman. The company's chief pilot, Captain Victor
Holyman, was on the flight as wireless operator.

Unlike the DH86 planes being delivered to Qantas, the
Miss Hobart only had a single pilot configuration in the
cockpit. The speculation was that the plane had plunged into
the sea while Holyman tried to swap seats with the pilot and
take the controls. An inquiry was launched into the mystery crash. It was adjourned to Sydney and two days in was
stopped again with the devastating news of the Qantas DH86
crash at Longreach.

The crash caused enormous concern both in Australia
and England. Fysh noted that Qantas, Imperial and de Havilland took the earlier successful delivery of its first DH86 by
reliable pilot Lester Brain as a reason not to lose faith. 'The
Director of Civil Aviation, Edgar Johnston, and his technical

staff were most unhappy and uncertain, and the public read the headlines in a state of shock. However, we had a signed contract,' he wrote.[3]

Qantas contacted de Havilland for tests to be carried out on the two DH86 planes that were successfully flying there. Both of those had the original single-pilot cockpit, which Qantas had now insisted be redesigned into a two-pilot configuration. The Air Ministry testers at Martlesham Heath, de Havilland and Imperial Airways reviewed the flight tests and sent back word to Australia that the DH86 was quite airworthy and there was no reason for the airline to discontinue flying it.

But in Australia engineer Arthur Baird was putting together another of the airline's new DH86s that had been delivered by sea when he found the fin post was cracked. The wreckage from Longreach had exactly the same problem. He concluded it was down to mis-rigging, but tests to show this was the cause of the crash were inconclusive. Of much greater concern was the lack of directional stability at certain speeds. Qantas engineers attempted to fix this by eliminating the servo tab from the rudder. Still, aviation watchdog Johnston was worried and would not let the airline carry paying passengers on its new mail route for the first three months of operation.

Australia's Civil Aviation Branch put aircraft designer Wing Commander Lawrence Wackett on the case. His report said: 'This type of aeroplane has inadequate fin and rudder area to ensure prompt recovery from a spin. It is recommended that the fin be increased by four square feet and the rudder by two square feet.'[4] His advice was ignored. Meanwhile, Qantas's fourth DH86 arrived from London and was found to have the same fin bias problems as the other planes. The aircraft's certificate of airworthiness was suspended, which was picked up by the media of the day as condemnation of all DH86 planes. Engineers from Qantas and Holyman worked hard at improving the mechanism, and found that very frequent oiling and cleaning would keep it correctly adjusted. Fysh wrote:

> Our people were really beginning to learn something about that DH86 fin assembly and how to humour it, but it was certain that the design had been hurried and was not of the best. Modifications got over this as they had in other types, but the QEA board were very upset and contemplated putting in a big claim against the company. They were wisely dissuaded by Imperial Airways, who made the point that the fault was not entirely de Havilland's. The DH86 was essentially a joint venture and Imperial and ourselves had pushed de Havilland unmercifully.[5]

The plane was given its airworthiness certificate and the airline began to run flights from Brisbane to Darwin and Singapore. The flights were trouble-free and the ban on passengers was lifted. Lady Louis Mountbatten and Major H. Phillips, en route to London, become Qantas's first overseas paying passengers on 17 April 1935. Later DH86 passengers on the route would include playwright Noël Coward and Hollywood actors Charlie Chaplin and Paulette Goddard.

Meanwhile, Holyman, having learned from the loss of the *Miss Hobart*, had ordered twin cockpit DH86 planes and announced plans to extend its routes from Tasmania to Melbourne through to Sydney. On the morning of the maiden flight, two silver DH86 planes left Essendon airport in Melbourne. The new *Loila* flew out to Sydney with four journalists on board for the inaugural journey. The *Loina* headed off to Launceston via Flinders Island on its regular morning run. Only one of the planes made it. When the *Loila* landed in Sydney the stunned crew were told the *Loina* had vanished. Another DH86 had gone missing. Holyman had scrambled an aircraft into the air to search for the *Loina* when it had not arrived in Launceston 45 minutes after it was due. The missing *Miss Hobart* was still raw in the minds of all the staff. The search plane reported wreckage floating almost ten kilometres out to sea from the Flinders Island landing strip. As the sea became rougher it washed ashore compelling evidence that the *Loina*, with two Sydney-bound passengers and two crew on board, had perished.

The wreckage included partially inflated life jackets, a pilot's uniform coat, newspapers from the day before, a felt hat with a railway ticket in the brim and, crucially, a large piece of plywood cabin flooring from the rear of the plane. Investigators puzzled over this. Part of the flooring, which would have been just outside the toilet door, was charred. There were carpet fragments stuck around the charred area and indentations indicating that attempts had been made to stamp the fire out. Witnesses, discounted as unreliable at the time, described the plane suddenly lurching to the left and then tumbling out of the sky, turning upside down twice, and falling like a 'tumbling pigeon'.[6]

Piecing the evidence together years later, former Civil

Aviation Senior Inspector of Air Safety Macarthur Job sur-
mised the likely events that caused the *Loina* to crash. The
evidence, he wrote, suggested that 'a discarded cigarette
might have set the cabin carpet alight in this spot . . . When
finally noticed towards the end of the flight, did two or more
passengers rush down the aisle to try to stamp it out? If this
happened unexpectedly as the crew were decreasing speed
preparatory to their approach to land, the resulting combination of aft centre of gravity and low airspeed would have
again duplicated the dangerous situation in which Brain
found himself en route from Benghazi.'[7]

Unfortunately air-crash investigators knew nothing about
Qantas operations chief Brain's problems with the first DH86
that he delivered to Australia from London via Benghazi.
Job himself uncovered that many decades later. At the time
the evidence of the burned carpet on the *Loina* was largely
dismissed and the mysterious problems plaguing the DH86
were allowed to continue. It was a cover-up.

Matters were not helped by the British attitude towards
Australia at the time. Royal Air Force (RAF) navigation
expert D. C. T. Bennett was visiting Melbourne after the
Centenary Air Race and said: 'Some sections of Australian opinion seemed to have jumped to the very groundless
conclusion that the DH86s have a serious defect. To say
that a machine breaks up in the air is a pretty grave accusa-
tion when there is really nothing to support it. I have also
heard the opinion that while the design might be satisfactory the construction could be faulty. But the inspection
routine at de Havilland – as in England generally – is so
searching that I do not think such a thing could happen. In

Australia, maintenance regulations are not nearly so rigidly enforced.'[8]

Civil Aviation director Johnston decided to call together as many experts as he could muster to try to establish 'that every feature, structural or otherwise, is beyond suspicion'.[9] Attending this conference were Fysh, Brain and Baird from Qantas, plus representatives from Holyman, de Havilland, Sydney and Melbourne universities, and just about every related government department, including the Royal Australian Air Force (RAAF). Wing Commander Wackett once again presented his doubts about the DH86, suggesting that the torsional bracing of the wings might not provide enough stability in situations where sideslip occurred. The Qantas view, expressed by Fysh with the entire Empire airmail service riding on the success of the plane Qantas had helped design, said that de Havilland and the Air Ministry in London knew best.

Johnston opted for a test of the DH86 to see if wing torsioning was a problem. Holyman's DH86 *Lepena* was emptied of her seats and fitted with monitoring equipment. A test crew was sent up with parachutes in case they did find what was causing the plane to drop out of the sky. After an hour of testing they landed, much relieved but no wiser. Similarly, a trip to England to tell de Havilland and the Air Ministry about Australian concerns regarding the DH86 was given a very cool reception. And then, two months later, the *Lepena*, on a routine flight from Launceston to Melbourne, sent out an emergency signal that the port lower wing strut had gone and made an emergency landing off Hunter Island. The DH86 certificates of airworthiness were suspended and

45

the plane was inspected to finally find out what was wrong. But there was nothing wrong with the *Lepena*. The incident proved pilots and crew also had their doubts about the DH86 but the certificates of airworthiness were reinstated.

Had Brain spoken up at the meeting of experts, there is every chance he could have prevented the final DH86 disaster. In 1942 World War Two was raging and Qantas was running on a makeshift number of planes, including two DH86s returned to it by the RAAF. On 20 February 1942, the day after the Japanese bombed Darwin, Captain C. H. Swaffield took off from Archerfield, near Brisbane in rain and low cloud with seven wartime priority passengers. The plane took off normally but minutes later plunged into trees on Mount Pirie on the outskirts of Brisbane. By the time a Civil Aviation Department official arrived to inspect the wreckage the next day, it had been burned. Queensland's Senior Department Aircraft Inspector had decided there was nothing to see because the plane was smashed to matchwood. The tail was found more than one and a half kilometres from the crash site and appeared to have broken away from the plane in flight, while under a heavy side pressure such as occurs when a plane spins out of control.

Fysh disagreed. 'After the flying boats came on in 1938 and our old pilots went to them, the DH86 aircraft continued to operate on the inland run between Brisbane and Darwin. This aeroplane required good pilot training and undoubtedly our standard had dropped on this secondary service. We experienced a number of accidents; but the only one which could be classed as a disaster was on the occasion when Pilot Swaffield took off from Archerfield aerodrome,

Brisbane, into heavy cloud and a few minutes later came out of it out of control. He crashed and all were killed. However, this accident was put down not to structural failure but to the effects of blind flying in cloud.'[10]

Fifty years later the British magazine *Aeroplane Monthly* revealed that the Air Ministry in Britain had ordered a number of investigations into the DH86 in 1936. The Aeroplane Armament Experimental Establishment at Martlesham Heath took on the investigations after three fatal DH86 crashes in Europe. The first involved a DH86 owned by Qantas business partner Imperial Airways just three weeks after the *Loina* had smashed into the sea off Australia. That same year a British Airways DH86 was lost in Germany and two weeks after that another British Airways DH86 crashed during take-off at Gatwick outside London. It is not known whether the results of the British tests were ever conveyed to Australia, but they emphatically condemned the design of the plane. Handling trials showed that when the plane was flying between 177 kph and 193 kph, there was a long interval between the pilot moving the control wheel and the aileron responding. When it did respond, it was erratic and not in proportion to the pilot's movements.

The British testers also confirmed the Australian findings that there was a marked twisting of the wing. The controls were not in harmony. Flying at up to 217 kph involved the plane moving bodily from side to side. When the centre of gravity was pushed to the back the plane rolled, dropping the outer wing, and became hard to control. The testers were so horrified they did not complete the airworthiness trials. Their report said: 'Night landing trials were not considered advisable. The aeroplane was only satisfactory to fly in calm air and for the gentlest of manoeuvres. In bumpy weather and when executing normal manoeuvres for the class of aeroplane, it becomes nearly unmanageable. It is recommended that the Certificates of Airworthiness . . . should be withdrawn pending remedial modification.'[11]

The manufacturer responded with a number of modifications, including an increased tailplane area and the addition of vertical endplates to the tail to counter the swing. It worked and the British planes were modified. Ten new planes were built, called the DH86B, and three of those flew a service between Sydney and New Guinea. None of the improvements were passed on to Qantas – if they had been and the planes modified, the final DH86 crash in 1942 need not have happened.

But if there was something the British needed to tell the Australians, there was something Qantas had been keeping under its flying hat too. In his book *Air Crash*, Macarthur Job produced a startling interview with Qantas Superintendent of Operations Lester Brain, conducted just before his death. Brain recounted how he went over to England to ferry the first DH86 out to Australia.

On arrival at Hatfield he found the only DH86 being tested had a single cockpit. Brain was horrified. Pilot fatigue on the three-and-a-half-day flight to Singapore made such an arrangement highly unsafe and he immediately made representations to Imperial's managing director, G. Woods Humphery, about redesigning the nose to allow side-by-side controls for two pilots. Humphery was 'a bit amazed', but talked to de Havilland, who said it would cost 10 kph in lost speed, add to the aircraft's weight and cause a six-to-eight-week delay. Brain cabled Fysh in Australia, who cabled back his rock solid support: 'If that's what Brain thinks, then that's what we want and we'll put up with the delay.'

It turned out that the two-pilot version was actually 8 kph faster because the longer new nose had better streamlining. Brain then picked up the remainder of the routine test flying of the plane. Initial testing had been done by de Havilland's chief test pilot, Hubert Broad, who cleared the aircraft for commercial flight. Brain felt Broad, who had a very high reputation in England as a test pilot, had 'let the show down'. Brain argued that it was not about how well a test pilot can fly a plane, but how the aircraft would fly in the hands of an average commercial pilot over an extended period. Broad should have 'corrected the details', argued Brain, before going on to list the flaws with the DH86:

> Apart from the DH86's very flat gliding angle and its need for some form of airbreak (necessitating the later fitting of flaps to the upper wing), the aeroplane was directionally unstable. Flying hands off, natural stability should have been enough to maintain course. But if you let the DH86 get down to about 90 mph [145 kph] in a slightly nose-up attitude, it was inclined to wander directionally and the variations tended to increase. Application of corrective rudder seemed to have no immediate effect until, with increased rudder deflection, the machine would suddenly flick from a turn in one direction to a turn in the opposite direction. This could be very frightening.[13]

Brain also took issue with the plane's primitive undercarriage, a cylinder containing an inadequate number of rubber blocks, which he described as making the plane behave like a 'cat on hot bricks' on landing. His letter of complaint to Woods Humphery was snubbed, with the Imperial chief deferring to the all-clear given by his own test pilot, Major Brackley, and de Havilland's Hubert Broad. Brain, however, was to be proven correct. The plane was to get its first real public test by flying the Minister for Air to Paris. Imperial pilot Captain Wilcockson had to test the twin-pilot version the day before the Paris trip. He landed and announced that he 'wasn't taking the Minister anywhere until something was done about that undercarriage'. Woods Humphery later told Brain: 'I thought you were a bit presumptuous, but evidently you were quite correct.'[14]

The first two Qantas DH86 aircraft were to be flown to Australia from England, with three more following by ship. Qantas was anxious to get on with crew training. Brain was taken aside by one of Imperial's senior pilots, Captain Prendergast, and asked if he could recommend him as the pilot to bring out the second aircraft. It would prove a fatal favour. Brain took the first plane with a young English first officer called Price and a flight engineer called Pink. Experts armed with slide rules and charts loaded the plane with spare parts, including a spare engine on a wooden trestle bolted and wired to the floor, all carefully checked to ensure that the centre of gravity remained within the manufacturer's guidelines. However, on take-off, Brain found the tail would not lift and he only managed to get off the ground with both hands pushing hard on the control column. In flight, it was also a problem and remained so all the way to Lyon in France.

He recalled, 'The first thing I did there was to get a ladder and remove all sorts of spare parts from the rear freight compartment. Then I transferred the magnetos and other heavy equipment to the nose locker in the long "snout". From then on the loading was reasonable and the aeroplane could be trimmed to fly hands off, though it was still not stable.'[15]

The DH86 flew on to Rome, Catania in Sicily, Benghazi in North Africa and then took off again on a beautiful morning with perfect visibility towards the RAF base at Mersa Matruh in Egypt. At 6,000 feet and half an hour out of Benghazi, Brain needed to use the toilet at the rear of the aircraft. Knowing it was already tail heavy, he handed control over to Price and got Pink to sit in his cockpit seat to counterbalance the effect of his weight going towards the rear.

Having 'tested' the toilet satisfactorily I sat down in the little folding seat near the door at the rear of the cabin. Sitting there enjoying the break, I felt the aeroplane begin to yaw to the left. I smiled to myself knowing that Price was about to keep a radio schedule, expecting he would correct the course. But instead the aeroplane suddenly yawed to the right. This continued to increase, then the machine swung rapidly back to the left as though beginning a flat spin. Luggage in the hat racks tumbled out on to the seats and I feared the spare engine might come adrift. I started back up the cabin as quickly as I could to the cockpit. 'Out of that seat and let me in,' I yelled at Pink. I never saw such scared looking fellows in my life – they were pale green.

I hopped into my seat and got the machine under control. By this time we had lost two or three thousand feet – it was plain that the directional problem was greater in a tail heavy aeroplane. I turned to Price and asked what happened. He said the controls must have carried away – they weren't working.

They seemed normal now, but there was a sliding panel in the bottom of the cabin door for dropping mail bags at outback places, so I sent Pink back to look through it to check the tail bracing wires were all intact. He reported that no wires were broken. Price still argued there was something wrong, but I believed he had let the aeroplane get a little nose up and it had got away from him.[16]

They landed at Mersa Matruh without further drama. But Brain later recalled: 'I remember this incident particularly because the second aeroplane followed about three weeks later, flown by my old friend Prendergast. After leaving Longreach for Brisbane on a lovely fine morning, his DH86 was observed to be flying along and then go into a flat spin. They were all killed.'[17]

Brain was in Brisbane when he heard of the tragedy and immediately jumped into a Puss Moth with Arthur Baird and flew eight hours to get there. As he was looking over the wreckage, a local man described what had happened. Brain thought quietly to himself: 'It nearly happened to me.'

Half an hour out of Benghazi, a few minutes out of Longreach! On each occasion a beautiful fine day, and in each case the same crew disposition and same cargo loading. I think the cause of the crash was identical to the problem we encountered – directional instability increased by tail heaviness, and the first officer distracted by having to keep a radio schedule.

I believe this proved beyond doubt that the aeroplane was dangerously unstable directionally. While it could be flown safely provided pilots thoroughly understood the features of the aeroplane, what it needed was more fin area. This was done on the DH86B which, in addition to the central fin and rudder, had two vertical fins, one at each tip of the tailplane. I never flew the DH86B but Captain Dick Man and others who flew them on the New Guinea run told me they never had any trouble.[18]

Brain knew there was a problem with the DH86. He never raised the alarm and, even after his friend Captain Prendergast died, Brain stayed silent. Job, the seasoned air-crash investigator, asks why Brain would not reveal the stability problems at the time. Why did he insist his delivery flight had been trouble free? Why did he offer no reason for the second DH86 going into a flat spin at Longreach? Job provides his own answer. 'Brain no doubt had his reasons – there was much at stake for him personally, for Qantas, for Australia's new venture as an international airline operator. For him, as he saw it, as indeed for Fysh, the DH86 "had to be right." '[19]

QF4

QANTAS AT WAR

'THERE WAS PRACTICALLY no warning. I heard the sirens and the roar of the Japanese planes almost simultaneously,' said Qantas captain Aubrey Koch. He was lying in a hospital bed in Darwin, recuperating after being shot down three weeks before. 'Three [bombs] landed very close. The walls shook and pieces of the ceiling fell in. One of the bombs had hit a wing of the hospital . . . After the first wave of bombers had passed I decided to make for the beach. I could only just walk . . . Some of the Jap machines were diving low and machine-gunning buildings. I could hear the crunch of bombs in other parts of the town. The machines were sweeping over ships in the harbour.'[1]

On 19 February 1942, the Japanese commander who

ordered the devastating attack on Pearl Harbor, Admiral Nagumo, despatched 188 aircraft into the bright, sunny sky. The fighters, bombers and dive-bombers leaving the decks of the four aircraft carriers were followed by a second wave of 54 land-based bombers. In radio silence they headed for a completely unsuspecting Darwin in Australia's Northern Territory.

Bobbing at her moorings south-east of the jetty in Darwin harbour was the Qantas flying boat *Camilla*. She was close to the 11,000 tonne ammunition-carrying merchant ship *Neptuna*, which was tied up alongside the wharf. The Qantas pilots were going about their normal business. Captain H. B. Hussey was sitting in the Roslyn Court building's barber shop waiting for his turn. Captain W. H. 'Bill' Crowther was in the middle of shaving.

As the Japanese planes began their deadly attack, Captain Hussey came flying out of the barber's, through the yard of the Victoria Hotel, looking for open space. Others, including a Mrs Hansen, joined him. Captain Hussey described in his official Qantas report seeing a second formation of bombers appear over their heads from where the sun was sitting in the south-east. When the bombs came down, he said they all sheltered in a concrete street gutter as debris flew through the air. Then, 'Captain Crowther appeared around the corner mostly sideways, trying to run, turn the corner and watch for falling missiles at the same time. With his shirt front open and soap around his ears, it was evident that he had been shaving.'[2]

Above them the Japanese planes were under the command of Captain Mitsuo Fuchida, who had led the attack on Pearl Harbor. He was backed by exactly the same crews that had so successfully hit the unsuspecting American fleet. They had five more planes than the earlier attack on Pearl Harbor and had as a target a relatively small harbour densely packed with 45 ships and very little air defence. The Japanese wreaked havoc.

Captain Hussey and his companions had to lie low to avoid the dive-bombers, who were now using their guns on ground targets. He and Captain Crowther had formed a small group of Qantas Empire Airlines staff. They bundled into a car and, with Mrs Hansen at the wheel, tore through the devastated streets to the Qantas base. There, to their astonishment, they found the *Camilla* afloat and untouched. But the *Neptuna*, outside the wharf, and the *Barossa*, on the inside, were both alight. Their smoke was hanging over the *Camilla*, hiding the Qantas flying boat from the attacking Japanese planes. The two Qantas pilots commandeered a launch that was unloading wet and injured men on the jetty and raced out to the *Camilla*. A quick check revealed only two small shrapnel holes in the elevators. Crowther took the controls while Hussey primed the engines, checked the petrol and cast off the mooring rope.

Crowther took up the story. 'I was figuring out the best way to get away from the *Neptuna* as quickly as possible. I became quite impatient as I had never seen such a holocaust before. The ship was burning most fiercely and with bright crimson colour.'[3] With the engines started they began taxiing down the east arm of Darwin Bay. At first they considered hiding out in the mangroves but abandoned the plan as unrealistic. Together they managed to remove all the ropes from outside the plane and secure the hatches. 'Just as we got over the mangroves,' he said, 'there was a bang and a bump downstairs, which gave us a fright, but on examination I found the pantry window open.'[4]

Just eight minutes after the *Camilla* took off, the *Neptuna*, laden with explosives, blew up with such force that she was shifted some 25 metres from the wharf before capsizing. All small craft in the area were sunk.

In total the Japanese attack sank nine ships in the harbour and badly damaged 13 others. Two Catalina flying boats were sunk at their moorings, many buildings in Darwin were damaged and the aerodrome and RAAF buildings, planes and hangars were all hit. An estimated 300 people were killed in the bombing raid. The Qantas building was also destroyed. QEA station engineer Norm Roberts was desperately trying to conceal the Qantas launch in the mangroves as a Japanese Zero strafed them in the water.

Hussey and Crowther at first pointed the *Camilla* towards the Alligator River but then, on reflection, instead turned to Groote Island, where they landed and took on 6,370 litres of petrol. Captain Crowther still had the dried soap from his interrupted shave on his ears. That afternoon, and in radio silence, they returned to the smoking ruins of Darwin ready for a dawn departure to Sydney. Among the passengers they safely conveyed to the harbour city was the badly injured Captain Koch.

The war ended what was a golden age of flying for Qantas. The airline had bought a fleet of flying boats that summed up the spirit and romance of exotic luxury travel. In *Qantas at War* Hudson Fysh describes the joy of travelling on a flying boat: 'Getting up out of his chair, a passenger could walk about and, if he had been seated in the main cabin, stroll along to the smoking cabin for a smoke, stopping on the way at the promenade deck with its high handrail and windows at eye level to gaze at the world of cloud and sky outside.'[5] It was not unusual to enjoy a game of quoits or mini-golf on the promenade deck to break up the monotony of the journey.

At fuelling stops, passengers and crew would hang fishing lines over the side in some of the world's most exotic locations. And it was luxurious. The cabin was made up with beds similar to a first-class rail journey for night flying. But more often the 15 passengers would overnight in luxury waterfront accommodation such as Raffles Hotel in Singapore. Hot meals were packed in thermos and vacuum flasks. Passengers would receive hot roasts for dinner and poached eggs for breakfast even though the plane did not have a galley. Oysters were packed on ice and portions were so big that they were often left unfinished. There was only one class – first – and the fare from Sydney to London was the equivalent of the average national wage. The service was so luxurious that Fysh felt Qantas had set a standard that would be an example the world over for service on airlines.

The British government wanted to run an airmail service to every corner of the empire using the flying boats. The dream was for all post to be carried swiftly by air at no surcharge. It never happened, but it did mean the business brains at Qantas knew there was a market for its services. There were problems. The Dutch airline KLM was making threatening noises about running its Indonesian service into Australia. Australia's government air watchdog, Edgar Johnston, was convinced the future lay in American-built land planes. The Australian government opposed the idea of flying boats, as did the RAAF. But Qantas knew the DH86 contract was due to expire by 1939 and there would be no real four-engined land-based planes ready in time to cross the seas.

Qantas chairman Fergus McMaster went to Britain, where Imperial had commissioned the Short Brothers to build 28 all-metal Empire-class flying boats, and returned convinced they were the answer to Qantas's problems. Chief pilot Lester Brain agreed and Hudson Fysh set off with Imperial's Major H. G. 'Brackles' Brackley on a flying boat route survey. They eventually chose a route to Singapore via Brisbane, Gladstone, an overnight stop in Townsville, across the Cape York Peninsula, to Karumba, Groote Eyelandt and on to Darwin. From there the route went across the Timor Sea, to Kupang, Bima, Surabaya and Jakarta and, finally, Singapore. British Imperial Airlines would then take over the plane and fly the rest of the route to London via India, the Middle East and Egypt. Although the two airlines operated the routes separately, the idea was that they would be interchangeable. Fysh shrewdly insisted that the Australian end have its own engine overhaul facility to prevent the problem of a four-month delay in shipping engines to England for repairs. Qantas decided it needed six flying boats for the job, at a cost to shareholders of £480,000. In January 1937 Australian Prime Minister Joe Lyons gave the scheme the green light.

Now Qantas needed to teach its crews how to handle flying boats. Chief pilot Brain spent £28 on a 12 foot (3.6 metre) sailing dinghy to give the crews some lessons in 'seamanship' on Sydney Harbour. According to Fysh, in most respects it was safer to land on water than on land, but because water could vary in terms of flatness and turbulence, great care had to be taken, especially when approaching or leaving the moorings. When the water was extremely flat and smooth, it was very hard for the pilot to see where its surface began.

The crews trained on a Cutty Sark amphibian flying boat purchased for £700 from World War One fighter ace Keith Caldwell when he joined Qantas. The plane came to an untimely end on the Brisbane River. Captain Crowther, who would later pilot the *Camilla* out of Darwin, landed on the river with the wheels extended and nose-dived into the water. No one was injured but the plane was written off by the salvage crew, which crushed the hull with the steel cable it used to lift it from the bottom. Despite the setbacks, and after full training in London, Qantas was ready to begin the service.

The flying boats *Coolangatta* and *Cooee* flew to the new Qantas landing strip – Rose Bay in Sydney Harbour – to begin the service. The official agreement, under which Qantas was to provide three return services a week from Sydney to Singapore, was signed on 23 July 1938. But the first flight left Rose Bay earlier, on 5 July. The *Cooee* went to Singapore under the command of Captain Lynch-Blosse and was then taken on by an Imperial flight crew to London.

Meanwhile, the Imperial flying boat *Challenger*, under the command of legendary Qantas Captain 'Scotty' Allan, arrived in Darwin on 4 July in darkness and during a gale. Customs officials in Darwin were ill prepared and the crew and passengers, including several journalists on board for the maiden flight, were left bobbing at the moorings in heavy swell. They all became seasick and, according to Fysh, 'were fairly ropeable . . . There was a hell of a row. The wires ran hot round the world. Darwin overnight became famous, or infamous, and such was the stir that when the next flying boat arrived the passengers were quickly whisked away to the Don Hotel, where they were put through their formalities.'[6] The next service ran into engine trouble at Bima on Soembawa Island in the Dutch East Indies and a spare engine had to be sent up from Sydney.

At a stately 240 kph, the flying boat service from Sydney to Southampton took nine and a half days, a day longer than the Dutch took to fly from Sydney to Amsterdam. Unlike Qantas in later years, Fysh embraced the rivalry. He felt it renewed determination within the company, and dealt with any adverse criticism about the length of the journey by emphasising how comfortable and spacious the Qantas flying boats were, as well as reminding passengers they provided a full meal service.

However, the flying boat service was not without incident. Qantas lost its first one, the *Coorong*, during the overnight stay in Darwin on 12 December 1938. Strong winds were pulling the plane against her mooring lines. The station engineer Norm Roberts, who later behaved so heroically during the bombing of the harbour, went on board to run the engines and take the strain off the lines. Once all was secure, he returned to shore. Despite his efforts, as the winds picked up later, the lines broke and the plane was washed onto the jagged rocks of the breakwater. Chief pilot Lester

Brain was once again on hand and was quick to begin salvage work that saw the plane dismantled, shipped to England and eventually put back into service.

Then, on 12 March 1939, Captain Hussey was taxiing the *Capella* after landing at Batavia when the wreckage of a submerged frigate ripped a hole in her hull. The plane was quickly beached before it could sink. She was then shipped back to England but salt water damage rendered her inoperable.

Despite these two incidents, Qantas ran its service to Singapore and Britain for just over 13 months, until the outbreak of war in September 1939. It carried more than 5,000 passengers, 500 tonnes of mail and 100 tonnes of freight, including 400 dozen oysters a week to Singapore. During this time Qantas learned the skills needed to run a major passenger service and laid down the foundations it would need to go aggressively into business when the war ended six years later.

Qantas chairman Fergus McMaster had suffered a heart attack in 1937 and, though nominally in charge, left much of the running of Qantas to Fysh. He was naturally anxious about the war and where it would leave his beloved company. By 1942, he could see opportunities that would allow Qantas 'to see the war out on a profitable basis despite our losses of aircraft'.[7] The airline was quoting on a cost-plus basis for its services. Fysh said one of the biggest problems was fixing the rate of profit for its flying and repair work. Qantas sought what Fysh considered 'a most inadequate' seven and a half per cent and finally settled for six per cent.

In 1939 the flying boat service was stopped for just six days before resuming its airmail runs to Singapore. In fact, rather than curtailing business operations in 1940, Qantas took a

23 per cent share in Tasman Empire Airways Ltd (TEAL) to fly two Shorts flying boats between Sydney and Auckland in New Zealand. Its partners were Imperial, which became the British government-owned British Overseas Airways Corporation (BOAC), the New Zealand government and Union Airways of New Zealand. It added another 2,170 kilometre long leg to the 20,816 kilometre route between Southampton and Sydney.

It was a fast-changing world and Qantas adapted rapidly to cope with it. Engineers stripped the luxury furnishings from the flying boats and installed long-range fuel tanks to run an extended service to Karachi. To avoid Italy, which had joined the war, BOAC then flew the mail on a 'horse-shoe' route to Cairo and then on to Durban, from where the mail went by ship to Britain. Qantas pilots also performed the third ever flight across the Pacific as its neutral pilots delivered 19 Consolidated Catalina flying boats from the US, which had not yet joined the war. Lester Brain, who had been restrained by Fysh from joining up at the outset of war, took the lead role in the operation. The airline then borrowed two of those Catalinas to fulfil the Australian government's request to open up a service to Portuguese Timor. Throughout the war many Qantas staff performed incredibly heroic deeds and Fysh lobbied hard for his people to receive official recognition. Such was the importance of civil aviation in Australia during the war that Qantas had grown, with staff numbers increasing from 290 at the start to over 400 when Japan joined the conflict. At that point, everything changed.

When the Japanese bombed Singapore, Qantas Empire Airways immediately cut its stops at Bangkok and Penang, and Fysh was tasked with finding a withdrawal route that avoided the coast of Burma. The Singapore route was still operating but pilots reported it was becoming increasingly hazardous. When Singapore was under air attack, they landed in 'funk holes' in the quiet bays to the south and waited for the all-clear. The flying boats were shuttling refugees out to Batavia. It was dangerous work and on Friday 30 January 1942 Qantas Empire Airways suffered its first casualty of war.

Captain Aubrey Koch was flying with four crew and 13 passengers from Darwin to Surabaya to collect women and children refugees when they came under attack by Japanese Zero fighters. As they neared the shores of the island, Captain Koch described, in *Qantas at War*, hearing a distinctive rattling noise in the fuselage of the plane as the air was filled with bullets from an overhead attack. Captain Koch opened the throttle and dived down to the water, swerving and zigzagging to throw off the tracer bullets. Inside the cabin the bullets tore through the hull as the Qantas pilot took desperate evasive action. Koch was aiming for the beach 24 kilometres away, but he realised they were not going to make it. Two engines were on fire and the plane was losing speed. As he touched down, the badly holed hull caught in the water and the plane was tipped on its nose. 'I was thrown over the instrument panel and out through an opening caused by the impact. I then came to the surface. The aircraft was floating with the wings afloat on the water. There were seven Japanese Zero fighters circling about 1,500 ft overhead,' he said.[8]

Satisfied the plane was about to sink, the fighters left and the seven surviving crew and passengers held a hasty conference to decide what to do. Despite a wound to his leg, Captain Koch and a passenger called Mr Moore set out for the shore eight kilometres away with the intention of finding help. It took them three hours and, upon reaching the breakers on the beach, the indefatigable pilot found he had to be helped out of the water because his leg would not support him. It was 'a graze on the knee', he later reported in something of an understatement.[9] Meanwhile, the flying boat had caught fire and the other survivors had also struck out for the shore using baskets and mail bags as flotation devices – two did not make it.

Once they had regrouped on the beach the survivors, including First Officer Lyne with a graze on his neck, agreed that two of the passengers would go for help. They swam a 360-metre-wide crocodile infested river to raise the alarm. The five survivors were finally evacuated by a Dutch flying boat. Captain Koch made it back to the hospital in Darwin just in time to give his eyewitness account of the Japanese bombing three weeks later.

As the Japanese pushed into Java, refugees gathered on the south coast at Tjilatjap, which became an evacuation point to Broome in Western Australia. Singapore fell, with Captain Bill Crowther flying the last Qantas flight out on 4 February 1942. On 19 February, the day Darwin was bombed, he also flew the last flight out of Batavia. A great deal of activity was now centred on Broome, with 8,000 refugees, many with dengue fever, and Dutch flying boats, military land planes, transports and bombers all crowded into the tiny town and its harbour. Qantas flying boats played a vital role in the hazardous operation. Two Qantas Catalinas, *Circe* and

Corinthian, left on the same day but only *Corinthian* made it back to Broome. *Circe*, with Captain Bill Purton in charge, was never found. It was presumed shot down by enemy aircraft. A search by Qantas flying boat *Corinthian* found no trace of *Circe* but located the crew of an American DC3 on an isolated beach north of Broome.

Qantas chief pilot Lester Brain had arrived in Broome on 21 February and reported that most of the refugees appeared jittery, 'as though the Japanese were close behind them'.[10] Although the Qantas planes were originally intended to take supplies into Java, it quickly became clear that it would fall and instead the flying boats went out empty and returned full with refugees. On one day alone there were 57 landings and Brain worried the activity could attract Japanese attention. He was right.

On the morning of 3 March 1942 Japanese fighters, gleaming silver in the early morning sun, flashed over Broome with machine guns blazing. Tracer bullets tore through the 15, mostly Dutch, Dornier flying boats, waiting to be fuelled in the harbour. The lead fighter took the Qantas flying boat *Centaurus*, which was under charter to the RAAF, as its first target. It burst into flames under a withering hail of fire. Captain Ambrose was refuelling the Catalina *Corinna*, as 25 passengers stood with their baggage on the jetty waiting to get on board and the Zeros, with the red rising sun insignias clear on their wings, swooped down. The Japanese bullets ripped it apart and, as he described in John Gunn's book *Challenging Horizons*, Ambrose witnessed the frantic rescue operation to save those who had already been loaded on to the flying boats. He was disparaging about the people of Broome, who fled as soon as the raid began, but he described how the flight crews and other personnel made valiant efforts to save passengers in peril from drowning or being burned to death, as they struggled to swim away from the fuel leaking into the sea out of tanks that had been peppered with bullets. None of the *Corinna*'s 25 passengers was harmed in the end.

Captain Brain, weak and ill from dengue fever and lack of food, looked out from his hotel window as the Japanese fighters wreaked havoc on the helpless flying boats. 'Shouts and screams can be heard coming across the water from the burning boats and it appears that when the Japs have finished there will be nothing left afloat to rescue the survivors,' he recorded in his diary.[11] Despite his weakened state he struggled to drag a rowboat down to the water's edge with the help of Malcolm Millar, who had been in charge in Java. 'After getting about half a mile out we could see heads bobbing in the water and hear shouts for help. On coming up we found seven Dutchmen, two of them supporting a Dutch woman who was in a state of collapse. Another was swimming on his back supporting a young baby and keeping its head above water. The others were keeping contact with a Dutch boy of about eight who was able to swim and support himself. We got the woman and baby, also the boy and three of the most exhausted men aboard the rowboat, and the remaining four clung to the edge. We could not handle any more, so returned to the nearest mangrove beach.'[12]

A 17-year-old Dutch girl swam for two hours to help her injured mother and another man to shore, and then told how she saw sharks take a woman and child who had been with them. The Japanese attack destroyed all the flying boats in the harbour, six land planes at the aerodrome, the Liberator that managed to take off and a Douglas DC3 96 kilometres north of Broome. Estimates suggest 70 people were killed. The Qantas flying boat *Camilla*, so bravely rescued from the attack on Darwin, was saved by Brain's caution. He told pilot Captain Sims not to return until 11 am, after the *Corinna* was due to have left for Sydney, because he did not want two company planes in the harbour at the same time. However, *Camilla*'s luck would also soon run out.

'Back in Sydney early in March 1942 we counted our losses, licked our wounds, and wondered how we were going to carry on as effective airline operators,' said Fysh.[13] The overseas service had been cut and half of the ten flying boats owned by Qantas and BOAC had been destroyed. Qantas was left with just its land plane service between Brisbane and Darwin, a couple of other provincial Queensland routes and three Empire flying boats: *Camilla*, *Corinthian* and *Coriolanus*. Matters became worse when the *Corinthian* crashed on landing in Darwin Harbour. Captain Ambrose was flying the plane with the equally experienced Captain Tapp as first officer. There were 12 US military passengers on board and a heavy load of gun barrels, ammunition chests and reels of wire. As the plane came in to land at 1 am on 22 March, the planing bottom broke up. Fysh believed it may have struck a submerged object that split the bottom; the heavy load then shifted and caused the plane to capsize. A rescue launch rushed to the scene and picked up survivors. Captain Tapp, realising that two people were missing, bravely swam into the darkened hull of the sinking wreck but could not find them. Their bodies were never recovered.

Fysh now had an airline with few aircraft. He was keen to re-establish a link between the two ends of the Empire route – a non-stop service of 5,656 kilometres between Ceylon and Perth. Qantas pilots Brain and Crowther thought it would be possible with American Catalina flying boats. Director General of Civil Aviation A. B. Corbett felt otherwise and wrote to Fysh: 'My reaction is that at present such a proposal would be little short of murder.'[14] McMaster and Fysh continued to lobby for it as the other work of the war carried on unabated. At one point, two Qantas DH86 aircraft were sent to Mount Hagen in the heart of New Guinea to bring out refugees. Their plight had been highlighted by a missionary called Father Glover, who used every conceivable mode of transport through enemy lines and across the sea to raise the alarm. Captain Orme Denny led the flights in, but found when he came to take off that the wheels sank into the soft ground. Undeterred, he encouraged the natives to perform a ceremonial 'sing sing' dance on the airstrip. Several hours later the landing strip was compacted enough for take-off. Qantas planes then joined the 'biscuit bombers' dropping supplies to Australian troops in Papua New Guinea. As operations continued, Fysh flew to London to lobby for the resumption of the Empire route.

On 22 April 1943 the redoubtable Captain Aubrey Koch was in command of the *Camilla*, flying from Townsville with 22 RAAF personnel and five Americans on a regular taxi flight. As he came to Port Moresby in light rain he found his way into the harbour and a safe landing blocked by dense black cyclonic cloud. Lester Brain's official report said: 'Thick weather intensified and spread. Koch was circling at low altitude on instruments [which was] unsafe and perhaps impossible. [He] turned and flew away over the water on a straight course on instruments, undoubtedly the correct action to take.' It was a dreadful position to be in. 'He had no option, and his final decision to land when his fuel was nearly exhausted was the only competent decision to make. [He] displayed sure, cool judgement and a very high standard of endurance and morale (two hours flying under extremely onerous conditions).'[15]

Landing on instruments in the darkness, Koch and his first officer misjudged the altitude and the plane stalled on landing, rapidly broke up and sank. Koch, who had already had to swim to shore after being shot down by Japanese Zeros the year before, spent 18 hours swimming before being picked up together with 17 other survivors in the afternoon of the next day.

On the same day *Camilla* crashed, Fysh's intensive lobbying at the very highest levels of British government was rewarded with news from the English director-general of Civil Aviation, William Hildred, that four Catalinas would be supplied for the operation of an Indian Ocean service from Ceylon to Perth. Qantas was back in business with the first Kangaroo Route.

Crew and passengers who took the flight were given a certificate as members of the 'secret order of the double sunrise' because they saw two sunrises on the same journey.[16] It was a marathon effort flown through enemy territory in complete radio silence and with so much fuel on board that emergency flying on a single engine could not be achieved until eight to ten hours into the flight. The lumbering planes had a top speed of just 204 kph. Qantas left the British roundels on its planes but gave them civil registration numbers and named them after stars: *Altair Star, Vega Star, Rigel Star, Antares Star* and, when a fifth plane arrived, *Spica Star*. The journey from the Qantas Empire Airways base on the Swan River in Perth to Koggala Lake in Ceylon was 5,652 kilometres, the longest journey undertaken anywhere in the world at the time.

The first flight left Perth on 29 June 1943 with Captain Russell Tapp in command. Fysh himself took the eighth service from Ceylon to Perth on his way back from England. Captain Crowther was commanding with legendary Australian navigator Jim Cowan charting the course. He would later use his skills to navigate routes for Qantas over the Indian and Pacific Oceans. The *Vega Star* left at 8 am on 30 August 1943. In his diary Fysh notes: '8.30 am. We are at 2,400 ft and our airspeed is 105 mph. Capt Crowther says it will be 11 hours before the aircraft has a single engine performance. This knowledge of twice the risk of a forced descent as compared with a single engined aircraft, plus the fact that we have no dump valves, plus the sea below, plus the fact that we are flying into Japanese patrolled areas lends a spice of adventure and risk to this trip.'[17]

It was a long, lonely flight. Fysh's diary captures a sense of the isolation experienced by the flyers as they drone steadily on over an empty, moonlit ocean: 'Midnight. The stars are shining bright and Crowther and Cowan have just taken a shot on *Vega*. Canopus is very bright and twinkling. Mars gleams steadily and I am told he is a most useful being, to the eye, hung in the midnight firmament at right angles to our course. Orion's Belt is rising, and the dagger of the handle of the saucepan is hidden by the big wing of the Catalina.'[18]

The Qantas Empire Airways Catalinas completed 271 of these long, dangerous crossings without the loss of a plane or life before the flights ended two weeks before the defeat of Japan in July 1945. However, Qantas continued to lose planes before then. On 18 January 1944 the *Clifton*, which had just returned from work with the RAAF, bounced, stalled and sank while landing at Rose Bay. Then, on 11 October 1944, the Empire flying boat *Coolangatta*, with Qantas hero Captain Brain in command, also stalled on landing at Rose Bay. The plane was lost and a passenger killed. Captain Brain survived. Years later, in 1968, Fysh reflected: 'This resulted in a further tightening of our Operations organisation in an attempt to put a stop to our dreadful run of accidents. In looking back I hope that all this pain, and experience, and groping for a better organisation has had some helpful part in the formation of the splendid operational organisation with which the present-day QEA is blessed.'[19]

QF5

THE BIG LIE

On 25 August 1960 Qantas Captain E. W. Ditton taxied the Lockheed Super Constellation onto the start of Runway 13 at Plaisance airport in Mauritius and opened the throttles to 35 inches of manifold pressure. The four supercharged 18-cylinder engines roared, spinning the propellers as the plane carrying 12 crew began to accelerate along the runway. The 38 passengers sitting behind in luxury were looking forward to the elegant cabin service and fully reclining seats after their stopover en route from Johannesburg to Sydney. Outside, the raindrops on the windows began to be pushed horizontally as the plane picked up speed. On the flight deck the first officer, S. D. Patrick, took over the duplicate throttles and pushed the plane to 112 knots – 207 kph. But instead of acknowledging take-off moments later, the flight engineer shouted: 'Failure number three!'[1]

Captain Ditton slammed off the power, braked hard and threw the engines into maximum reverse thrust. The giant plane with its 59,850 kilogram weight was not stopping. The captain applied maximum braking as the flight engineer feathered troubled engine number three and then shut it off. The Super Constellation slipped along the wet concrete runway and, still travelling at 75 kph with the engines howling at maximum reverse thrust, overshot the end. It ploughed through the grass safety strip, bumped over an embankment and plummeted, nose down, into a rocky gully 100 metres from the end of the runway. The port wing-tip tank burst on impact and a fire began, inflamed by aviation fuel pouring onto the ground from other ruptured tanks. Thick black acrid smoke rose into the air.

The tower controller immediately despatched fire trucks towards the stricken plane. They were overtaken by the Qantas Mauritius base staff, former navigator Jim Cowan and engineers D. J. Kennedy and R. P. Barrett, who had seen the plane get into trouble from the balcony of the terminal building and raced downstairs to hurtle towards it in the company car. The aircraft was fully laden with fuel and the wing tanks, with extra fuel pods on the wing tips, were ablaze. Captain Ditton came into the cabin where the passengers were badly shaken up but not injured. 'All out,' he commanded.[2] Pandemonium ensued. Children screamed, doors jammed and the crew dashed back to help. There were no emergency slides. Passengers and crew had a three-metre jump onto rocks.

When the ground crew arrived they found the crew

struggling with a large lady who had broken her ankle jumping from the emergency exit at the rear of the plane. Scrub
was burning around her. Cowan immediately helped to move
her while the two engineers fearlessly climbed back into the
blazing fuselage and ran the full length of it to make sure
no one was left on board. A threatening rumble reverberated
through the stricken Constellation. Although fire crews had
started spraying foam on the plane, they could not reach the
front and there was 5,000 litres of highly flammable aviation
fuel on board. 'Time to go,' shouted Kennedy.[3] They jumped
down to the rocks and sprinted through the burning scrub
to safety. The company coach ferried the badly shaken passengers back to their hotel, where they were treated for cuts,
abrasions and burns. A six-year-old child had her fractured
arm strapped and the woman with the broken ankle was
taken to hospital.

The Australian Department of Civil Aviation's expert on
Super Constellations, Jim Brough, investigated the crash.
The failure of engine number three to reach full power had
precipitated the accident. But it was the failure of the flight
engineer to call out a warning in time and then the captain's
delay in applying reverse thrust and full braking power that
had greatly contributed to the ensuing accident. On receipt
of the comprehensive report, the department's director-
general, Donald Anderson, said: 'This was a "cheap" accident
for Qantas . . . the important thing is to ensure the company
acknowledges the weaknesses involved in bringing it about
and is made to see it was completely avoidable.'[4]

His comments could so easily have applied to the runway
overrun in Bangkok 39 years later, in which an even bigger

jet would have remarkably similar problems, as described in chapter 1. Had Qantas learned anything from the mistakes of the past? As crash investigator Macarthur Job pointed out in his flight safety report on the 1960 crash: 'Spared what could so easily have been tragic consequences by a frighteningly slim margin, Qantas's public composure seemed unaffected. But behind the scenes the accident was a serious affront to the airline's pride after so many years of accident-free flying – especially so in light of its expanding jet network.'[5]

It was ironic that almost at exactly the same moment the Super Constellation VH-EAC *Southern Wave* was burning on the end of a runway in Mauritius, the Australian Minister for Civil Aviation, Senator Shane Paltridge, was tabling the Qantas Annual Report for 1959–60 extolling its safety record. The report boasted that the airline had flown 238 million kilometres since 1946 without a major incident or fatality. However, the families of the seven people who died on board Qantas flight VH-EBQ on 16 July 1951 when the centre propeller of their de Havilland DHA-3 Drover failed, causing the plane to crash into the Huon Gulf near Papua New Guinea, may have had cause to argue with Senator Paltridge's assessment.

Even before World War Two had ended, the governments, airlines and aircraft manufacturers of the allied victors were jostling for position and dominance in the newly peaceful world. Naturally the Americans thought they should run everything. The British were leaning heavily on their colonial past and pushing strongly for Australia to use British planes in partnership on the Kangaroo Route. In Australia the Curtin government was making no secret of its plans to nationalise the Australian domestic and international airlines.

Hudson Fysh continued to fight ferociously for Qantas and its future. In October 1944 he flew to London to discuss the airline's next steps, taking one of two Qantas-owned Liberators on its regular service across the Indian Ocean. 'Our two Libs are the world's oldest and worst Libs on the world's longest air hop,' he noted.[6] On arrival he discovered: 'Britain had nothing but second-rate aircraft to offer for use on overseas routes.'[7] Undaunted, Qantas decided to make do with converted Lancaster bombers until a better option became available. The nose and tail-gun turrets were stripped out and nine seated or six sleeping passengers crammed uncomfortably into the fuselage. The biggest benefit came from the four Rolls-Royce Merlin engines, which powered the planes from Sydney to London in just 67 hours – a dramatic improvement on the nine and a half days it had taken in 1939.

Qantas operated the planes from Sydney to Karachi and BOAC took over from Karachi to London. In 1946 one of Qantas's 'most able commanders' was flying the Lancaster G-AGLX from Ratmalana in Ceylon (now Sri Lanka) to the scheduled stopover on the Cocos Islands.[8] As per routine, he called in his position and reported the flight was normal. There were some showers at the Cocos Islands, 1,111 kilometres ahead. And then nothing. The aircraft was never seen or heard from again. Ten passengers and crew were on board, including the son of Sir Roy Dobson, head of the Avro Company, which built the plane. 'We felt quite upset about it all,' said Fysh in his book *Wings to the World*.[9] Thirteen aircraft were scrambled to look for the Lancaster but nothing was found. Fysh speculated that the cause could have been light-ning coupled with a fuel leak – the converted bombers often smelled strongly of fuel at the rear of the fuselage.

The loss of the converted Lancaster came just before Qan-tas resumed its Singapore service. It now ran an express mail service with the fast Lancasters, and a slower but more luxu-rious service taking five and a half days with Hythe flying boats – an improved version of the old pre-war Empire flying boats. At the close of World War Two, Fysh noted that Qan-tas had come out of the war with a profit and a good 'scratch' operation of aircraft and routes, as the battle for the future of civil aviation loomed.

The world was changing. The charter of the United Nations was signed and in April 1945 31 nations met and signed the articles of association of the International Air Transport Association (IATA). In Australia the Labor government of Ben Chifley passed the Australian National Airlines bill to nationalise the aviation industry. The domestic carrier Aus-tralian National Airways fought it, but for Qantas the die was cast. Stopped from nationalising Ansett and ANA, the gov-ernment set up Trans-Australia Airlines (TAA) to operate domestic routes and recruited the loyal Qantas hand Lester Brain to run it. The government then set its eyes on Qantas. Against this backdrop of political and financial manoeu-vring, Fysh had his sights on something that would be equally important to Qantas's future – Lockheed Constella-tion aircraft. Britain was pushing for Australia to take what Fysh called 'forlorn hopes': the Yorks, the Hermes, the San-dringhams and the Tudor IIs.[10] At Australian government level Fysh's case for Constellations was greatly helped when the Air Ministry in London sent 'misleading figures' comparing the as yet unflown Tudor II with the Constellation.[11]

In September 1946 Fysh managed to secure a meeting with Prime Minister Chifley. In his Qantas history, *Wings to the World*, Fysh recalled the meeting with the Prime Minister at Victoria Barracks in Melbourne. The minister responsible for the upcoming government purchase of Qantas, Arthur Drakeford, went in first:

> Then a long fidgety wait before at last I was ushered into the presence. A visit to any PM is always something of great import to a person such as myself. Such a man has the weight of the country's affairs and problems on his mind.
>
> Smoking his pipe as usual, his puffs floating upwards in the still, rarefied air of the Barracks, Chifley invited me to sit down. In front of him on his pad lay the leaves of an urgent telegram. He did not waste words. He and Drakeford had made up their minds and did not want to hear any more.
>
> Said Chifley, fingering the telegram, 'You see this? It is an urgent telegram from Clem Atlee, Prime Minister of England, begging us not to go on with those Constellations you want.'
>
> A pause, a smile, and then he said: 'Well, anyhow, I have decided. We'll give it a go.[12]

Fysh, giddy with success, hung on the strap of the tram back into the city, where he went to the GPO to send a telegram to Sir Fergus McMaster in Brisbane, notifying him of his success. Ironically, and despite the intense pressure from the British government, BOAC itself went ahead and bought the superior American planes. It ordered the bigger and more expensive Boeing Stratocruisers after first asking Qantas if it would buy Constellations on its behalf because the Australians had negotiated such a favourable price!

Buying the Constellation fleet, and thus securing the competitive edge of the organisation by equipping it with the same planes bought by rival airlines, was the last major deal Qantas did as a private concern. Shortly afterwards, the Australian government took over the UK shareholding in Qantas Empire Airways and then the private Australian shareholding. McMaster, in increasingly poor health, resigned as chairman but remained on the board. Fysh took over as executive chairman and managing director, transferring those positions to the new government corporation that would run the national flag carrier when the deal was finally sealed in September 1947. The original Queensland and Northern Territory Aerial Services company that had begun it all was liquidated. Qantas, like many other newly government-owned airlines around the world, was taking off into a new era of aviation.

The first Lockheed 749 Constellation, the *Charles Kingsford Smith*, took 29 passengers and food parcels to London on 1 December 1947 to inaugurate the postwar Kangaroo Route. It took four days, with passengers spending two nights in Singapore and Cairo and two in the air.

While passengers to London were enjoying first-class luxury, the airline was also returning to its pioneering days with a service to Papua New Guinea. On these trips, operated by a mixed bag of de Havilland Otter and Beaver land and float planes and a Catalina flying boat, passengers climbed in with their luggage and were handed a thermos of tea as their in-flight hospitality before take-off. Pilots reported the clouds over Papua New Guinea, which has a spine of mountains rising 15,400 feet, as being like a box of chocolates: 'Some have soft centres and some have hard ones, and you don't know which is which.'[13] The technical term for those hard clouds is cumulus granaticus.

This service proved an excellent training ground for Qantas pilots looking to move to the more prestigious routes flying the new Constellations. The New Guinea operation was built up to be an important part of the Qantas empire, with four-engine Douglas DC4s being brought in to fly the Sydney–Port Moresby–Lae service in 1950. The airline also worked on developing the de Havilland Drover aircraft, one of which crashed in 1951 killing all seven on board following a series of non-fatal accidents involving the centre propeller. In 1959 the Papua New Guinea operation was providing Qantas with eight per cent of its total revenue. However, it was brought to an end when the Australian government, as a result of intense lobbying, decided the service was really domestic and handed it over to TAA and Ansett.

Qantas was growing rapidly and security was becoming an issue. Thefts and petty pilfering started to be a problem. When a director's wife left her fur coat in the luggage rack of a flying boat at the Rose Bay base and it went missing, Fysh knew the time had come to act. The director was particularly unhappy because his suitcase had been dropped overboard during his last visit! A security team was set up, which Gordon Fraser, who was poached from the airline department of the New South Wales Police Criminal Investigation Branch, joined. He was soon to put those skills he learned in his 11 years with the police force to good use.

At this time Qantas was also expanding its services, with a route into Lord Howe Island. The airline was in direct competition with a start-up airline called Trans Oceanic Airways (TOA) run by former World War Two pilots under the guidance of aviation pioneer P. G. Taylor. On 23 June 1949 the Qantas Catalina broke her moorings in a 'blow' on Lord Howe Island and was washed ashore. Only the previous night the same thing had happened to the TOA Catalina, but the crew had remained aboard and been able to salvage the situation. An investigation was launched into why the galvanised steel mooring cable, which had been tested and passed as fit by the Civil Aviation office three weeks earlier, on 1 June, should break. The Defence Research Laboratories tested the cable, which had a breaking strain of 17,532 kilograms, and found that all the galvanising had been removed and a 'red corrosion product' had appeared between the strands.[14] Foul play was suspected but could not be proven.

'This loss placed us at a great disadvantage but we were able to continue with the service until, at 2.22 am on Saturday morning, 27th August 1949, the Catalina VH-EAW blew up at its Rose Bay moorings with a roar that woke me in my home at Wallaroy Road,' wrote Fysh.[15] Security chief Fraser at first thought the explosion was the result of an accident, but when the wreckage was dragged from the bottom of Sydney Harbour, a device was found under the flight engineer's seat and the New South Wales Police Arson Squad was called in. 'Following salvage operations a piece of fruit case board was found under the seat of the flight engineer attached by string and fishing line, and there was an alarm clock, a six volt battery and a vibrator coil,' said Fraser.[16] There was speculation that this apparatus was designed to throw a spark and ignite the fuel that had drained into the engineer's compartment from the broken locking device on the port side fuel gauge. 'It was a very neat job but the perpetrators had not expected the apparatus to be recovered virtually intact,' said Fysh.[17] The subsequent investigation put the managing director of TOA, Bryan Monkton, into the dock but he supplied a strong alibi with the help of P. G. Taylor and was acquitted. He may have survived but his airline did not.

The security service was also important because Qantas was transporting a great deal of gold mined from Papua New Guinea. The importance of the new security service was emphasised when, just as it was formed, a BOAC security guard in London was offered a £1,000 bribe to put sleeping pills into the meals of staff handling the strongroom at London airport. The guard tipped off Scotland Yard, which replaced the airport staff with police officers who pretended to be asleep. When the gangsters entered the secure area they were all arrested and subsequently received lengthy jail terms. The BOAC security guard who raised the alarm was given a job at one of Qantas's most remote bases under an assumed name.

These diversions aside, Qantas was concentrating on the

business of building a global airline. The service to America was key because there was little time difference between flying to the UK via Asia and the Middle East, or via the US. The fear was that, if the Commonwealth countries did not offer a service, the Americans would clean up. Pan American had already opened up the route over the Pacific in 1947, flying into Sydney with a glamorous 'sleeperette' service. Naturally Qantas wanted to run the operation across the Pacific, basing its argument on the fact that it had successfully flown the route to deliver Catalinas during the war. But the Australian government, having just bought Qantas, then baffled most observers by going into competition with itself. It bought half of British Commonwealth Pacific Airlines (BCPA) in partnership with the British and New Zealand governments. The new airline, which did not have any planes at that point, was to fly to England via New Zealand and America. It was an ill-fated idea. The new airline struggled and, when a BCPA aircraft crashed on approach to San Francisco airport in 1953, what was left of the airline's morale was destroyed with it. The airline was cleared of any blame but BCPA was finished. The Australian government bought out the British and New Zealand governments' shares and vested them in Qantas.

In May 1954 the first Qantas Super Constellation, *Southern Constellation*, flew from Sydney to San Francisco and opened the way for the Australian national carrier to circle the globe. But Qantas had not forgotten its outback routes. It was operating the Flying Doctor Service with de Havilland Dragon aircraft, a successor to the ill-starred DH86 planes. The airline had also worked on the development of the de

Havilland Drover for the service, which suffered a string of crashes before the faults were ironed out. As the aviation industry prepared for the revolution of the jet age, Qantas had a good, but far from perfect, record.

Today the Qantas Public Relations department is keen to gloss over some of the biggest incidents in the airline's history. The slick PR department would like to foster the public's misapprehension that Qantas is the airline that never crashes. This is the big lie that came about thanks to a Hollywood movie. In 1988 Dustin Hoffman played autistic savant Raymond in the hit film *Rain Man*. In the best free publicity any airline ever received, Raymond tells his avaricious brother Charlie, played by Tom Cruise, that he will only fly Qantas, because Qantas never crashes.

Respected aviation crash investigator Macarthur Job has a forthright view on Dustin Hoffman's character in *Rain Man*: 'He was wrong,' he said by telephone from his home in Victoria. 'That's a bit of a furphy – they have had quite a lot of crashes.' And he was disappointed that the Qantas PR department was happy to perpetuate the line. A report by Bloomberg saying Qantas had never lost a passenger went uncorrected. 'It's plain dishonesty. They want to make it sound good and make much of the fact,' he said. 'I have tried to point it out to the PR department but they don't seem to be interested. The record is a myth – it's a myth that needs exploding.'

He wrote to the Bloomberg reporter, Laura Cochrane, saying the statement that: 'the carrier, founded in the Queensland outback in 1920, has never had a fatal accident',[18] could not be allowed to go unchallenged.

I have been involved in the Australian civil aviation industry for many years (as a qualified commercial pilot, as an air safety investigator with the aviation regulator, and as an aviation writer specialising in air safety) and am reasonably familiar with Qantas' history.

Some of us in the industry have been concerned for several years that Qantas PR have been 'stretching the truth' in perpetuating the myth that the airline has never lost a passenger. Certainly Qantas has a very fine record and has never experienced a fatal accident to a jet aircraft, but the truth is that the airline has lost around 65 passengers and crew in nine fatal accidents over the years – the last in Papua New Guinea in 1951.[19]

Putting it into perspective, Mr Job said: 'Qantas has a superb record, and, in its 50-year history of operating modern jet aircraft, has never experienced a fatal accident. This is indeed an achievement that few, if any, world air-lines can approach. It is therefore a pity that Qantas media releases are not content to rest on the fine laurels of this fine record . . . Instead, Qantas PR has sought to perpetuate this myth, thereby compromising the plausibility of its other releases.'[20]

Why would Qantas seek to gild the lily so unnecessarily? The only conclusion that can be reached is that, as it suffered a spate of near disasters and mid-air crises in recent years, it wanted to cement in the public's mind its brilliant safety record. When tackled head-on about this issue the PR department stressed: 'Safety is, and always has been, our highest priority. Our system of airworthiness checks is as rigorous as ever and we continue to invest heavily in engineering, maintenance and training.' The statement also confirmed the details of previous fatalities and the Mauritius crash. It added the disclaimer: 'We have never promoted claims made about our safety record, such as in the film *Rain Man*.'[21] But Qantas has not gone out of its way to correct those claims to its benefit when made erroneously. As one member of the PR team confided: 'Why should we?' The problem with the repetition of the *Rain Man* myth that Qantas never crashes is best summed up by Macarthur Job: 'He was wrong.'

QF6

EXTORTION

'IT'S AN ANEROID bomb and it's incredibly, appallingly effi-cient. It seems to me that any major airline that can afford to spend hundreds of millions of dollars on a fleet of 707s could certainly afford to divest itself of a few hundred thousand dollars, especially to save one of those shiny aeroplanes,' said the telephone voice in the 1966 movie *The Doomsday Flight* starring Jack Lord.

For the Qantas chief executive, Captain Robert Ritchie, the movie became a nightmarish reality at 12.20 pm on 26 May 1971. Captain Ritchie had been a major player in bringing Qantas into the jet age – now he faced losing one of those planes in the most horrific circumstances. Police offic-ers at Sydney airport had received a call from a Mr Brown saying there was an altitude bomb hidden on a Qantas Boeing 707 that had just left Sydney for Hong Kong with 127 passengers and crew on board. If the plane dropped below a certain altitude the bomb would automatically explode. The police had been guided to a locker at the airport in which they found a vinyl bag containing a sample bomb and three letters. The first letter explained how the bomb would detonate at a certain altitude, the second that a similar bomb was on the Hong Kong flight and the third was addressed to Captain Ritchie. It demanded $500,000 in used notes before 4 pm. Mr Brown promised to tell Qantas how to find and defuse the bomb once he had the money. While police confirmed the airport bomb would work as promised, Qantas ordered the Hong Kong flight into a holding pattern above 19,500 feet while the crew methodically searched it for the bomb. Nothing was found.

Captain Ritchie faced an awful dilemma. The police did not want him to deal with an extortionist who had effectively hijacked the Qantas jet by remote control. But he did not want to lose the lives of the 127 people on his plane. He called Qantas finance director Bill Harding, who went to the Reserve Bank and returned with the money in bundles of $20 notes. Meanwhile, up in the sky, the plane was running out of fuel and would have to land by 7 pm. Captain Ritchie controversially chose to deal with the extortionist and pay out the money. He personally handed over the cash in two suitcases to a man in a yellow van outside the Qantas building in the middle of Sydney. Frustrated police officers found they were trapped in a lift that stopped at every floor of the building as Mr Brown calmly drove away. Once clear, he called Qantas and told them there was no bomb on the plane. It was an elaborate and expensive hoax. The plane landed safely, but where was Qantas's half a million dollars?

Mr Brown was in fact a 36-year-old English migrant called Peter Pasquale Macari. He had been arrested in England on homosexuality charges and had absconded to Australia, where he had briefly run a fibreglass factory at Brookvale on Sydney's northern beaches and driven a taxi. Those who knew him by the alias Peter King at the Bondi gymnasium where he regularly worked out described him as sly, witty, restless and generous. They also noticed, after the Qantas extortion, that he had a lot of money. So did his accomplice, 28-year-old Sydney barman Raymond Poynting.

Macari went on a spending spree. He bought a 1967 white E-type Jaguar with black leather upholstery for $5,000. Then he added to his collection a Mini Cooper for $1,900, a Morris Cooper ERW 306 for $800 and a Ford Transit van for $1,800. He paid $41,000 for a three-bedroom top-floor unit in Bondi with panoramic ocean views, and flew to the Gold Coast to get a sample of carpet he had seen and liked in a motel there. He put down a deposit on a $14,750 former butcher's shop and residence in Annandale, in which he stashed some of the Qantas ransom money. Macari then sold the E-type to Poynting, who had already spent $4,300 on a tangerine Ford Flacon GT, and instead bought a 1967 Chevrolet Camaro. Ron Phillips, owner of the Five Dock car yard where Macari bought the car, told the *Sydney Morning Herald*: 'It was what we call a pose car. A young bloke who wants to be noticed might buy it. As it drove past, you'd turn and look, that's for sure!'[1] Mr Phillips said Macari haggled the price of the car down by

$500 to $5,500. The Camaro was hard to miss. It was iridescent blue with bone white upholstery and had red wall tyres on its US magnesium alloy wire wheels.

On 4 August, less than three months after the Qantas hoax, an anonymous tipster called police and told them a man had been spending a lot of money and was now driving around Bondi Junction in a blue Camaro. The hoax had attracted plenty of media attention and the caller wondered if it was Mr Brown. Detective Ross Bradley and Detective Sergeant Mervyn Brazel did not find the car hard to spot and tailed the Camaro to St Vincent's Hospital, where they spoke to Macari, who claimed he was Raymond Poynting because he was using Poynting's licence.

Macari was a promising suspect. After a preliminary interrogation at CIB, Detective Sergeant Brazel told the head of the Consorting Squad, Detective Sergeant Jack O'Neill: 'He's English, hasn't worked for about eighteen months, and for mine he's Mr Brown from Qantas.'[2]

Even before police stopped Macari in his flash American car, the police investigation was closing in on him. Officers were looking for him under one of the many aliases he had used, they had his fingerprints from England and patient checking of gelignite and typewriters was starting to provide new leads. Macari maintained there was a mastermind behind the bomb hoax, known to him only as Ken, who had taken all but $125,000 of the ransom money. It was Ken who had been inspired by the movie *The Doomsday Flight* and had told him what to do. 'He threatened me personally and spoke of what some of his mates would do to me,' Macari told police.[3]

After Captain Ritchie had handed over the money, Macari claimed he took it straight to Ken, who was waiting in a white Valiant. 'The agreement was $125,000 and he gave me or he took out of the bag approximately that amount. Seven bundles, I think. Removed the suitcases to the boot in the car. They drove off.'[4] The police officers did not believe him for a minute. Macari was a proven liar. When the police asked for his date of birth he said: 'I don't know. I've told people that many things about my birthday, I can't remember the right one.'[5]

At his court case it became clear that Macari had watched *The Doomsday Flight* with a friend on the portable television in the back of his black and cream Commer van while on a trip to Townsville in Queensland. Afterwards he told the friend: 'That would be a good way to make money.'[6] He bought gelignite in Mount Isa and an altimeter in Sydney, and recruited Poynting to help him type out the letters.

Macari pleaded guilty to extortion and was deported to England after serving nine years of his 15-year sentence. Poynting served four of his seven years. Police recovered $138,240 of the ransom money stuffed behind the fireplace of the former butcher's shop in Annandale and managed to recoup some of the stolen cash from the cars and properties Macari and Poynting had bought. But almost half – $239,000 – of Qantas's money was still missing. Macari and Poynting had taken a skin-diving course, and police believe they put the money in two corruption-proof safes and sank them in the sea – probably within sight of Macari's ocean-view flat. The money has never been recovered.

The bomb hoax became known as Australia's most

audacious crime and inspired a movie of its own, *Call Me Mr Brown*, and a copycat crime by a 17-year-old in 1997, which was quickly revealed by security checks as not serious. Meanwhile, the film that inspired the hoax, *The Doomsday Flight*, was taken off the air for several years. Macari was later linked to the mystery of the murder of Billy Day, 24, who went missing after taking a trip to Queensland in a camper van with a 'Peter Brown' in 1970. English Detective Chief Inspector Andrew Ravassio interviewed Macari about it on his return to England. 'When I suggested he knew what happened to Day he said, "You prove it",' said DCI Ravassio.[7]

For Qantas the missing money was the least of its problems. The start of the 1970s saw an oil crisis, a worldwide economic slump and an airline industry geared up for high capacity with wide-bodied jets holding seats that few people could afford. It was just one in a series of economic problems the airline had encountered since ushering in the jet age.

In the 1950s Qantas had realised its propeller-powered Super Constellations would soon be outmatched by bigger and faster passenger jets. Chairman and Managing Director Hudson Fysh had seen the British-built de Havilland Comet I at the Farnborough Air Display in 1949 and been hugely impressed. 'What a thing of beauty it was,' he wrote.[8] But it had serious shortcomings. Despite Qantas's partner BOAC ordering the Comet, Fysh and the experts at Qantas did not believe the plane would work over the longer distances required for Australian routes.

His fears were then compounded by a series of Comet crashes. The first came in 1952 in Rome when a BOAC Comet failed to achieve full take-off and crashed at the end of the runway. It was followed by a Canadian Pacific Airlines Comet 1A crashing on take-off from Karachi on its delivery run to Sydney in 1953. All aboard were killed. Then a BOAC Comet broke up in the air in bad turbulence soon after take-off from Calcutta, and again all aboard were killed. In January 1954 a BOAC Comet crashed into the sea off the island of Elba and in April another Comet crashed into the sea at Naples. In those four accidents 24 crew and 85 passengers were killed, and after the fourth the Comet's certificate of airworthiness was withdrawn. Tests found metal fatigue had led to the pressurised cabins collapsing. The Comet was modified and put back into service, but its reputation was damaged and de Havilland's time advantage over the American passenger jet manufacturers was lost.

Meanwhile, Qantas was coming under increasing pressure from its competition. Pan American had ordered Boeing 707s and would be flying them by 1959. The new jets would easily leave the Super Connies trailing in their wake. The 707s travelled 200 kph faster and carried 120 passengers. Fysh had also been at the roll-out of the Boeing 707 in 1954 and was caught up in the possibilities of such a machine. At this time Qantas had the tough C. O. Turner as its general manager. He and Fysh had already clashed, but Turner's shrewd analysis of figures, routes, operations and aircraft performance gelled well with the extremely technical knowledge of pilots such as Scotty Allan and Bert Ritchie, who would later go on to become chief executive himself. Turner pulled off a masterstroke of diplomacy in his dealings with Boeing. He personally called William Allen, the president of Boeing, and they struck up a rapport. It was a big deal at the time. One Qantas executive recalled that the mood of buying the new jets was 'like a flea going to his bankers to buy his own dog'.[9]

When Qantas chose the Nadi to Honolulu route as crucial for its network, it needed changes to jet airliners to meet its needs. US aircraft manufacturer Douglas refused to change the specifications of its DC8, which had been built for the US domestic market. But Boeing agreed to shorten by 3.5 metres its standard 100 series 707 and equip it with the more powerful US military version of the Pratt & Whitney engine.

Turner and Qantas were convinced and in September 1956 the Australian government minister for civil aviation announced Qantas would buy seven Boeing 707-138 aircraft, making it the first non-US carrier to operate American jets. With its new aircraft, Qantas could carry 104 passengers at 880 kph from Sydney to London in 27 hours – a massive 21 hours faster than with the Super Connies. The flight from Sydney to San Francisco was cut from 28 hours to just 18. Cruising at 35,000 feet above sea level the 707 was also a great deal more comfortable because it was literally flying above most of the weather. The jets would become known as V-Jets – the title taken today by rival Virgin for its service across the Pacific from Australia to America.

In the 1960s the arrival of the Qantas 707 V-Jets heralded the arrival of the swinging jetset era, bringing Australia a lot closer to the rest of the world. Business people considered trips to Europe and North America viable, investors could come to Australia to look at opportunities and rock stars could include Australia on their concert schedules – starting with the Beatles, long before they were popular in the US. European migrants, attracted by the cheaper tourist-class fares offered by the new bulk carriers, could seriously contemplate a return visit to see families left behind. Up until then the journey had been a once-in-a-lifetime boat trip that took a month each way. Migrant travel became increasingly important to the airline. In 1967 Qantas brought 47,600 migrants to begin their new lives in Australia.

The first Boeing 707-138, named *City of Canberra*, arrived in Sydney from the Boeing factory in Seattle on 2 July 1959. Its flight time was a record 16 hours and 10 minutes, beating the previous record set by a DC7 by 11 hours and 20 minutes. Crowds flocked to see it, but residents near the airport were appalled at the thick black smoke trails left by the jet engines. Bean counters in Qantas head office were more concerned about the high fuel consumption. The engineers at the rapidly expanding Qantas Jet Base at Mascot quickly retrofitted new fan bypass engines to the Qantas jets, which ducted air around the body of the engine, increasing thrust and swallowing noise from the jet powerplant to make it quieter and more powerful. The increased performance meant there was no need to have water injections on short runways and ended the unpopular sight of greasy black smoke trails following Qantas jets into the sky.

Of course not everything with the 707s went according to plan. Two days before the Christmas of 1964 Qantas Captain R. C. Houghton was bringing his Boeing 707-138 jet in to land at Singapore when things went badly pear-shaped. An error of judgement by both pilots caused the plane to bounce. Incorrect technique in attempting to re-land the plane on the runway put it in such a severe nose-down attitude that the nose wheel touched the runway before the main wheels. No one was injured but the nose landing gear suffered extensive structural damage. However, incidents such as this were rare.

The arrival of the jets also marked a bigger change within Qantas. The pioneers were retiring and younger pilots, managers and technical experts were taking up the reins. These were the years when Qantas built up its enviable reputation for safety. Incidents on Qantas planes were virtually unheard of. The airline itself would traverse some rocky economic times over the next few decades under the stewardship of some remarkable men. Sir Cedric Turner, who was responsible for the dramatic postwar expansion and the arrival of the jet age, retired from Qantas in June 1967 and was replaced as chief executive by Captain Bert Ritchie, who guided the airline into the world of mass-market travel. Qantas even went into the hotel business, opening the luxury 450-room Wentworth Hotel next to the company's headquarters in the heart of Sydney's central business district.

Ritchie saw Qantas through the change of three governments and applied his common-sense approach to show that the supersonic Concorde would not be economically viable flying from Europe to Australia. He was at the helm for the oil crisis of the early 1970s and to report a $6 million loss in 1971–72, partly brought about by passengers flying to Singapore and then taking cheaper charter flights to Europe. He introduced new low fares on the new Boeing 747 jumbo jets to stop the rot. In fact, he showed nerve, not taking the first 747 series of jets but holding out for the 747 B series, which was better suited to Qantas's unique long-haul conditions. It meant other airlines had a two-year lead on Qantas in operating the new wide-bodied jets. But once the jumbos were introduced, with lower charter-style fares, the gap was quickly made up and Qantas leaped ahead.

Ritchie was also in charge when Cyclone Tracy swept through Darwin in 1974. The airline evacuated 5,000 people in six days, setting records for a single 747 jet, which carried 673 people and a 707, which carried 327. However, the boom in low fares presented Ritchie's successor, Keith Hamilton, with problems – the airline was flying a lot of people but not making any money. He brought in a team of management consultants, trimmed the number of bosses and offered staff a voluntary 'separation' (redundancy) plan. It was the mid-1970s, the Whitlam Labor government had fallen and Qantas had been building its headquarters, the Qantas Centre, on a complete city block on the site of the Wentworth Hotel, with an early giant computer called Qantam taking up seven whole floors below ground level. Hamilton immediately cut back on the airline's commitment to the industrial-action-prone building project.

As recession loomed, Qantas reported a loss of $19.5 million in the 1981 financial year. Hamilton sold off the new Qantas Centre, its holdings in the Wentworth Hotel and property in San Francisco to restore the balance sheet. Qantas also cut airfares by up to $200 to 'fly its way out' of the recession.[10] Even so, the 1982–83 financial year saw a loss of $34.4 million and a cut in staff numbers of 1,000.

Hamilton died suddenly at home in 1984 but had set

Qantas on course to become what chairman Jim Leslie described as 'a leaner, tougher and smarter airline'.[11] The following year, under Chief Executive Ron Yates, Qantas introduced Boeing 767s and began the process that would eventually lead to privatisation.

One of the reasons Qantas gave for the financial loss of the early 1980s was an industrial dispute over the crewing levels of the Boeing 747SP, the shorter special performance version of the 747, designed to carry fewer passengers than the standard jumbo. Over the decades Qantas had struggled with its employees over pay and staffing levels. In the 1960s old hands such as the airline's founder Hudson Fysh clashed with a new breed of executives, particularly over the issue of pilot pay. Qantas pilots were meeting their well-heeled American counterparts in luxury hotels on stopovers all over the world and wondering why they did not get paid as much money for flying exactly the same planes. Across the globe other pilots were feeling the same way. Even some of the American pilots felt hard done by. BOAC, Pan American and Eastern Airlines pilots decided to take industrial action. Fysh said: 'We thought in our false pride [Qantas] was different, and it just could not happen to us.'[12] But this was not the case.

In April 1957 Qantas pilots went out on strike for nine days, with navigators and flight engineers going out in sympathy. Little was resolved. In February 1964 the pilots went out again for three days. Fysh was dismayed. 'These differences with the pilots caused me much anguish of mind, especially as I felt that I was one of a small group of us who understood the pilot's position; but I was frustrated and unable to do anything about it. I was accused of favouring the pilots in the critical early days of the first strike when I felt future trouble might have been avoided,' he wrote in the third of his memoirs chronicling his 46 years with Qantas.[13]

Even his patience became exhausted when the pilots went out for 28 days in November 1966. 'This strike took place after my retirement, and resulted in a disastrous loss of revenue to the company and also to its pilots.'[14] The new executives did not like the fact that the pilots were so well paid. Fysh said: 'One of the mainsprings of misunderstanding was the fact that senior pilots received a higher remuneration than many hard-working senior executives. This of course was a tradition from the old Air Force days, and so also was the fact that an air pilot was a man of great independence, a man who could not be ordered about as others could. In fact they were damn difficult, as I suppose I was.'[15]

Difficulties over the pilots and Fysh's views about these heroes of the air made his last days at Qantas unhappy and unpleasant. The World War One aviator and bush pilot was reluctantly pushed into retirement in June 1966, leaving the airline he had built to a future in which bureaucrats would run it without any of that romantic nonsense about pilots being men of great independence who could not be ordered about.

In fact, it would not be until two decades later that Australia's pilots would be finally put in their place by a politician who called them glorified bus drivers. Prime Minister Bob Hawke's attack on pilots at the outset of the domestic pilots' pay dispute in 1989 finally showed pilots what politicians and the business community thought of them. The dispute would have far-reaching consequences for Qantas and its future, ultimately helping to push it towards privatisation.

Australia's domestic airline pilots, employed by Ansett, East West Airlines, Ipec Aviation and the government-owned Australian Airlines (previously TAA) demanded a pay rise of 29.47 per cent. When it was rejected, all 1,647 domestic airline pilots resigned, prompting what Qantas historian John Gunn described as 'the worst crisis ever faced by the aviation industry'.[16]

In solidarity with their colleagues, all Qantas pilots refused to carry domestic passengers. But the government was resolute. The Royal Australian Air Force was drafted in to carry domestic passengers to Australia's capital cities using aircraft including Hercules transports and a Boeing 707. The RAAF had to refuel at military bases because Transport Workers' Union members refused to touch them. Fourteen overseas airlines with domestic legs in Australia also agreed to carry domestic passengers, but even so passenger numbers were down by more than 75 per cent.

The Labor government remained firm, with Prime Minister Hawke staking his own survival on beating the pilots. Using highly charged rhetoric he warned that the pilots' action threatened 'Australian life as we know it'. Should the pilots win, he said, 'The whole wage system is dead and Australia is dead'.[17] What quickly became clear was that the pilots' decision to resign had left them badly exposed. Transport Minister Ralph Willis said: 'They have resigned on absurd advice from their union. The organisation has virtually committed suicide. It is now a matter between individual pilots and their companies.'[18] He was right, the pilots had lost their collective power.

James Strong, the chief executive of Australian Airlines,

became the effective mouthpiece of all the airlines and offered the pilots individual contracts based on productivity – more pay for more flying. Strong refused to negotiate with the Pilots' Federation. He had been hired three and a half years previously to turn the nationalised domestic airline that was TAA into the more competitive Australian Airlines. His brutal economics had been a culture shock to the loyal staff of TAA, who prided themselves on providing the nation with a safe and reliable domestic airline.

Strong, who left Australian Airlines during the pilots' dispute, had no words of sympathy for the pilots. 'I get pilots ringing me or writing saying "How could you do this to us? What a terrible thing for all the loyalty we have given the airline",' he told the Melbourne *Age*. 'Not one of them ever stops to think that the airline has given them a wonderful career, the best training in the world, made them the pilots they are, given them good salaries, wonderful superannuation schemes – and they have put the airline on the ground, costing it millions and millions of dollars.'[19] Qantas pilots, crew and staff would do well to heed those words and sentiments – James Strong was the man who would later be appointed to step in and ramrod Qantas into the cut-throat private sector.

If the pilots thought they could salvage a victory from the dispute they were sadly mistaken. After a month Hawke declared a state of national emergency and backed the airlines by waiving any fees, such as airport landing fees, that they owed the government. Australian Airlines started to put on a service using management crew and Ansett announced it had hired back 50 of its pilots on individual contracts. The airlines then began to advertise for pilots overseas and took out newspaper advertisements to warn Australian pilots that there were only jobs for six out of every ten pilots who chose to come back on individual contracts.

By December it was clear the Pilots' Federation was a spent force. It was no longer recognised by the airlines and did not represent the many pilots who were now flying domestic routes. By Christmas the federation was broken and domestic air services were slowly returning to normal. For Qantas crew, pilots and staff enjoying the last Christmas of the decade, the dispute was the first warning of the next winds of change that were about to come howling through the airline.

QF7

PROJECT SUZIE

QANTAS CAME OUT of the pilots' strike at the start of the 1990s with a dramatic restructure. It was designed to cope with the sudden drop in demand for its own services, which flowed on from the domestic dispute that had hit Australian Airlines and Ansett so hard. Inadvertently this restructure, particularly with its focus on new routes into Asia, put the Australian airline ahead of its international competitors when the economic slump doused the world economy a couple of years later. It meant the airline was better placed to deal with the first Gulf War and the quadrupling of fuel prices that cost the airline industry $US15.6 billion in the first three years of the decade. But it still carried debt.

The Qantas board had long been begging the government

for capitalisation – a cash injection to invigorate the air-line – but it was not forthcoming. Without that, the board argued, the only way forward was privatisation and a cash boost from the share-buying public. It also lobbied for an end to the longstanding restrictions that prevented it from operating on domestic routes. Qantas CEO John Ward called for 'the winds of competition' to blow through Australian aviation.[1]

The big change came after Paul Keating took his seat in the prime minister's office. In February 1992 he radically changed the government's policy on Qantas in his ground-breaking One Nation statement. 'Qantas will not be able to compete effectively in international markets unless it is given the same opportunity as its foreign competitors . . . the restrictions on Qantas operation . . . forming and cementing an alliance with an Australian domestic carrier will therefore be removed,' he said, making the New Zealand trans-Tasman operations part of a single market.[2] Keating was ending decades of careful segregation of the domestic and international markets. He was also paving the way for an end to government-controlled aviation companies, instead allowing those winds of competition to set the pace. Australia's skies were up for sale and the race was on to see who would emerge with the rights to fly them.

There was a great deal of jostling over which airlines would team up. The mood was reflected in the questions posed by the *Sydney Morning Herald* in March 1992:

What bidders want to know is what they will be buying: will Qantas be buying into Australian? Will Australian seek to take a bigger stake in Qantas than is now being seriously considered by the airline? Will Air New Zealand get rights to fly passengers onwards from Australia? Will it be flying domestic routes in Australia? Will Ansett bid into Qantas? Who will buy News Corp's 50 per cent share in Ansett, and, most importantly, what will the rules be for Australian and Ansett's access to international routes?[3]

At one point Ansett and Australian teamed up with their own proposal to take a lucrative slice of Qantas's international routes. The unlikely alliance was brokered between Ansett's bosses – TNT's Peter Abeles and News Corp's Ken Cowley – Australian Airlines' chairman Ted Harris and ACTU secretary Bill Kelty. It put the old domestic rivals together and cut out new start-up airline Compass. Ansett followed this up with a proposal that effectively would have given it control of Qantas. That idea never took off. Ultimately it came down to three serious contenders: British Airways wanted to buy a combined Qantas and Australian; Singapore Airlines was interested in a prime stake in Qantas; and Air New Zealand-Brierleys wanted a prime stake in Australian.

Publicly the sale of Australia's international and domestic airlines dragged on. Behind the scenes frantic and complex negotiations were taking place. The government finally acted. On 26 May 1992 the Qantas directors received a short and startling message: 'There has been an important and urgent development concerning privatisation. In short, Qantas has an immediate opportunity to purchase all the shares of Australian Airlines. The government is seeking a signed agreement from Qantas this evening.'[4] The price was $400 million – a great deal more than the $150 million Qantas had first offered for the loss-making domestic airline. But CEO Ward, a mathematician, had crunched the numbers and knew that the deal, like the airlines, would fly.

On 2 June 1992 Mr Keating announced a 'little bit of history' to the assembled Canberra press gallery.[5] The government would sell 100 per cent of Australian Airlines to Qantas for $400 million and then offer 100 per cent of Qantas for sale by public float and trade sale, retaining a golden share to safeguard the national interest.

The aviation industry approved. The regulations that had kept Australian domestic and international flights strictly apart for so long had been swept aside. *Aircraft* magazine described the government's move as 'breathtaking' and said it would ensure Australia had 'at least one airline strong enough to compete in an increasingly concentrated international market dominated by a few mega-carriers'.[6]

The combined airlines had 84 aircraft, and passengers immediately felt the benefit as Qantas put Australian jets on some of its routes. As the two airlines merged the obvious cost savings came into effect. Significantly the key job losses were from the board of Australian, with Qantas chairman Bill Dix asking for the resignation of Australian chairman Ted Harris and all the board apart from himself, Qantas CEO John Ward, and managing director and former Qantas man John Schaap, who remained as managing director.

Now the Australian government had to find a trade investor to buy into Qantas. The same three bidders remained in the race: British Airways, Singapore Airlines and Air New Zealand. To sweeten the deal the government promised to pump over $1 billion into Qantas, finally granting the Qantas board the taxpayer capital injection it had pleaded for, just in time to benefit the new private shareholders. British Airways quickly emerged as the most serious contender, despite losing Lend Lease as a potential partner. The loose alliance between the builder and the airline was only revealed by incompetence, when a confidential facsimile from the chairman of the Australian government's Asset Sales Task Force, Harold Heinrich, intended for British Airways, was accidentally sent to a Sydney stockbroking house.

Despite the long history of a mutually beneficial partnership between the two airlines, Prime Minister Keating had to reassure the Cabinet that Qantas would not fall completely into foreign hands and John Ward had to reassure the public. 'There's no contemplation of letting control leave Australia,' he told the *Sydney Morning Herald*. It was not a sentimental decision; if there was foreign control 'we could well find we lose all our operating rights. By all means, we could have some foreign shareholding but not foreign control – that just can't be contemplated.'[7] That foreign shareholding came into being when British Airways paid $665 million in return for a 25 per cent share in Qantas on the proviso it was given three seats on the board. When the trade sale went through in February 1993, the government pumped $1.35 billion of Australian taxpayers' money into Qantas.

The question at the time was whether Qantas could have picked a better, or at least ethically cleaner, partner. The month before British Airways handed over the cash for its share in Qantas, it had been forced to hand over £4 million – $9.3 million – to tiny British rival Virgin in an out-of-court settlement, after a British Airways dirty tricks campaign went horribly wrong. Virgin boss Richard Branson was given a public apology and $500,000 compensation for personal libel, which he split among his staff. The *Sydney Morning Herald* suggested the 'matter inevitably raises questions as to whether Canberra might have chosen a different big brother for Qantas had it known the extent of BA's shenanigans with Virgin'.[8]

British Airways boss Lord King disingenuously suggested he had been too caught up in the buy-up of Qantas to pay full attention to what had been happening at home. But the dirty tricks began as far back as 1988. That was when Virgin's flamboyant chairman was reading through some of his first-class passengers' comments and noticed one said she had been called at home by a British Airways official and asked why she had chosen to fly Virgin. She was not the only one. British Airways officials had accessed the Virgin passenger lists. They were also harassing passengers at the check-in and offering free British Airways air miles to swap flights. The British Airways officials were even calling passengers and lying that Virgin flights had been delayed in order to get them to transfer to British Airways. Meanwhile, British newspapers were running stories about Branson's finances as part of a smear campaign by slick PR man Brian Basham. All this to compete against a start-up that was 30 times smaller than 'the world's favourite airline', as British Airways liked to call themselves.

When a television documentary caught British Airways staff haranguing Virgin passengers, the company denied it in its newspaper, publicly branding Branson a liar and providing him with the legal grounds to fight. It was war. Branson, with advice from ruined rebel airline boss Freddie Laker, went to the courts backed with funding from the $US1 billion sale of his Virgin Music group. Meanwhile, British Airways suspected there was a Virgin mole in its ranks and launched the £50,000 Operation Covent Garden to find the leak. There was no mole.

Also underway was Operation Barbara, a disinformation and muck-spreading campaign against Virgin that was authorised from the very top. By the time British Airways had reached the stage of shredding documents and attempting to stall the Virgin court case, it was no longer considered 'the world's favourite airline' by many British customers. The dirty tricks campaign had driven disgusted passengers straight into the arms of the rival it was trying to stop. Lord King admitted he had 'underestimated' Branson. Qantas may have wished it had been saddled with a different partner.

Despite these nefarious doings, British Airways was credited in the Australian media for having the 'ear' of the Australian government and for bringing in former Brambles chairman and Qantas director Gary Pemberton to replace Bill Dix as chairman.[9] In August John Ward stepped down as chief executive, with Pemberton holding the reins until October, when James Strong, the former chief executive officer of Australian Airlines, was handed the top job of managing director.

The choice was a deliberate attempt to build solidarity between the merging staff of Qantas and Australian Airlines. Things had not been running smoothly. 'There was an initial feeling in the Australian Airlines camp that this isn't a merger, it's rape,' Julia Fellows, the Qantas human resources director charged with making the marriage work, told the *Australian Financial Review*.[10] The airlines had vastly different cultures. Little things like the Qantas staff being paid fortnightly and the Australian staff being paid weekly became major bones of contention. Things came to a head when, at a Christmas party in the city, Qantas staff refused to let Australian staff onto the guest list.

To show its solidarity with Australian Airlines staff, Qantas bosses chose the same stewardess, Cindy Mackenzie, who had appeared in the Australian TV ads, to be the new face of the combined airlines in the new Qantas ads. It was now called Qantas, The Australian Airline. That did not help the former Australian Airline steward ordered to shave off his beard to conform to Qantas regulations. The steward, one of four bearded employees, went to the union and was advised it was discrimination against bearded employees.

The niggles were eventually worked out and years later Qantas staff looked back on the influx of domestic airline managers and thought that perhaps it was the international arm that had been 'raped' after all. 'When we merged with Australian they brought in all those domestic managers and the cost-cutting began, it was the end of the glory days for Qantas,' lamented one flight crew member.[11] It began with the arrival of Strong. 'He is a Trojan Horse,' grimaced one onlooker.[12]

The future was signposted less than three weeks after Strong's appointment, when the merged company announced a loss of $376.8 million and Pemberton signalled staff cuts and the axing of marginal routes as the way ahead. Strong cemented his position by bringing in two former Australian Airlines hands to undertake two more of the most senior jobs. Former Australian general manager of marketing Geoff Dixon quit his job at Ansett to head the Qantas commercial team and join former Australian colleague Gary Toomey, who took the job of Qantas chief financial officer. As the *Australian Financial Review* noted: 'Australian Airlines is rapidly taking over Qantas – from the inside out.'[13]

Qantas staff were not the only losers. The Bureau of Transport Communications and Economics concluded that post-deregulation airfares were more expensive for passengers. Economy fares in the December quarter of 1992 were up 14 per cent, business class were up 12 per cent and first-class fares had risen six per cent. The forthcoming float of the airline was also subject to tough economic pressure, with the prospect of market share being slashed by Air New Zealand's promised entry into the Australian market. The key stakeholders held a secret meeting in Canberra. Gary Pemberton took the floor on behalf of Qantas. Federal Transport Minister Laurie Brereton and British Airways' Sir Colin Marshall listened as he spelled out the airline's predictions of exactly what Air New Zealand's arrival in Australia would do to business. By the end of the meeting the government's pledge of a single trans-Tasman air market was a dead duck. Naturally Air New Zealand was not happy.

Other problems with the float were gradually buffeted aside. The Trade Practices Commission allowed British Airways and Qantas to pool their resources on the Kangaroo Route, and the federal government agreed to raise the level of foreign ownership of the airline from 35 to 49 per cent. This decision effectively allowed a further 24 per cent of the airline to be sold into foreign hands in addition to British Airways' quarter share. The Qantas bottom line was also given a boost to make it attractive to investors by the government's decision to switch two of its busiest travelling accounts, the Department of Defence and Department of Education, from Ansett to Qantas. Everything was in place. When the now familiar strains of 'I Still Call Australia Home' played out from television sets on the first Sunday in June 1995 and Aussie icon Smoky Dawson urged Australians to 'pick up a prospectus' it was no wonder the telephone lines ran hot. Even Olympic gold medal winners Hayley Lewis and Jane Flemming were pressed into service, along with Australian of the Year winner Mandawuy Yunupingu, to sheet home the green and gold message. Over 100,000 people called the hotline in the first two weeks of pre-sale publicity. Those who studied the prospectus closely were also bolstered by the federal government's decision to settle a $100 million tax dispute between the Australian Taxation Office and the airline rather than have it drag down the profit projections before the sale.

When the share offer was finally opened to the public in July 1995, over 600,000 potential investors had applied for a prospectus. The $1.45 billion float was a huge success, with small investors quickly offloading their $1.90 shares to make a short-term killing. The embarrassment came in August when the Australian Stock Exchange released figures showing foreign investors held 517.5 million shares, breaching the federal government-imposed limit of 494.88 million shares by 22.62 million shares. In other words, the airline was 52 per cent foreign owned rather than the government's prescribed limit of 49 per cent. Even so, it was not as bad as earlier figures had indicated. Pemberton reassured the Australian public: 'Foreign ownership is starting to look manageable. A twenty-two million overhang in a company the size of Qantas, in terms of our daily turnover, is clearly manageable. And we have taken steps to ensure that, by allowing at least ninety days for the situation to work itself through.'[14] He also took the opportunity to have a pop at the media for its portrayal of British Airways' influence on the Qantas board. 'The reality of the situation is quite the opposite to what has been portrayed publicly,' he said, pointing out that the requirement for a two-thirds majority on decisions made it quite hard for British Airways' three directors to swing things their way.[15]

Qantas had successfully gone from having one owner, the Australian government, to British Airways and about 117,000 mostly Australian shareholders, with the sale. It had floated successfully but was now exposed, without government protection, to the realities of life in the corporate world. The wolves were circling. In the gleaming offices of Macquarie Bank, Australia's home-grown 'millionaire factory', heavy hitter Nicholas Moore had his eyes on Qantas. Macquarie had already come up with a debenture called Qanmac, which overcame the foreign ownership constraints of the Qantas Sales Act and allowed overseas investors to buy the Aussie airline. Moore, according to a bank insider, believed Qantas could be 'geared up to a greater level'.[16] The idea did not get past the concept stage and was never put to the board of Qantas, but the seeds were sown for the development of a later takeover bid called Project Suzie.

Sydney Morning Herald journalists Kate Askew and Scott Rochfort uncovered the details of Project Suzie in 2007 when Macquarie again took a tilt at buying Qantas. In 1998 Project Suzie was to be a leveraged buyout that would involve Macquarie, Kerry Packer – Australia's richest man – and one of the world's biggest private equity operators, Texas Pacific Group. It was the idea of Nicholas Moore's young protégé, Ben Brazil, who had been recruited straight out of university and, at the age of 26, was known in the corridors of the millionaire factory as 'Brains'. He was ambitious and persuasive enough to convince the head of the Packer family's private company, Consolidated Press Holdings, Ashok Jacob, to take the idea to the big fella himself. Kerry Packer loved it. He told Brazil the industry needed to be shaken up and echoed former Prime Minister Bob Hawke's view that pilots were just glorified bus drivers.

Busy Brazil managed to get David Bonderman's Texas Pacific Group on board with a promise of a repeat of the riches it achieved when it bought bankrupt Continental Airlines five years earlier. Continental earned Texas $US600 million – just think what Qantas could chalk up, given that it wasn't even bankrupt! Bonderman loved airlines. He had also bought 20 per cent of low-cost Irish airline Ryanair, which became Europe's major economy airline and provided the inspiration for Jetstar in later years. Bonderman also loved Suzie.

Macquarie was keen to take the third, smaller split in addition to pocketing the fees for brokering the deal. Brazil's idea was a basic bit of engineering – not of the planes but of the balance sheets. Qantas planes were undervalued.

According to the *Herald* investigation, the idea was to transfer the planes off the Qantas books for refinancing through New York, freeing up the extra loot for the three new shareholders. Today we know that kind of thinking leads to global financial meltdown, but back then greed was good and it seemed like a first-rate idea. Project Suzie was a go.

Then the unthinkable happened. First, Packer senior got cold feet. According to the *Herald*, 'the big fella could foresee problems in the country's richest man buying Qantas. It was never going to be easy to convince the public.'[17] His son, James, was also reportedly reluctant to get into the airline business. Then Qantas shares started to go up in value, adding a dollar to the $2.40 share price by the end of the year. No one in Macquarie knew about Project Suzie. The bank had kept the deal so ultra-secret it had not even listed Qantas as a no-go zone to its acquisitions and mergers team. Was there a leak? A huge number of shares were traded in a single transaction and the Macquarie board went 'apoplectic', according to the *Herald*.[18] Already stung by insider trading charges over the TNT takeover, it did not want to risk news of a hostile bid for Qantas getting out and damaging its profitable aircraft leasing business. The pin was pulled.

The Qantas board was oblivious to the scheming. Director Jim Kennedy said, 'I have no such recollection of any bid coming forward. I'm sure Gary [Toomey, Qantas finance director] would have told us at the time.'[19] Packer is understood to have told Qantas executives just before he died that he had looked at the airline. But, eight years after Project Suzie bit the dust, it would be his son and heir, James, who had a seat on the Qantas board and a spot at the helm of another, this time friendly, Macquarie bid for the Australian airline.

Qantas was really playing with the big boys now.

QF8

ANGEL AND DEMON

A MONTH AFTER Geoff Dixon took over as CEO of Qantas in March 2000, the Michod family were sitting on a Qantas 747-300 jet at Rome airport, waiting to return home after a European vacation. QF16, with 303 passengers and 19 crew on board, was taxiing in preparation for take-off. Jonathon Michod noticed something was wrong. 'The plane started to turn and I had said to Dad that the plane, you know, it felt like the plane was turning around the wheel. It was a really tight turn. I hadn't seen a turn as tight as that,' he told ABC television's *The 7.30 Report*.[1] Philip Michod said: 'Whilst doing that turn, there was a number of squeaky noises which were not that unusual, but then there was a very loud clunk and the plane had jolted, almost as though it had run over a very large rock, and then it settled, but it settled on [an] angle and we could see that the engine was touching the ground.'[2] The undercarriage had collapsed. The pilot made a brief announcement. Jonathon said: 'We were told that the engine had touched the ground and there was a problem with the landing gear and that was all, really. I was scared, basically, 'cause I thought that, when he had mentioned the fire crews, that the plane could have burst into flames, with all the fuel on board.' When he tried to take photographs, the Qantas crew became 'quite aggro' with him.[3]

No one was hurt but it was embarrassing for Qantas. David Forsyth, Qantas Aircraft Operations manager, was fielded onto the ABC to placate an anxious public. 'We're treating it as a very serious accident and we've got our investigating team up there. We've asked Boeing to send a team down from Seattle to assist us with the assessment of the repair and obviously we'll be doing everything we can to cooperate with the authorities to make sure we find out the cause,' he said. 'There's been three or four incidents of this type of fracture of an undercarriage component on the 747. Other aircraft types have also had fractures of the undercarriage. They're always treated seriously by airlines. Qantas hasn't had one before. But this is our first and we want to make sure it's our last.'[4]

Just six days later the pilots of a QantasLink BAe 146 aircraft flying from Brisbane to Canberra were warned of undercarriage problems. The plane landed safely and the problem was fixed, only for the pilots on the same aircraft to be warned of undercarriage problems as the plane came in to land at Hamilton Island a month later. Qantas assured an anxious public that it was just a wiring problem and not an issue with the undercarriage. If people were concerned it was understandable. Newspapers reported that the QF16 Qantas jet that suffered the undercarriage collapse in Rome was 14 years old and the strut that collapsed was more than a decade older. It had also been used on at least five planes before it was fixed onto the Qantas jet. Once again Mr Forsyth was wheeled out, this time to tell the *Age* that the use of reconditioned parts is standard in the airline industry. But it was still embarrassing, given the fact that US regulators had withdrawn approval for Qantas to repair US aircraft after a routine audit had found problems in the standards of the bearing and seal shop.

When pushed on the maintenance of QF16's broken undercarriage strut on the ABC, Mr Forsyth explained to Quentin Dempster: 'Well, when you're twisting a cylinder, the undercarriage strut is a cylinder, and when you're twisting it during taxiing, it puts very high torsional loads on the top of the strut and that's the failure mode that's occurred here.'[5] The Australian Manufacturing Workers' Union raised its concerns over the airline sending maintenance overseas. Union spokesman Julius Roe told *The 7.30 Report*: 'If the public are to have confidence in Qantas, then Qantas needs to have full control over the maintenance operation. We've got to reverse the trends that have occurred since privatisation and corporatisation.'[6]

The Rome incident was minor compared with the other factors affecting Qantas at the start of Geoff Dixon's reign.

Qantas had to deal with the fallout from the September 11, 2001 terror attacks in America, the Bali bombings, severe acute respiratory syndrome (SARS), bird flu in Asia and the start of the Gulf War in Iraq, all of which affected the public's confidence in flying. They may explain why, when asked to reflect on his early days at the head of Qantas, he said: 'When I took over they thought I had been handed the proverbial shit sandwich.'[7]

Dixon is not a man to mince his words. Profiles of him during his tenure at the top of Qantas portrayed a tough, ruthless businessman who ground opposition from his path, and a loyal friend and family man devoted to charitable causes. Angel and demon in the same package; which one you thought he was depended on whether you were his friend or in his way.

Geoff Dixon was brought into Qantas before the airline was privatised as part of James Strong's loyal coterie. The two men had formed a close friendship when they worked together at the bauxite mining company Nabalco in Gove in Arnhem Land in the Northern Territory. Dixon had gone there to work in the public relations department; Strong, four years his junior, was already the industrial relations manager. 'We liked each other immediately; we were sort of from similar backgrounds,' Strong told the *Australian Financial Review Magazine*.[8] Strong was from a dairy farm in Lismore and Dixon from the rural New South Wales town of Wagga Wagga. Despite being younger, Strong became a mentor to Dixon, leading him to some of the key jobs in his life and ultimately to the top job at Qantas. 'He's a good man and he's done a great job. In every organisation there's the right man for the right time, and I think he's been that man. He's a tough dog for a hard road,' said Strong of his protégé.[9] And Strong should know. He tested his own mettle at the mine in the 1960s by leading the management team onto the floor when the mining and process workers demanded higher wages. For 13 weeks the white-collar team produced the alumina, with women from the offices greasing the machines, and the mining unions were defeated.

Dixon, who would also become known for his tough dealings with unions, had grown up in a staunch Labor household, the son of a wool and skin buyer and founding president of Wagga Leagues Club. Born in December 1939, he was a wiry five-eighth for the Wagga Wagga Magpies and lifesaver with his older brother, Terry, at the local lifesaving club on the banks of the Murrumbidgee River. He left school at 17 after his Intermediate Certificate and became a trainee journalist on the local paper. 'I didn't like school, I wanted to earn money. I had a chance to get a job as a cadet at the *Wagga Daily Advertiser* and I took it. Simple as that,' he was reported as saying in 2002.[10] He quickly impressed, becoming the chief of staff by the age of 21, before realising there was no money in journalism and heading into public relations.

It was on his way to his new job at Nabalco's mine in the Northern Territory, on the tarmac of Alice Springs airport, that he met Dawn Lowe, who was ten years his junior. She had been Miss Wagga 1969 and was also going to join the mine in the information technology department. They married at Sydney's Wayside Chapel in 1971 and have two children together, Ben and Jessica. Like Strong, Dawn has been a key figure in Dixon's life. She was diagnosed with Parkinson's disease several years ago and her care has been intrinsic to Dixon's life during and after Qantas. 'One thing I am committed to is going on the board of the Garvan Foundation. Medical research resonates with me because my wife's got Parkinson's and that's how we got engaged with the Garvan because of their research into Parkinson's, among other diseases,' he told the *Sunday Telegraph* in 2008.[11]

Dixon also keeps in contact with his friends back in Wagga, who still know him as Dicko. When his old mate Col Turvey was in trouble Dixon offered to bail him out and set him up in business. 'I hit some hard times and I was on a disability pension a while back. Geoff wanted to lend me money, but I wouldn't take a loan – so he bought the pub and said: "We'll give you a share of the profits", said Col, from the Turvey Tavern.'[12] Even when they were young Col knew his mate was headed for the big time. 'He always had exceptional ability. My father said to me, "They'll be shining the big chair up for that bloke". That was 40 years ago,' he said.[13] Dixon also sponsors the Ronald McDonald House in Wagga and has worked on a number of Indigenous causes after his father pointed out the inequality and unfairness of the lives of Aboriginal Australians when Dixon was growing up.

After leaving the mine Dixon joined the diplomatic corps in Canberra and was posted to the Australian consulate in New York in 1976. Liberal MP Bruce Baird was there as a trade commissioner at the same time and has been regularly quoted in profiles on Dixon, talking about sharing Bloody Marys and hamburgers together behind the Rockefeller Centre. 'I always found him very personable. He has a strong social conscience and strong political views and was concerned about Aboriginal reconciliation and apartheid and so on. He also had a great sense of humour and was quite funny. *Grease*, the movie, had just come out and so we [Australians] were pretty fashionable then,' he said.[14]

In later life Baird would find himself at odds with Dixon because of the large number of Qantas employees living close to the airport in his Sutherland Shire electorate who feared for their jobs. He still gave his old drinking buddy the benefit of the doubt. 'I've spoken to Geoff about it many times because I've got more Qantas employees down in my area than anywhere else. But Geoff believes those issues will be looked after and I've found him to be a man of his word in the past,' he said in 2007.[15]

It was diplomat Richard Woolcott who told Dixon his strengths lay elsewhere, prompting him to write to his old workmate James Strong and congratulate him on taking over at the Australian Mining Industry Council. Nine months later Dixon was on his way there too. And when Strong was given the top job at Australian Airlines he took Dixon with him to run commercial operations. They were joined by Gary Toomey as chief financial officer and Doug Gillies as operations manager. It was the birth of the team that would ultimately end up running Qantas. But before that Strong took at job at law firm Corrs Chambers Westgarth, and the others went their separate ways, with Dixon going to Ansett. There he honed his skill at developing compelling advertising, including the airline's memorable Enya campaign. Naturally, when Strong joined Qantas he put his old Australian Airlines team back together, with Dixon at the top of the list.

The arrival of the Australian Airlines team left little room for the old Qantas hands. Within a year of Strong's arrival nine senior Qantas executives had resigned or moved to other positions. 'I don't get shy about the fact that those things have to be done,' said Strong. 'We do not have anywhere near enough sense of urgency or hunger for business.'[16] Five of the departed Qantas executives' replacements had come in from Australian. Among the Qantas casualties were deputy managing director Julian Hercus, group treasurer Allan Brown, group quality director Ed Denny and human resources director Julia Fellows, who had said the Australian staff felt the merger was more like rape. Her departure helped underline exactly who was 'raping' who.

Qantas's Hong Kong-based Orient director, Alan Loke, and tour operations director, Ron Rosalky, both resigned and went to Ansett. Former Australian chief John Schaap also resigned. He had a history with Dixon from their time together at Australian when Schaap had come in as CEO and told Dixon he couldn't work with him. 'I'm not one for hanging around. John and I did a deal in about half an hour and I was in the pub by 5.30,' Dixon said of the move that sent him to Ansett for a spell.[17] Certainly Schaap did not last long when Dixon came in to Qantas. Deputy managing director Ted Radford was also moved out of his role into another job.

From the original Qantas team in place when Strong arrived, only three remained a year later, all in executive general manager positions: Rodger Robertson as head of corporate planning, Ian Riddell in information technology and Trevor Crabtree in engineering and maintenance. Another executive general manager, Ken Gilbert, executive general manager of customer and staff services, brought embarrassment to the airline when it emerged that he had awarded lucrative training contracts to consultants linked to his own private company. Two days after it became known that Gilbert had awarded the contracts he was clearing his desk and Strong had called in the auditors to overhaul the rules governing contracts for outside consultants. Bow-tie-wearing Strong, who had been angered at a newspaper description of him as a Ken Doll, was quickly showing he was more of an Action Man with a tough new broom.

Previously, Strong had moved on fairly swiftly, so there was always jostling to be his successor. CEO Dixon and deputy CEO Gary Toomey emerged as the front runners, creating tension among the divided executive team. The tension was illustrated in an off-the-record recollection given to the *Australian Financial Review* by one of the senior management team who was staying with the executives at the InterContinental hotel at Hyde Park in London. 'Toomey went into Geoff's room and said, "You've got a bigger room than mine." Dixon said, "Do I? It looks OK to me," and Toomey said, "Of course it does. It's bigger." I had to go to the hotel management who said the rooms were exactly the same in square metres, just different shapes. But Toomey had his nose out of joint for the whole trip. And when there wasn't a bellhop to meet him when he checked in, he bunged an act on. Geoff would never do that; he'd just go and check in, no worries.'[18]

While the executives bickered, the airline was locked in a battle for domestic market share with Ansett. It was frustrating Strong, who hit out at the domestic rival in 1996 for agreeing to an eight per cent pay increase for staff over two years that would become a benchmark for the Australian airline industry. 'Here you've got a company that is probably losing money, agreeing to a set of wage increases that are not related to its profitability and how the company is going nor are they apparently related to how they think they're going to fund it,' he said at the time, before outlining the thinking that would dominate staff and union negotiations with Qantas for the next two decades. 'I find that interesting. Unfortunately there is still too much of a sense in Australia of a comparative wage justice without looking at the welfare of the corporation that is going to be paying it and by whom people are employed and its future.' And he warned: 'Significant cost reduction is going to be an ongoing feature of the operation of this company.'[19]

This cost-cutting culture was ultimately blamed for creating the environment that resulted in QF1 skidding so disastrously off the end of the runway in Bangkok in 1999. That incident brought the question of cost-cutting into the public eye for the first time and led to the questions about safety and maintenance that have dogged Qantas for the last decade.

In addition to cost-cutting, a significant weapon in the Qantas armoury was its advertising campaign with the children from the Australian Girls Choir and National Boys Choir singing 'I Still Call Australia Home'. One of Dixon's closest friends, advertising guru John Singleton, took a call from Dixon one Christmas morning asking him if he had seen the choir on Carols By Candlelight. He wanted Singleton to put them at Uluru, on the Brooklyn Bridge and in front of Big Ben singing the heart-stirring Peter Allen song. It cost $3 million but was the defining ad of the Sydney Olympics when it first aired in 2000, helping to steal the thunder from official carrier Ansett. 'He's a genius. I mean it, he understands far and beyond what makes all aspects of the company work,' said Singleton.[20]

It was a good ad, but the battle with Ansett was far from over. It should also be noted that Singleton, who at the time of the comments was dining with Dixon on a weekly basis, had felt the savagery of his business acumen when he axed Singleton's agency from the Ansett account. However, he gave Singleton the Qantas account when he started working there. He also hired Sydney chef Neil Perry to create the first- and business-class menus, combating the tired old jokes about airline food by getting a celebrity chef to attach his name to the Qantas brand.

There were other examples of Dixon's uncanny marketing nous. When the new Airbus A380 came on line he called in brand expert Hans Hulsbosch, the designer responsible for rebranding Woolworths, and sent him to the Airbus factory in Toulouse to see if there would be a problem with using the famous flying kangaroo logo on the new planes. Hulsbosch walked back into his office two weeks later and placed on Dixon's desk a hand-drawn cartoon of a kangaroo sitting in a wheelchair with its legs amputated. 'What better way to explain it to a CEO? They have a million things going on in their heads, so you have got to hit them between the eyes, it makes them instantly focus on what you are doing," said Hulsbosch.[21] The problem was that, unlike older jets, the entire rear stabiliser on the tail of the A380 moved up and down, effectively slicing off the legs of the traditional kangaroo. 'We would have had a national icon without any legs. That's why it had to change,' said Hulsbosch.[22] He said it took him ten minutes to redraft the kangaroo with its legs forward to avoid the moving stabiliser. But that was the easy part. The new kangaroo then had to be redrawn and applied to the whole Qantas fleet, plus every single branded Qantas item – stationery, baggage carts, napkins, you name it. Just designing the new look is estimated to have cost Qantas $2 million – implementing it cost a great deal more.

Another Dixon marketing coup was to sign up Hollywood star John Travolta as a Qantas ambassador. The plane-mad actor had his own vintage Boeing 707 and lived at a pilots' resort in Ocala, Florida, which had a double garage for two jets and, instead of a driveway, a runway that could land a 747 jumbo jet. Travolta explained during a 2004 promotional tour for the movie *The Punisher* how the unlikely partnership came about: 'I went to them and said, "I love your airline, it has a perfect safety record for 84 years and I would like to be part of it somehow," and they came up with the ambassador idea. They offered me to get my 747 wings and I did then I flew around the world twice for them and I enjoyed every second of it. I love being their ambassador.'[23]

Travolta, the self-confessed airline geek, had clearly studied the Hollywood version of Qantas's safety record. He sealed the deal by painting his former Qantas jet in Qantas colours, wearing a Qantas pilot's uniform and flying his vintage 707 from Los Angeles to Sydney, Melbourne, Perth, Singapore, Hong Kong, Tokyo, London, Rome, Paris, Frankfurt and New York on The Spirit of Friendship Tour in 2002.

The exact financial nature of the relationship has never been made public. Qantas would only say that the details of their arrangement were confidential. But there is speculation that, in return for his endorsement, Travolta receives Qantas landing rights at airports, and possibly other advantages such as fuel and insurance. He certainly uses the Qantas facilities to keep up his own and his co-pilots' 747 pilot proficiency levels. 'There's a big Qantas building at the airport and in that building there's the latest up-to-date simulators for the 747 and we go over there and do it,' Travolta said. 'They throw simulated dangers at you. One after another. All day long you are bombarded by fake emergencies, but you have to treat them as though they're really happening to you so your heart pounds, your adrenalin goes but you handle it.'[24] He explained that his love of flying was the reason he only ever acted in movies. 'That's why I don't produce or direct because the time I take to keep up my hours and professional profile as a pilot would be the time I would be producing and directing. You can't do both. You can be a hired actor and be a professional pilot, but you can't be a hired actor, producer, director and still be a professional pilot. There's not enough time in the day. Whenever I'm finished with a movie then I have to dedicate so much time to the flying to keep proficiency.'[25]

He also has to devote time to helping Qantas promote the airline. In October 2008 he turned up in full uniform with Australian *Grease* co-star Olivia Newton-John at Los Angeles airport to give the new Airbus A380 super jumbo a Hollywood red-carpet welcome. His attendance helped generate worldwide publicity for the airline. Dixon was on hand to tuck into meat pies and sausage rolls with the Hollywood mate to whom he first presented a pair of Qantas golden wings in 2002.

Meanwhile, back in the less glamorous world of running

an airline business, and before Travolta came on board, Strong and his team had won a lot of admirers for the way they steered Qantas through the Asian economic crisis of 1998 without a loss. In fact Qantas profits rose on average 15.5 per cent a year from the time Strong took over. In 1999 the cost of fuel around the world increased by 44 per cent but Qantas managed to offset that by putting in a hedging strategy that cut the effect of the hike in fuel costs by 80 per cent. The net profit after tax for that year was a record $517.9 million.

Even so, Qantas faced a number of challenges. Richard Branson's Virgin Blue started up, joining Impulse Airlines in battering Qantas and Ansett with cheap fares on major domestic routes. Costs started to rise with landing charges at Sydney airport going up and the airline needed to commit itself to upgraded planes, which cost an awful lot of money.

Little wonder that when Dixon won the internal fight with Toomey and succeeded Strong in the CEO's office, a cartoon at the time depicted Dixon at the joystick of a flaming Qantas aircraft with Strong wearing a parachute and preparing to jump out. It was the 'proverbial shit sandwich'. But Dixon had been hoping and longing for the role. His mate Singleton said: 'It's not often when you're older than the CEO you'll ever get the chance, you know; and Geoff and I often discussed the frustration of him probably never getting a shot at this and, if he didn't what he would do. We discussed all sorts of options and then, when he got the job, it was like someone who makes the Australian team when they didn't think much of their chances.'[26]

Former Qantas company secretary Stephen Heesh told the *Australian Financial Review*: 'There was a sense of "I wonder how he'll go?" Personally, I thought, "You poor bugger; you've inherited a real can of worms here." But he made it work. There were some pretty tough decisions that had to be made, and I don't think James would have been the right man in the job at the time. Geoff is not unreasonable, but he's a tough little character.'[27]

He needed to be. The wiry rugby five-eighth had grown into a fiercely competitive man. The Zegna suits sat well on a fit frame pounded into shape with a 5 am run along Balmoral Beach whenever Dixon was not on a plane somewhere.

He was about to have his first really major test as the head of the nation's number one airline. The first thing he did was follow Strong's lead and bring in his own team. Two hundred management staff were shown the door but three were promoted – Denis Adams, John Borghetti and Paul Edwards now reported directly to Dixon himself. They joined an elite team loyal to Dixon that included Steve Mann, David Burden and Peter Gregg.

Qantas's major international competitor, Singapore Airlines, announced it wanted to increase its stake in Air New Zealand to 49 per cent. Air New Zealand owned Ansett. If Singapore Airlines pulled off its bid, it would be able to take on Qantas on its domestic Australian routes with devastating effect. Dixon went on the offensive, telling anyone who would listen that the deal would marginalise Qantas. He knew the people in the corridors of power and he used every contact and emotional tool at his disposal to stymie the Singapore Airlines proposal. Chairwoman Margaret Jackson joined him in the Oak Room restaurant in Canberra when he argued the Qantas case to Deputy Prime Minister John Anderson, tourism minister Jackie Kelly and Max Moore-Wilton, the influential head of the Department of Prime Minister and Cabinet. It was a private company's convincing rallying cry to the Australian flag. 'Qantas, through Margaret Jackson and myself, had every right to the point of view, which we held strongly, that the airline industry in this country would not be best served by allowing Air New Zealand, Singapore Airlines, Ansett all to get together,' said Dixon.[28] So persuaded of the case was the previously doubtful Anderson that when he crossed the Tasman to argue the point to New Zealand finance minister Michael Cullen, he was dubbed 'Minister for Qantas' by the Kiwis.

Dixon was also lobbying hard. He made a counter offer to buy Singapore Airlines' share of Air New Zealand and for Singapore to buy Ansett. When it was knocked back Dixon was resolute. Jim Farmer QC, then chairman of Air New Zealand, said: 'His words were to the effect that he did not believe that the Australian Government, in particular the Foreign Investment Review Board, would approve of Singapore Airlines obtaining such an increased presence in the region. If that wasn't their view, Qantas would certainly consider taking legal action to ensure that that view prevailed,' he told the *Australian*.[29] Farmer was in no doubt about what Dixon was doing. 'He did run interference and it undoubtedly had the effect of creating a degree of uncertainty and instability in the market, which affected Air New Zealand's share price, which then snowballed into the ultimate result,' he said.[30]

Air New Zealand needed a rescue package from its

government and Ansett collapsed, going into voluntary administration the day after the September 11 attacks in 2001. It had operated for 66 years. Qantas helped ferry 100,000 stranded Ansett passengers to their destinations and then set about capitalising on the huge gap left in the domestic market. 'You can say, well, why shouldn't he?' Farmer said of Dixon's actions. 'But the question really is, they haven't thwarted us through fair play in the marketplace, they've done it through political mechanisms and processes, and that's a matter, I think, of criticism.'[31]

Farmer was not alone in this view. The Australian report that carried the interview with him concluded with new market research from a Melbourne institution, which used Qantas as a benchmark. It seemed that by 2002 the research was throwing up the usual words associated with Qantas – Australian, safe, flying and kangaroo – plus one new one: arrogant. The airline's slide from public favour was well underway. Staff morale was being badly affected by the rounds of cost-cutting and no one in the airline's management seemed to fully understand what a special place Qantas held in the hearts of the nation. Unusually for a company, Qantas was a source of national pride. Losing that badge of honour took quite a few years; getting it back would be the really hard part.

QF9

TOXIC AIR

Qantas flight QF26 left Los Angeles airport under maximum thrust on Saturday 28 July 2007 bound for Auckland, New Zealand. As the plane climbed through 8,000 feet on its way to its cruising altitude, the cockpit filled with a pungent odour similar to blue cheese or vomit. All the air vents in the cockpit on the Boeing 747-338 series jet were directed onto the flight engineer sitting behind the two pilots. He began to struggle. His eyes were watering, his chest tightened and he fought for breath. As he ran through the emergency checklist with blurring vision, he became confused as to whether he had checked an item or not. The flight engineer, captain and first officer put on their oxygen masks in order to continue flying the plane safely. Two non-operating Qantas crew members – relief crew travelling in the cockpit – headed back into the main passenger cabin to try to identify the source of the smell. They came back to say it had also spread through the jumbo's upper deck and part of the lower passenger area. The crew traced the source of the smell to the air conditioning unit.

After eight minutes the smell had cleared and the operating crew were able to take off the oxygen masks. But the flight engineer was so badly overcome, his heart beating erratically and eyes watering, that he had to go back to the passenger cabin for 15 minutes until his head cleared. The plane carried on to Auckland, where it landed and the flight engineer visited a doctor. None of the passengers who breathed in the same fumes on the flight was told anything was wrong. One of the off-duty Qantas staff who had gone into the passenger cabin had not used an oxygen mask at any time and was exposed to the fumes on the upper deck, flight deck and passenger cabin. When he got to Auckland he felt ill and had to be flown home to Sydney. Once home he spent three days violently vomiting, giving himself a double hernia, and had to seek workers compensation before finally being able to return to work several weeks later.

The toxic fumes event suffered by the flight engineer was not uncommon. It is part of an international aviation scandal that is equivalent in scale to the discovery that smoking or asbestos is bad for you. The truth is only just emerging and no one in the aviation industry wants you to read it. When confronted with these details, Qantas stated that it operated all cabin-air systems within the manufacturer's guidelines and complied with CASA directives. It pointed out that toxic air instances are very rare – that if there were 13 in a 12-month period, this would equate to one event around every 24,000 flights. But what if you were on one of those flights?

All over the globe, flight crew, pilots and flight attendants have been mounting legal campaigns because their lives have been ruined by inhaling toxic fumes. These are professionals who can no longer work, in some cases can barely function, because of their exposure to these fumes. Others are dying. The flight crews can mount a case and point to individual incidents, but what about the passengers? Many of them have been unknowingly exposed to toxic fumes on aircraft and as a result are struggling with health and mental problems that go undiagnosed for years.

The problem is a cost-cutting design flaw present in almost all modern passenger jet aircraft. It is not possible to pump air for people to breathe straight from the outside of a jet into the pressurised cabin. At the altitude modern jets fly the air is too cold. Originally, on the early Boeing 707 aircraft, the air was pumped through a small compressor on top of the engine. But on later aircraft, such as the classic 747, designers instead chose to overcome the problem by taking air straight from the compressor inside the hot jet engine. This superheated air is then cooled to cabin temperature in an air conditioning unit and pumped into the cabin. At no time is the air filtered.

Problems arise when there is any kind of oil leak in the front of the engine. A worn seal and a small leak are enough. Mobil Jet Oil 2 is harmless enough in a can, but superheat it in a jet engine and it breaks down into a deadly cocktail of airborne carcinogens and organophosphates, including the particularly nasty tricresyl phosphate, or TCP, which attack the nervous system and can cause long- and short-term brain damage, and motor neurone disorders such as Parkinson's disease. When cooled and pumped into the cockpit and cabin of a modern jetliner, this chemically laced air smells oddly like blue cheese or vomit.

Airlines have long disputed these claims, which are now being independently researched at the University of Washington. The Civil Aviation Authority in Australia has also set up an independent panel of experts to determine the extent of the problem and to decide if further investigation is necessary.

On a new plane toxic air is not usually a problem because there is little wear and tear and consequently few leaks. In fact, the new Boeing 787 Dreamliner does not use 'bleed' air, cabin air bled directly from the engines, at all and so it will never pump toxic air into the cabin. But if you have an aircraft operator with an existing and ageing fleet, who is on a cost-cutting drive and may not be doing the maintenance quite as quickly as desired, an oil leak can be pumping chemically laced fumes into a cabin for days, weeks or even months.

The Qantas Boeing 747 that operated as QF26 out of Los Angeles has the registration number VH-EBW and a shocking maintenance record. The problem on VH-EBW was an oil leak in the auxiliary power unit (APU), a tiny jet engine in the tail of the plane that provides power to the electrics and air conditioning while the plane is stationary and waiting for the engines to be started for take-off. 'These units are not really important and are usually just run into the ground,' said a Qantas technician who did not want to be named. 'When the oil leaks it flows to the air condition-ing unit in the middle of the plane and settles on the water separator. The air conditioning unit separates the water from the air that is pumped into the cabin. The separation process dislodges the oil, which is then turned to gas by the superheated air that comes in from the engine. That gas is then pumped into the cabin with the cooled air.'[1] The APU is turned off before the plane takes off so the smell in the cabin only lasts as long as it takes to burn off the leakage from that sector.

Qantas keeps thorough logs on all its planes. The techni-cal defect log for VH-EBW shows the APU needed to have a quart of oil added on 11 October 2006, nine months before the flight engineer was overcome on the flight from Los Ange-les to New Zealand. Another quart was added a week later on 18 October 2006. On 15 November it needed 1.5 quarts of oil. Then the fault light started flashing – and kept flash-ing. On 19 January the APU was topped up with 1.5 quarts of Mobil Jet Oil 2, two quarts on the 24th and 1.5 litres on the 31st. Month by month the engineers kept topping up the oil. Where was it going? They checked for external leaks and replaced the oil tank cap but still the oil level kept dropping. More oil was poured, quarts and quarts of it. The APU oil tank only held four quarts of oil. In April 2007 it burned through almost two full tanks of oil. In July it went through two more tanks.

Four days before the Los Angeles toxic fumes incident, the log showed that an inspection of the APU found the cooling air manifold and APU firewall were wet with oil.

The air cooling fan seal was replaced and the tired old APU pushed back into service. On 10 August, less than two weeks after the fumes incident, two quarts of oil were needed and two days later another two quarts were added. On 17 August the technical log finally considered the APU might be the cause of several complaints of fumes in the cabin. On 18 August a suspected rear bearing leak was identified as the possible cause of the leak. That was almost three weeks after the flight engineer had to be laid off work because of fumes in the cockpit and at least nine months after they started topping up the oil. In the meantime the plane had still been flying – turning oil into toxic gas on every sector.

It is not as though the alarm was not being raised. Technical logs filed by the crew reported the smell of jet oil fumes in the cockpit when the plane flew from Auckland to Melbourne – the day after the flight engineer was sent home sick. On 31 July the flight crew reported that MJ II oil vapour was coming through gasper outlets. For three weeks after the flight engineer fell sick the plane kept flying – Auckland, Melbourne, Perth, Sydney, Los Angeles. Pumping carcinogens and organophosphates into the cabin air every time the engines started.

Qantas finally swung into action after complaints by aircrew led to WorkCover NSW issuing an improvement notice on the airline relating to two incidents of fumes on aircraft flight decks. News of that prompted Qantas to say: 'Instances such as these are extremely rare and we take them seriously. In accordance with WorkCover requirements we are reviewing our occupational health and safety procedures and are in the process of discussing these procedures with our people. WorkCover fully supports this approach. There is no evidence to suggest that cabin air quality is an issue in any of our aircraft.'[2] When presented with all this information in September 2009, the airline remained dismissive. 'Odour or fume incidents are generally short in duration and it is not always possible to identify the source. In relation to the QF26 incident referred to, extensive checks were carried out but the source could not be identified. At the time, the aircraft was climbing at 8,000 feet in the vicinity of bushfires in California, and one theory was that it flew through a smoke plume. Oil usage in the aircraft's APU in the prior months was always within manufacturer limits. At the time of the incident, the APU had been shut down for around 20 minutes and therefore could not have caused the event.'[3]

But it was not an isolated incident. The fumes on the Qantas Boeing 767 with the registration VH-ZXA were also reported to WorkCover. Other technical logs show that a Qantas classic Boeing 747 with the registration VH-EBV also had fumes in the cockpit in February 2008.

Globally, flight crew are so concerned about toxic fumes that they have united, behind their employers' backs, to take swabs from the walls inside commercial airliners on three continents, including Australia. In 85 per cent of cases they found positive traces of the chemicals generated by superheated jet oil. The Australian and International Pilots' Association, which represents Qantas pilots, does not want to create a panic, but

Association General Manager Peter Somerville said: 'People don't need to stop flying but there is a problem and it needs to be fixed.' For flight crew it is a workplace health and safety issue. 'It affects the flight crew more because they receive a lot more oxygen and they fly more often,' he said. [4] But it is a bigger issue than simple occupational health and safety. CASA has deemed that 'smoke, toxic or noxious fumes inside the aircraft' are a 'major defect'. [5] Australian Federation of Air Pilots spokesman Lawrie Cox warned: 'If we get a major incident where two pilots are affected, the outcome would be a disaster.' [6]

Flight crews felt for a long time that Qantas maintenance standards were not being monitored closely enough by CASA. A Senate inquiry into the administration of the authority highlighted the problems. One submission by retired airworthiness inspector David Klein said that only 20 per cent of Qantas operations overseas had been checked and that 'total faith' was placed in Qantas's ability to regulate itself. He said more inspectors were needed.

In fact, the authorities do not appear to know about many of the instances of toxic fumes leaking into the cabin. On many affected flights an Air Safety Incident Report was not sent to the ATSB because the captain filling out the report did not tick the box at the bottom marked 'ATSB Reportable'. No tick and it goes into the bottom drawer at Qantas HQ, never to be seen again. No paper trail. No CASA or ATSB involvement. It is simply monitored by the Qantas safety team. No problem. When challenged, Qantas said: 'It is both the law, under the Transportation Safety Investigation Act, and Qantas policy for any employee, including our pilots, to report safety occurrences via the well-established Air Safety

Incident Report (ASIR) system. In fact, our internal reporting system goes beyond the requirements of the Act. If a pilot "ticks the box" on an ASIR, it is automatically forwarded to the ATSB. If a pilot does not "tick the box" when we know of an incident, we will still notify the ATSB. Following the QF26 event referred to, the ASIR was forwarded to the ATSB.'[7] So, definitely no problem then.

Except something is going wrong in the system, because many of these instances do not appear on the ATSB website, which records the progress of all incident investigations. The problem is a lot worse than Qantas maintained in its disingenuous statement when it said that instances such as this are 'extremely rare', after the QF26 event was exposed in the Australian media. It might also explain why it can happily maintain there is no evidence to suggest air quality is an issue on any of its aircraft.

Qantas keeps an internal Fumes Event Register, on which crews can file an Accident/Injury Reporting System (AIRS) Injury-to-Personnel Report if they are concerned they have been exposed to fumes and might need to make a workers compensation claim at a later date. The register from July 2007 to July 2008 itemises a shocking 31 separate AIRS incident notifications on 13 different jets for exposure to toxic fumes by Qantas crew, starting with QF26 out of Los Angeles. On 8 November one notification was filed when fumes were smelled in the cabin of a Boeing 737 registered VH-VYH during take-off and descent. Two notifications were filed on 7 December after fumes were detected when Boeing 737 registered VH-VXF was locked down for five minutes during a thunderstorm. On Christmas Day one notification was filed after fumes were detected and Boeing 747-300 VH-EBY was pushed back to the blocks. Two months later, on 25 February, three more were filed when the cockpit of the same plane, VH-EBY, filled with fumes and the flight crew had to put on their oxygen masks. One was filed when fumes were detected on Boeing 747-400 VH-OEG on 2 January and two on 18 February when fumes were smelled on Boeing 747-300 VH-EBV. An engine wash on Boeing 737 VH-VYD led to fumes during the take-off roll on 28 February. There were three incident notifications on 7 April from crew on Boeing 747-400 VH-OJC and one on 8 June from Boeing 767 VH-OGN. On 15 June three crew filed notifications after inhaling smoke in the cabin of Boeing 747-400 VH-OGS and two after breathing a 'slight haze' on boarding Boeing 737 VH-VXC on 4 July. On 17 June Boeing 767 VH-OGR had two notifications filed and the same plane had one case medically treated on 1 July.

The worst offender was Boeing 737 VH-TJZ. It appeared no less than three times on the Fumes Event Register. On 23 November one crew member filed a notification for breathing in toxic fumes, on 9 January two people filed notifications for breathing fumes during take-off, and two more crew members filed notifications for the same thing on 16 January. The technical log for VH-TJZ is even more damning. It first reports a complaint of an oil smell in the cockpit and cabin on 20 November 2007. On 23 November the APU was found to be leaking oil into the air conditioning system and was changed. On 16 January, when two crew members had filed AIRS notifications for breathing toxic fumes, the engines were checked and run at 90 per cent of power. The mechanics could not smell any fumes. Five days later, on 21 January, the smell was recorded again and the engineers finally found that oil was leaking in the middle of engine number one. The jet was cleared to fly from Brisbane to Melbourne, where the leaking engine was taken off and replaced on 23 January. Qantas had let the jet fly with oil being superheated into toxic gas and pumped into the cabin for over two months. In that time five Qantas crew members had been affected by the fumes badly enough to file incident notifications. Qantas only conceded: 'Our records show that fewer than five claims were submitted by employees in the period July 2007 to July 2008 related to cabin-air quality issues. These generally involved small claims for costs associated with doctors' visits and days off work.'[8] While only fewer than five were sick enough to go to the doctors, the afore-mentioned 31 were affected badly enough to register the event on the AIRS Injury to Personnel Report. Qantas added: 'Protocols are in place to ensure appropriate support is provided to flight or cabin crew members in the event of an incident, including assistance with medical checks where necessary.'[9] But, and this is the most telling point of all, none of the passengers on any of the flights had been told of any problem.

The ATSB appeared to be investigating just one of the incidents – VH-EBY on 25 February. Clearly the Qantas captains had not ticked the little box, even though CASA indicated fumes events were a major defect. No wonder efforts to find out how many fumes events really happened were met with calming platitudes. CASA spokesman Peter Gibson said there had been six cases of toxic fumes events in Australia the year before. Six? And he was not particularly worried about them either. 'No health and safety authority anywhere in the world has anything to prove there is any danger,' he said.[10] Now we know why – they don't know about most of them. In response to concern over the issue, CASA has now set up an Expert Panel on Aircraft Air Quality, which is expected to report back on the issue by the first quarter of 2010.

University of New South Wales toxicologist Chris Winder said: 'The industry has been running silent on this issue. They need to acknowledge it is a problem. Oils in jet engines are toxic. It's OK if they stay in engines, but if it comes out of the engine and gets into the bleed air system crew, pilots and passengers can get sick.'[11]

Australia led the world with an investigation into the effect of toxic fumes suffered by Ansett and Australian Airlines crew flying on the notorious BAe 146 jet in the early 1990s. That plane pumped noxious fumes into the cabin so frequently that the crew only noticed when it didn't smell. A survey by the University of New South Wales of 242 BAe 146 pilots found that eight out of ten breathed toxicants during flight and six out of ten of those suffered short-term consequences such as memory loss. A quarter of them suffered such bad long-term effects that they can no longer work. The fact that today there is little faith in CASA to control this issue is based on past experience. The Senate inquiry into the BAe 146 criticised the authority for dismissing fears about the safety of the toxic aircraft that had been raised by its own staff. Committee chairman John Woodley told the Melbourne *Age* that CASA and British Aerospace's evidence that the aircraft was safe was 'unconvincing'. 'The problem is described by some specialists as

Qantas founder Lieutenant W. Hudson Fysh of 1 Squadron, Australian Flying Corps, standing in front of his Nieuport Scout aircraft, in France, *c.* 1918. (Australian War Memorial, negative number P00342.001)

The first Qantas office, Duck Street, Longreach, Queensland, 1921. (National Archives of Australia; B941/2)

Part of the Qantas de Havilland fleet in front of the airline's Brisbane hangar, 1934. The *Atalanta* on the far right was destroyed in an accident near Winton, killing the pilot and two passengers. (Macarthur Job)

A Qantas DH86 refuelling at Cloncurry. The plane was plagued with problems due to the hurried design process, which Qantas insisted on in order to land a vital and lucrative airmail contract. (Macarthur Job)

Wreckage of the DH86 that crashed outside Longreach on its delivery flight from England, killing all four on board. (Macarthur Job)

The Coolangatta, one of the Qantas Empire flying boats that ushered in a new era of luxury flight on the Kangaroo Route between Australia and England. (Lionel Perry/Gold Coast City Council Local Studies Library)

The smoking salon on an Empire flying boat. After a visit passengers could adjourn to the promenade deck for quoits. (Hulton-Deutsch Collection/Corbis)

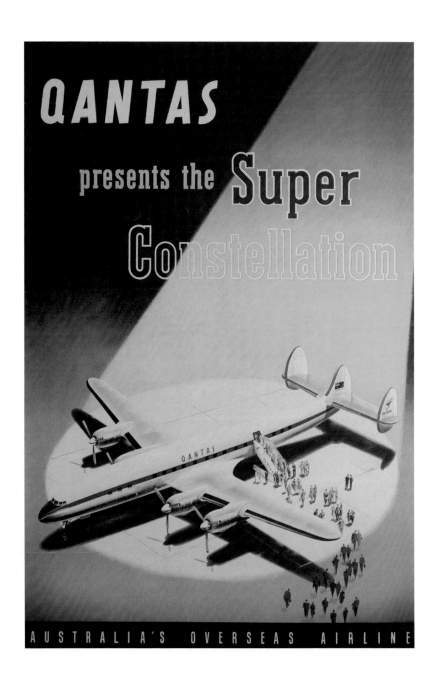

In May 1954, the first Qantas Super Constellation flew from Sydney to San Francisco. (Josef Lebovic Gallery)

Wreckage of the Lockheed Super Constellation VH-EAC, which suffered an engine failure on take-off from Mauritius in 1960. The Department of Civil Aviation's Director of Air Safety Investigation said, 'This was a "cheap" accident for Qantas . . . the important thing is to ensure the company acknowledges the weaknesses involved in bringing it about and is made to see it was completely avoidable.' (Macarthur Job)

Peter Macari, a.k.a. Mr Brown, who extorted $500,000 from Qantas by claiming he had placed a bomb on a Hong Kong-bound jet in 1971. The claim was a hoax and he was caught after going on a spending spree with the money. (Fairfax Photos)

QF1 at Bangkok Airport in 1999 after hydroplaning along the wet runway and ending up nose down on the next-door golf course. Cost-cutting measures by management were blamed for the crash. The jet hull was eventually repaired and put back into service. It is claimed aircrew have since nicknamed it the golf buggy. (Sukree Suplang/Reuters/Picture Media)

New broom . . . James Strong, who swept out many of the Qantas old guard, pictured here at the Qantas AGM in 1999. (Fairfax Photos)

Qantas chief executive Geoff Dixon displays his marketing flair introducing new Qantas ambassador, Hollywood star and aircraft fanatic John Travolta, in 2002. (Krista Niles/AP)

Qantas ambassador John Travolta launches Jetstar with Alan Joyce (in front of Travolta to his left) and Magda Szubanski, in Sydney, 2004. (William West/AFP/Getty Images)

Woman of steel: Qantas chairman Margaret Jackson as seen by the *Daily Telegraph*'s Eric Lobbecke in August 2004 as she battled the Federal Government for what she called a level playing field – Qantas paying the same low tax as other international airlines. (Newspix/News Ltd)

The hug that said it all . . . Qantas chief executive Geoff Dixon and chairman Margaret Jackson at a news conference to announce the proposed sale of Qantas to TPG/Macquarie. (Newspix/News Ltd)

Lisa Robertson, *English Patient* star Ralph Fiennes's favourite hostie. She was sacked after her mile-high-club antics with the actor appeared in the press. It later emerged she had supplemented her hostess wages by moonlighting as a prostitute. (Nigel Wright)

Designer Hans Hulsbosch displays his new, streamlined kangaroo logo on a model of a Qantas Airbus 380, Sydney, 2007. The latest variation on a theme, originally adapted from the old penny coin, was first painted beneath the cockpit of a Qantas Liberator aircraft in 1944. Qantas became known as the flying kangaroo when wings were added to that design in 1947. (AFP/Newspix/News Ltd)

New generation . . . Qantas CEO Alan Joyce attends a press conference in Toulouse, France, in 2008, before the delivery ceremony of the first A380 to Qantas. (Pascal Parrot/Getty Images)

The damage to the fuselage of a Qantas 747-400 in 2008 after the number four oxygen tank exploded in the hold, causing rapid depressurisation in the cabin and forcing the pilot to drop from 10,000 to 3,000 metres. The pilot landed safely in Manila on back-up controls.

The damage inside the aeroplane after the oxygen bottle had punched through the floor, hit the door handle and smashed into the overhead locker, before being sucked back through the hole and being lost, probably in the South China Sea.

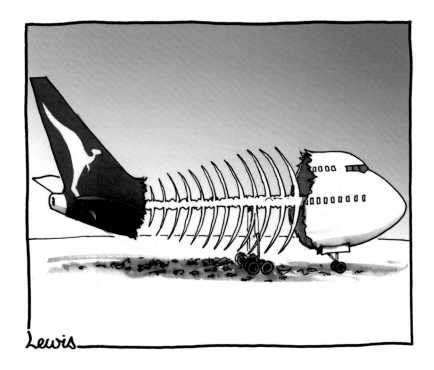

Cutbacks . . . there is concern about just how much can be trimmed off the airline. (Peter Lewis/*Newcastle Herald*. www.peterlewisart.com)

aerotoxic syndrome and warrants further extensive clinical and technical investigation,' Mr Woodley said.[12] His concerns were justified.

The claims of the flight crew were stymied when the two airlines dropped their complaints against the manufacturer of the BAe 146 and instead pursued the American manufacturers of the faulty components. Documents tabled before the Senate in 2007 showed that Ansett and East West were paid more than $2 million in hush money by British Aerospace to go after the component manufacturers instead. Labor Senator Kerry O'Brien said: 'There is no doubt there has been a cover-up. Australians now need to be reassured these sort of contamination issues are not currently endangering crew and passengers.'[13] When that evidence was sent to the House of Lords in Great Britain, Lord Tyler told the House: 'Pilots, cabin crew and passengers have been denied information. It seems that BAe were more concerned about the leak of this document than the leak of toxic fumes into aircraft, with a potentially devastating result.'[14] The British government, in an echo of the tone of aviation industry officials in Australia, said that only one in 2,000 flights were affected by fumes. Lord Tyler replied: 'The Committee on Toxicology has refused to take evidence from the group representing pilots who are affected. In any event, one in 2,000 is hardly a drop in the ocean when there are some 2.5 million flights taking off across the world every month. Just one fatal incident would be one too many.'[15]

Susan Michaelis was a BAe 146 pilot flying QantasLink passengers up and down the east coast of Australia for National Jet Systems. An experienced pilot, the day she stepped into the cockpit of a BAe 146, she questioned the smell of 'old socks and vomit'. After a while her voice became husky and then she started to suffer nausea, headaches, dizziness, tiredness and had trouble concentrating. At 35 years old and at the height of her flying career, she went home one night and collapsed. She was suffering from what would become known as aerotoxic syndrome. 'The extent of the injury is shattering. I can never fly again. After years of visiting specialists I now know that the damage is irreversible. I have lung function and neurological abnormalities, permanent head pressure, I have difficulty concentrating, suffer chronic fatigue and chemical sensitivity, scans have shown brain damage and I have beryllium – the metal in BAe 146 engine bearings – attached to my DNA,' she said.[16] Michaelis has gone on to become a campaigner to highlight the dangers of toxic air in modern jets. 'This is the asbestos of the skies. My determination to be a pilot has been replaced by a determination to bring about a change in an industry and stop others suffering what I have to live with for the rest of my life.'[17]

The first step in that fight would be for airlines such as Qantas to be honest about toxic fumes incidents that occur on its aircraft.

QF10

JETSTAR

In July 2004 passengers on Jetstar flight 711 to Sydney had just taken off from Hamilton Island in Queensland's Whitsundays when they were thrown sharply to the left. 'I felt my stomach go down, and the people said to me, "Oh, did you see that?" and I said, "No", and they said, "Oh, it was a Qantas plane really close,"' said New Zealand tourist Wendy Stevens.[1] Fellow passenger Alan Bowler, travelling with his wife and children, was sitting on the other side of the Jetstar Boeing 717 and was also suddenly jerked to the left. The horizon disappeared. 'All we could see was the water shimmering, and we were getting closer to it,' he said.[2] The larger Boeing 737 of Qantas flight QF1174 from Brisbane was coming in to land at exactly the same time as the Jetstar flight was taking off. Both planes were under the control of the Hamilton Island tower as the drama unfolded. 'The Qantas flight crew could see the Jetstar aircraft at all times,' Qantas reassured the travelling public in a statement. Many experts had predicted low-cost start-up airline Jetstar would collide with its rich parent Qantas when it was launched in 2004, but no one expected anything quite that dramatic.

Jetstar was born out of Qantas's need to maintain a foothold in the ferociously competitive budget airfare market. At the start of the millennium Qantas was looking for ways to hold market share against Richard Branson's budget airline Virgin Blue. The dogfight was a battle for more passengers on lower fares, with $1 one-way trips grabbing front-page headlines. And it did not take long to get dirty. Virgin Blue's chief executive, Brett Godfrey, accused Qantas of 'blatant capacity dumping' after Qantas added another plane to Virgin's new Brisbane to Adelaide route in January 2001.[3] Virgin had just put two planes on the route, adding to the Qantas and Ansett flights already servicing it daily. Virgin's flights had already increased capacity by 90 per cent. More importantly for customers, Virgin was offering fares that, at $118 one way, were half the price of a Qantas fare. Godfrey felt it was 'very cynical' of Qantas to then put on another plane, increasing seating capacity yet further, and offer a new $117.70 fare that undercut Virgin by 30 cents. He complained to the Australian Competition and Consumer Commission.

Meanwhile, of course, passengers were delighted. Their joy at Australia's domestic market finally becoming affordable was echoed by Commission chairman Allan Fels, who said: 'The process of getting more competition in the airline industry is of great importance.'[4]

But inside the boardroom of Qantas the problem of how to deal with Virgin, which was based in Brisbane and armed with a war chest from the Queensland government, was vexing the men and women in grey suits. Qantas had already seen off the threat of Impulse Airlines, which had been targeting its business travel market. Qantas had solved the Impulse problem by agreeing to 'wet lease' – hiring the plane, crew, maintenance and insurance to fly under the Qantas flag for a short, fixed term – Impulse's aircraft and crew in return for a cash injection and an option to buy the airline if it wanted. By November 2001 Qantas had taken the option and absorbed the Impulse planes and crew into its QantasLink fleet. Virgin's Brett Godfrey vowed to keep fighting. 'Virgin Blue does not want to go the same way. They do not want to be absorbed into another carrier or disappear from the face of the earth. We came here, we now see ourselves as the only low-fare carrier in this country and we are the ones going to keep the buggers honest.'[5]

However, Qantas's reputation was tarnished by the Impulse deal, not through any wrongdoing but simply by association. Impulse boss Gerry McGowan told flamboyant Sydney stockbroker Rene Rivkin about the impending merger. Rivkin bought 50,000 Qantas shares based on the information and made a trivial $346 profit. He was investigated for insider trading by the Australian Securities and Investments Commission (ASIC) and in May 2003 was sentenced by the New South Wales Supreme Court to nine months of weekend detention and fined $30,000. Media reports frequently mentioned the words 'Qantas' and 'insider trading' in the same breath, which cast an unfair shadow on the airline.

Rivkin also helped drag another Qantas name through the mud. Order of Australia recipient Trevor Kennedy was forced to resign from the Qantas board after it was revealed that he, Rivkin and Labor king-maker Graham Richardson had shareholdings in a printing company called Offset Alpine, which they had hidden offshore in a secret Swiss bank account. The printing plant of Offset Alpine had burned down in 1993 and the insurance premium had paid $53 million on assets valued at just $3 million. Five days after ASIC investigators raided Kennedy's home in November 2003, he resigned his Qantas directorship plus those of several other companies. 'I am resigning my directorships of all public companies forthwith. This is not a result of pressure from any of the fine companies and wonderful colleagues I am associated with. It is quite the contrary. I do not believe that I have broken any laws, nor that I have done anything dishonest at all, but the speculation in relation to the allegations against me leads me to the view that these companies will suffer,' he said in a statement.[6]

Qantas came under fire for failing to boot him out. Opposition Finance Spokesman Stephen Conroy told the ABC: 'Well, I was disappointed last week by the reaction of some of the companies he's involved in, particularly Qantas, who said that it's none of their business to ask any questions or seek any information on these matters. I think there's a real question of governance when a board chooses to ignore the sort of revelations that took place in the last two weeks.'[7]

The Offset Alpine saga continued to roll on for years

with the pursuit, trial and eventual jailing of Rivkin's driver, Gordon Wood, for the murder of his girlfriend, Caroline Byrne. She was thrown off The Gap in Sydney for knowing too much about the Offset Alpine deal. Rivkin committed suicide in 2005 and as recently as 2008 Kennedy was hit with a multi-million-dollar tax bill by the Australian Taxation Office for his part in the scandal.

Virgin Blue continued to go from strength to strength, cutting down to 60 per cent Qantas's 90 per cent share of the domestic market it had at the time Ansett failed. Qantas needed to compete without damaging its premier brand and alienating its all-important business clients, who paid a premium to sit at the pointy end of the plane at short notice. An attempt to put all economy jets on certain routes had backfired, with passengers angrily complaining at the lack of their customary luxury perks. The solution was a budget carrier. But other airlines, including Qantas partner British Airways, had tried to launch low-cost options and failed spectacularly. British Airways' Australian-born boss Sir Rod Eddington, formerly executive chairman of Ansett, said he knew British Airway's Go Fly budget brand was not going to work when he heard the chief executive of Go talking on the radio about the routes she intended to target. They were all British Airways' most profitable routes and British Airways had no way of stopping her. British Airways sold Go Fly in 2001 after just three years of the botched experiment.

Geoff Dixon needed to make a Qantas low-budget airline work by learning from the mistakes made elsewhere. He needed someone with previous experience who understood the problem. Fortunately for him he already had that man on the staff, hired from the ashes of Ansett. Dixon had given him a job in 2000 in the route-planning department on the recommendation of Eddington. 'I thought he was terrific,' Eddington told the *Australian*. 'He was well respected and well liked at Ansett. He had very good analytical skills. He was very knowledgeable and he had his ego under control – which is important.'[8]

The man was Alan Joyce, who would go on to be Dixon's successor. Joyce recalled his interview at the Qantas Melbourne office: 'Geoff interviewed me, with his feet on the table, for about fifteen minutes.'[9] He got the job. Geoff Dixon was an unusually decisive man.

Irish-born Joyce was perfect for the role. Born in 1966, the first of four highly successful siblings, he achieved a double major in physics and mathematics and a masters in management science at Trinity College, Dublin. His father worked as a postman and in a cigarette factory and his mother as a cleaner at a sports centre to help put their four children through university. He first went into computer programming before joining Irish national airline Aer Lingus as an operations research analyst. 'It was the job that attracted me rather than the airline, [but] I got kerosene in my nostrils,' he told the *Australian*.[10] He actually wanted to be a pilot but his eyesight wasn't good enough. Instead he was tasked with coming up with finding a way to meet the threat of Ryanair, which Michael O'Leary had turned into the pin-up hero of cut-price airlines the world over. Joyce's detailed analysis of the sector came to nothing then, but it was the perfect foundation when, years later at Qantas, Geoff Dixon called him in to look at how a low-cost carrier could be set up to match Virgin Blue.

Joyce already knew what not to do. 'There were two types of failures. The ones that compromised on cost base and ended up not having the advantage to compete against the others. Ted [United Airlines] and Song [Delta Airlines] and a lot of the American carriers fall into that category. They were too expensive,' said Joyce.[11] 'On the other side were the Go-type airlines, which got the cost base down but which were completely independent of the parent and the cure became worse than the disease,' he said.[12] Dixon had already told him not to base Jetstar in Sydney, in order to maintain its independence – Joyce chose Melbourne – and never to put it before Qantas. 'If I wanted to do a Qantas route, we had to debate it. We made sure we never competed,' Joyce said.[13] Every decision was put before a board chaired by Dixon and featuring Joyce and Executive General Manager John Borghetti.

Joyce went away and spent a week 'pressure testing' a business model with old Aer Lingus boss Conor McCarthy, before putting a detailed business plan before the board in October 2003. It was given the go-ahead, using the old Impulse Boeing 717 fleet as the basis of the new airline. Joyce took inspiration from the hugely successful Ryanair, even employing a couple of its former executives to help build the business model. 'Jetstar sought to adopt the efficiency of Ryanair,' Joyce said. 'Ryanair has also achieved notable success with their direct ticket sales via the internet.'[14] He mimicked the lightning fast 25-minute plane turnaround of Ryanair, which was five minutes faster than Virgin Blue and ten minutes faster than Qantas. This maximised the use of the plane and cut down on crew stopovers.

Free seating also helped. 'Our free seating process saves

THE MEN WHO KILLED QANTAS

Jetstar around five minutes on each aircraft turn, helps return a flight crew to its home operating base by shift's end . . . and overall allows for tighter scheduling across our network,' Joyce said. 'Despite free seating being an entrenched feature of some of the world's most profitable carriers outside of Qantas – such as Southwest, Ryanair and most recently Air-Asia – the net benefits to Jetstar and our customer base have far outweighed the negative PR the procedure originally produced.'[15] It was all about timing. Making customers collect their own bags and check them in again for the next flight also saved Jetstar vital minutes. 'The infamous Irish boss of Ryanair, Michael O'Leary, has proclaimed he would rather catch a social disease than introduce connectivity on his airline,' Joyce told assembled aviation hacks at the National Aviation Press Club. 'Whilst I don't feel that level of passion about this issue, non-connectivity is core to our low-cost culture at Jetstar.'[16]

The major thing that Jetstar did not take from Ryanair was its customer service policy. Jetstar spokesman Simon Westaway said: 'Ryanair is notorious for its level of customer service – or lack of it. We sought not to go down that path. We are very aware of our customers and their needs and you just wouldn't get away with what Ryanair does in Australia.'[17]

Jetstar was jubilant, with roaring internet sales even before a white and orange jet had left the hangar. 'We had the most successful launch of any low-cost carrier, we believe, in the history of aviation,' said Joyce, pointing to the 98,000 bookings taken on the website on the first day of its launch.[18] Virgin Blue's head of communications, David Huttner, begrudgingly snarled: 'If you were gifted fourteen aircraft that moved out of the mother fleet, you would have some success. For a rooster that is yet to fly, he [Joyce] is doing a lot of crowing.'[19]

Jetstar was launched on the back of a funny and popular $15 million advertising campaign featuring the comedienne Magda Szubanski. Qantas ambassador and Hollywood star John Travolta was on hand to unveil the first Jetstar jet – although, for a while, it looked as though the veil would never come off, and Travolta had to ad lib until it finally slid away to reveal the new plane. Two weeks later the first Jetstar flight, JQ371, took off, flying from Newcastle to Melbourne on 25 May 2004. By July Jetstar was flying over 100 flights a day with an average of three-quarters of the seats full.

But there were niggling problems. Passengers complained when they failed to check in 30 minutes before the flight and automatically forfeited their cut-price ticket. The internet ticketing also upset travel agents. Jetstar, sticking to its European model, refused to give agents significant commissions. Graham Turner, boss of one of Australia's biggest travel agencies, Flight Centre, hit back. He arranged with Google for the first internet search of Jetstar to be connected to Flight Centre. The site then said that to make a Jetstar booking you had to call the agency, where it was unlikely that a travel agent on zero commission was going to push the Jetstar flight over a similar Virgin Blue flight that paid the agent five per cent commission.

There were also problems on the ground. In June, a month after the airline was launched, six flights had to be cancelled when a ground handler accidentally used the wrong remote control on an aircraft. He had meant to activate the push-back on one Boeing 717 but instead activated it on the 717 next door, which was still loading passengers. The plane moved back with the airbridge still attached; no one was injured but the front cabin door was badly damaged. Transport Workers' Union official Glenn Nightingale said: 'Questions must be asked if training in this new technology is adequate when this guy made a blunder using the wrong remote control.'[20] Naturally, Jetstar's Simon Westaway was on hand with a reassuring answer: 'The training on these units is not two hours. The training which consists of both practical training and classroom briefing . . . is the equivalent of up to one week's training.'[21] That may well have been the case, but it did not address whether this was an individual blunder or whether a week's training was sufficient.

Then a baggage handler fell off the back of a Jetstar jet while loading luggage and injured his arm, prompting the union to complain of 'sweatshop conditions' and 19-hour shifts. TWU official Nightingale alleged that while Qantas and Virgin Blue had six workers to unload a plane, Qantas subsidiary Express Ground Handling had six workers unloading three Jetstar aircraft. 'It's the epitome of exploitation of workers under sweatshop conditions. It's only a matter of when someone will be killed. Essentially, you have six workers doing the work of what should be 18 workers, with horrendous shifts of 19 hours duration straight.'[22] Jetstar's Westaway offered the reassurance: 'Safety is just simply not compromised.'[23]

How anyone could tell which were Jetstar planes anyway was tricky. At the time of the launch only one had been painted in the airline's orange colours. All 14 Jetstar Boeing

717s had been stripped of their QantasLink designs and some had a temporary decal advertising the website, but they would not all be painted until December. Joyce said it was too costly to take them all out of service at once to paint them. Aviation consultant Hugh Ritchie told the *Sydney Morning Herald* that the blank jets gave passengers a message that 'this organisation hasn't got any brand name. And worse, it's blank. It doesn't bode well for the start-up with the aircraft coming into new ports painted white.'[24]

Despite these problems the public voted with their wallets. For the first time ever the flight was cheaper than the taxi fare to the airport. Jetstar already had plans to expand its services beyond the shores of Australia. Central to that was replacing the ageing 125-seat 717 jets with new Airbus 320s, of which 23 were due for delivery by mid-2006. The first A320 was flown to Melbourne from France in June 2004, only for the CASA inspectors to 'fail' the Jetstar crew that made the flight. 'There were certain issues raised by us in relation to the operation of that flight which Jetstar are addressing,' said CASA spokesman Peter Gibson.[25] Jetstar's Simon Westaway felt it was 'inappropriate to comment on matters between the regulator and the licence holder'.[26] Not that Jetstar had an air operator's certificate for the A320s, only for the 717s, and it needed to put on a series of up-to-scratch flights to get it.

Earlier, CASA had ruled that it was okay for Jetstar pilots rather than engineers to carry out pre-flight safety inspections. The Australian Licensed Aircraft Engineers' Association federal secretary, David Kemp, said it was the same as asking a bus driver to do the work of a mechanic.

But CASA's Peter Gibson argued: 'To use David's analogy, it's no different to asking a bus driver to walk around a bus to check the tyres are in good condition, that there's no obvious damage and that there are no fuel or oil leaks.'[27]

At the heart of many of these publicly raised issues was the anger of Qantas staff that Jetstar was eroding standards of pay and conditions that had taken years for Qantas staff to build up. One Qantas flight crew member recalled: 'When Jetstar started up there were some very ugly scenes in hotels when Qantas and Jetstar crews stopping over would meet at the check-out. The Jetstar crews were working for a lot less money so resented us Qantas high-flyers and we resented them for taking jobs on the cheap.'[28] Jetstar pilots were usually not members of the union and were earning around 40 per cent less for flying the same routes as their Qantas colleagues.

But those pesky unions and all their high-minded ideas of fairness and equality were not going to be the problem to Jetstar that they were to Qantas. By 2007 Jetstar was looking to get as many staff as possible out of the union and on individual contracts. 'Jetstar as an organisation needs the flexibility to grow and we believe that a flexible workplace agreement allows us to do that,' said the indefatigable Jetstar spokesman Simon Westaway.[29] The plan to get as many pilots and engineers as possible on individual workplace agreements was described by the Australian International Pilots' Association as 'a union-busting activity'.[30] Association General Manager Peter Somerville said: 'It has nothing to do with flexibility, it's about peeling employees from their collective representatives.'[31]

In the spring of 2007 the airline set up a subsidiary called Team Jetstar to recruit flight attendants on new, 'flexible' terms and conditions. A recent enterprise bargaining agreement meant that Team Jetstar staff would be paid a lower base wage but have incentive payments for working longer hours. The model was put in place to compete with the in-flight staff cost of new competitor Tiger Airways, which was backed by Singapore Airlines. 'We have to be competitive against new entrants,' said Joyce. 'Tiger had Australian workplace agreements with terms and conditions that are more competitive than Jetstar. Team Jetstar matches those conditions. Through this we can create over 500 new jobs based in Australia.'[32]

But what the unions were worried about was these crews then being used on Qantas routes. A precedent had been set by the Qantas-owned Australian Airlines. Qantas had long ago spotted the advantage of having direct links to more international markets. It had joined with partner British Airways in launching the Oneworld alliance in 1995. American Airlines, Canadian Airlines, Cathay Pacific, Iberia and Finnair had all quickly joined later that year. The alliance gave passengers greater freedom to choose routes across the globe where Qantas did not traditionally fly, increasing the number of people who could use the airline on one straightforward ticket. Qantas had also seen another niche in the tourism market and in 2002 launched a Cairns-based international leisure brand called Australian Airlines. The carrier started flying at the end of 2002 with trips from Cairns to Japan, with Singapore, Thailand, Bali and Hong Kong quickly following.

However, the airline was not a success, despite paying its

staff less than those employed by Qantas and having a cost base 20 to 30 per cent lower. By 2005–6 passenger numbers were dropping – down by 3.6 per cent in a year – and Australian Airlines had lost $11.6 million before interest and tax. It had to go. Qantas wanted to focus instead on launching Jetstar Asia. There was a small overlap, but the domestic Jetstar model had proved to be the example of how a cheap international alternative could work; Australian Airlines had not.

The five Australian Airlines Boeing 767s were repainted in Qantas colours and the 370 employees absorbed back into the airline under their existing workplace arrangements. And that's what the unions did not like. Documents filed by the Australian and International Pilots' Association in the Federal Court in February 2007 alleged that former long-haul Australian Airlines pilots were now flying Qantas jets on Cairns–Tokyo and Sydney–Manila routes. While a Qantas pilot would be paid up to $187 an hour for the job and a Qantas first officer $123 an hour, the Australian Airlines crews were doing it for 20 per cent less. There were 94 Australian Airlines pilots in Qantas uniforms working for less money, said the Association as it sought recompense under the Workplace Relations Act.

Australian Airlines' problems had begun as early as its inaugural flight from Melbourne to Honolulu, when the aircraft was delayed after fuel loaded into the centre wing tank leaked onto the tarmac. The leak was eventually traced to faulty seals and proved another public embarrassment. And slipping through almost unnoticed at the time of its launch were the activities of Australian Roger Donazzan, who had seen the business opportunities on offer in the Japanese ski resorts of the island of Hokkaido. He bought up land there before Qantas announced that Australian Airlines would be flying there direct. As 50,000 Australian skiers, including *Matrix* star Hugo Weaving and his family, headed to the new Japanese ski fields on Australian Airlines jets, Donazzan teamed up with Colin Hackworth, the former director of the Mount Hotham and Falls Creek ski resorts in Australia, to announce the development of an ambitious 8000-bed ski village and resort. It was a sure-fire winner and they would ultimately sell it to a Hong Kong development company backed by billionaire Richard Li for an undisclosed, but presumably extraordinarily large, sum.

Questions were raised by the media when it was revealed that Donazzan's wife and business partner was Margaret Jackson – chairman of Qantas. Harmony Resorts Niseko was registered in November 2003 and was a quarter owned by Donazzan and Jackson. Donazzan had 1.75 million shares and Jackson one million. In June the following year Qantas announced that Australian Airlines would be running a twice-weekly service to Hokkaido during the ski season. Jackson told the *Sydney Morning Herald* that she had advised the Qantas board of her husband's position and had excused herself from any meetings when Japan was discussed. Therefore she had no knowledge of the impending flights to Japan.

Nor did she have a problem telling the board about flying four directors of her husband's company out to Japan with Qantas for free. In the annual report for 2005–6 the fine print revealed that Qantas had 'sponsored' four economy airfares for directors of the ski company Donazzan chaired. Jackson maintained her position that she had done nothing wrong and the board apparently agreed. As did the company, which, in September 2009, stressed that the decisions to fly to Sapporo in 2004 and then stop flights in 2006 were management decisions supported by the board on commercial grounds. It confirmed the annual reports of 2006 and 2007 included disclosure entries with regard to Roger Donazzan and his position as chairman of Harmony Resorts Niseko Pty Ltd. In response to questions it said: 'Qantas upholds the highest standards of corporate governance and rejects any suggestion of governance issues in this specific instance.'[33]

QF11

FREIGHT CARTEL

Bruce McCaffrey looked at the human resources woman in stunned disbelief. For 26 years he had been the efficient head of Qantas freight in America. Now this woman, flown in especially from Australia, was telling him his job was finished, 'based on performance'.[1] But his performance had been exceptional. His performance reviews year after year were excellent. He had built the Qantas share of Australian freight flown through the United States from 15 per cent to 25 per cent and had hit budget for 24 of his 26 years in the top job – one of those he missed was during 9/11. How could he be sacked based on his performance? 'Actually, we don't have to give you a reason,' she said.[2]

McCaffrey did not have to wait very long to find out. The

169

next day Qantas in Australia announced that it had been involved in a price-fixing cartel between 2000 and 2006 and agreed to pay a $A68 million fine to the United States authorities. In return for rolling over, the airline secured an agreement with the US Department of Justice not to prosecute company executives or employees. Six employees were exempt from the deal not to pursue a criminal prosecution – one of those was McCaffrey. He was being thrown to the wolves.

'Maybe I should have seen this coming,' 65-year-old McCaffrey said in an interview with the US trade journal *Air Cargo News* before he was jailed:

> Qantas management called me six months before I was terminated and offered me a buyout, but I refused. I guess when you look at the landscape of executives in air cargo that are now taking the package and getting out, I should have gotten out then too. As it turns out, now I am retired from Qantas having earned (and fought) for my pension.
>
> I just thought that everything would be OK, even with the ongoing investigations, and I thought that Qantas would handle all the price-fixing allegations. I went about my business as usual, reporting everything just as before.[3]

McCaffrey, a straight-talking former Vietnam War helicopter pilot, was clear: he had done nothing that the cargo bosses at Qantas in Sydney did not know about. He was just following orders.

The freight cartel had its origins in 1996, when Qantas's former head of freight, Peter Frampton, flew to Europe for a series of business meetings. The price of jet fuel was jumping and the hot issue of the day was whether to add a surcharge to cargo. If Qantas did and none of the other airlines followed suit, the flying kangaroo would price itself out of business. In Paris Frampton called his secretary and asked her to send him the contact details of all of the Australian airline's cargo competitors. Shortly after receiving the numbers Frampton confidently informed Qantas's freight managers that he believed eight other airlines would be imposing a fuel surcharge on cargo.

The following year the International Air Transport Association started to look at some kind of mechanism or index that would give a trigger point for fuel surcharges to be automatically applied by all airlines. It started to publish an index, despite the Association's lawyers warning that such a fuel surcharge index would be viewed with 'great suspicion'.[4] The lawyers were right. The US authorities rejected the index as 'fundamentally flawed' in 2000 and at a meeting of the Association's air cargo committee they agreed to stop publishing it.[5] Frampton, however, was not giving up. He walked out of the meeting with the clear belief that it was alright to consult other airlines about imposing a fuel surcharge, providing the trigger point was measured on an 'independent fuel index'.[6] He clearly missed the point made so strongly by the US authorities. By the end of 2000 Qantas and its competitor airlines agreed to consult each other about imposing a fuel surcharge once fuel had reached a certain price on an index published by German airline Lufthansa. It was a price-fixing deal that would come badly, expensively and very publicly undone for Qantas.

Price-fixing in America, unlike in Australia at the time, is a criminal offence. In 2006 investigators from the Department of Justice raided Bruce McCaffrey's office at Qantas Freight in Los Angeles and took away paperwork and computers. It is understood they were acting on information passed on by 'low-level types' who had been promised immunity.[7] McCaffrey believed Qantas bosses in Sydney would take care of it. They did, but they did not take care of him.

The American case was simple. 'American consumers were forced to pay higher prices on goods they buy every day as a result of the inflated and collusive shipping rates charged by these companies,' said Scott D. Hammond, Acting Assistant Attorney-General in the US Department of Justice Antitrust Division.[8] The investigation found more than 30 airlines were involved in the cartel. German airline Lufthansa was granted conditional immunity for being the first to give information on the secret price-fixing deals. Qantas pleaded guilty to a criminal offence for fixing charges on the trans-Pacific route and agreed to pay $A68 million in fines. In return, the Department of Justice agreed not to prosecute any company executives or employees – with the exception of six people.

Stephen Cleary, group general manager of freight, and Harold Pang, general manager of freight sales in Singapore, were still employed by the company and had Qantas's unswerving support. 'This does not mean the individuals have been involved in any illegal activity nor that the Department of Justice will prosecute them. Both of the current Qantas employees deny involvement in any illegal conduct,' said a statement issued by the airline.[9] Also exempt were four former employees: Peter Frampton, former general manager of freight sales and marketing; John Cooper, former vice president of freight for the Americas; former employee Desmond Church; and Bruce McCaffrey. The difference between McCaffrey and his five co-conspirators was that they were in Australia and he was a US citizen living in America. Because competition offences were not criminal in Australia then, there was no prospect of the other five Australian residents being extradited to face court in the US. McCaffrey was on his own.

He told *Air Cargo News* that Qantas had abandoned him. Debilitated by a stroke, suffering from arthritis and in need of a kidney transplant, he needed to raise $US500,000 to defend himself in a case he had no guarantee he would win. He said Qantas told him it would share his legal fees if he fought the case and won. If he lost, he would be on his own to face over a million dollars in fines and possibly ten years in jail.

Qantas denied McCaffrey's claim and insisted it had stood by him. Its general counsel, Brett Johnson, told the *Australian* it had introduced white-collar-crime specialists to McCaffrey, but at arm's length, and had never attempted to influence his decision. Nevertheless, McCaffrey felt his only option was to cooperate with investigators.

In the US District Court in Washington DC, Judge John Bates sentenced him to six months in jail – two months fewer than the plea deal he had agreed with investigators because he had been such a vital prosecution witness. McCaffrey was also fined $US20,000 for his part in price-fixing at least

$US244.4 million worth of air cargo between January 2000 and February 2006. Prosecutor Katherine Schlech told the judge: 'Defendant McCaffrey has provided a wealth of information regarding specific meetings and discussions with competitors about surcharges, rates and other competitively sensitive business information. The information he provided about these contacts has been corroborated by other witnesses and contemporaneous documents from Qantas files as well as those of US-based competitors.'[10]

McCaffrey's New York-based lawyers, Jeffrey Udell and Thomas Fleming, said the ailing 65-year-old was simply a middle manager and that blame needed to be levelled at his bosses in Sydney. 'At Qantas, the plan to engage in price-fixing emanated from Sydney, which gave direction to Qantas managers around the world, including Mr McCaffrey, to co-ordinate certain aspects of pricing with their colleagues at other airlines.'[11]

His sister-in-law, Cindy McCaffrey, wrote to the judge: 'It saddens me greatly that this man has been used as a scapegoat for the failing of his corporate bosses and is being sacrificed on their behalf.'[12] 'By following their policy decisions he became their victim. We, his family and friends, are devastated knowing he was the one taking the brunt of the blame for this crime. Why is it that senior management, the ones making all the decisions, are not forced to face these charges?'[13] Judge Bates agreed: 'Most responsible from his company will never face these kind of consequences,' he said.[14]

Afterwards McCaffrey said:

The jail time can't be easy, but I'll be damned if I let the time define me. I will define my time and my life by taking the opportunity to think about my life and reflect on my air cargo career.

My case is not the end of the price-fixing investigations. I believe that there are many more cases yet to be raised.

I just spoke to investigators from Canada this afternoon. Recently I was interviewed by investigators from New Zealand. As often as I am approached now I cooperate because of the offer of immunity. Investigators want to know about the business of air cargo. Fasten your seat belts, there's a bumpy ride ahead.[15]

He was right. In America, British Airways and Korean Air were each fined $US300 million and Japan Airlines $US110 million. Qantas, along with the other airlines, was being pursued around the world and announced it was putting aside $40 million to cover penalties in Australia, Europe and New Zealand. The question quickly came up as to whether that would be enough. The Australian Competition and Consumer Commission (ACCC) pursued the airline doggedly into the Federal Court and succeeded in slapping a $20 million fine on Qantas.

In an agreed statement at the end of the Australian Federal Court case, the ACCC said Qantas 'expects to pay a very substantial penalty in Europe at the conclusion of European Union investigations'.[16] It then faced fines in the High Court in Auckland in New Zealand for operating an 'extensive and long-term cartel' in the global freight market.[17] Qantas was also named in a US class action estimated to be worth $US1 billion and an Australian class action worth $A200 million. The Australian action was put together by Melbourne class-action specialists Maurice Blackburn Cashman. The legal eagle was using the airlines' cooperation with authorities, in return for smaller fines, to bolster its clients' case. Qantas was targeted together with British Airways, Japan Airlines, Air New Zealand, Cathay Pacific, Singapore Airlines and Lufthansa.

After Qantas and British Airways were fined in America the legal firm's principal, Kim Parker, said: 'These guilty pleas will certainly be tendered as evidence against the airlines in the class action. Air freight customers will now have even greater confidence in recovering the hundreds of millions of dollars spent on fuel and other surcharges over the last seven-year period in question.'[18]

Qantas boss Geoff Dixon told the National Aviation Press Club in August 2007 that the airline did not know how much cash it was in the hole for. 'As you know, we had said there was a potential liability, but we've not been able to quantify it as yet and we're still in discussions with a range of authorities on the issue,' he said.[19]

Apart from the financial damage, the price-fixing scandal had also damaged the airline's reputation. What it told people was that Qantas, together with every other airline, had ripped off its cargo customers. That meant every single person who bought something that had been shipped by air freight between 2000 and 2006 had paid over the odds for it. It also said the Qantas board had nothing to do with it. ACCC chairman Graeme Samuel backed Qantas's statement that the price-fixing had been arranged in the freight department and was not known to the board. 'As soon as the Qantas board learned of the conduct, it instructed its legal department and staff to make an exhaustive investigation and to provide full assistance. Qantas has continued to assist and provide evidence both in relation to its own conduct and that of others. Its behaviour after learning of the conduct in its freight division has set a standard we would hope all companies finding themselves in a similar position would follow.'[20]

Not everyone saw it that way. 'Plain and simple, price fixing is theft,' wrote University of New South Wales competition and fair trade Associate Professor Frank Zumbo in the *Herald Sun* after McCaffrey was sentenced:

While Qantas itself pleaded guilty and paid a $US61 million criminal fine for its role in the conspiracy, other Qantas executives or employees involved in the cartel have escaped a jail term.

First, the question arises as to what kind of corporate culture allows illegal behaviour to emerge among corporate executives and continue for extended periods of time. If these corporate leaders promote a cut-throat culture where anything goes in order to maintain record profits, then it's not too long before corners are cut and executives get tempted to start 'crossing lines'.

Clearly, knowing when the rot in corporate culture is starting to set in remains a central personal challenge for any CEO and board. Second, while a CEO and board may not be directly involved in cartel behaviour or other wrongdoing, they must always be ready to take moral responsibility for the failure of their executives to comply with the law.

Did the CEO or board know of the possible wrong-doing or did they just fail to spot the warning signs? Did they simply not care because their only focus was with maintaining record profits?'[21]

The question remained unanswered. The entire sorry saga said a lot about Qantas at the time – none of it good. The corporate culture within the company encouraged price fixing, cargo customers were ripped off. That spoke volumes about the management's attitude and love of profit. It said even more to the people working within the airline. A long-standing and loyal member of staff had done what he was told, even though it was wrong. When the company was caught out, it abandoned him. After McCaffrey was thrown to the legal wolves, the worrying seeds of doubt were sown within Qantas's once loyal staff. The message to them was clear – if something goes wrong, you are on your own.

QF12

MENTAL

'THIS IS A momentous day in the history of Qantas and I'd like to wish you all a very Merry Christmas, our customers a very merry Christmas, and our shareholders a very merry Christmas.'[1] Qantas chairman Margaret Jackson closed the press conference and embraced the airline's chief executive officer, Geoff Dixon, as the cameras flashed. 'I wasn't going to intrude,' laughed Airline Partners Australia (APA) spokesman Bob Mansfield, who was happy to watch from the sidelines, looking all the while like the cat who swallowed the canary.[2] It was an eyebrow-raising $11.1 billion hug that said everything about one of the most controversial and badly botched takeover attempts in Australian corporate history.

In 2006 Macquarie Bank put the old Project Suzie band

back together. By November the new consortium, called Airline Partners Australia, was knocking on Dixon's door with a $10.9 billion offer to buy Qantas's publicly listed shares and put the airline into private hands. The deal was not considered good enough and so the consortium went away and returned in December with an offer of $11.1 billion – $5.45 a share plus a 15 cent dividend. The clincher was that the consortium wanted to keep the Qantas senior managers in place. On top of that it agreed to underwrite future aircraft purchases, providing Dixon and his team with a perfect answer to how they would pay for a new Qantas fleet. The capital investment program would help buy 70 new planes over five years. When Jackson, Dixon and consortium spruiker and ex-Telstra boss Mansfield held that first very huggable press conference to announce and endorse the bid, Qantas shares were trading at $4.10. The buyout seemed like a good idea at the time.

At the press conference Dixon assured passengers, shareholders and staff that it would be 'business as usual'. He said: 'It should be absolutely seamless for passengers and I am quite sure it will be.' And he said the management restructuring program and changes planned for the airline would go ahead, including a $3 billion cost-cutting program: 'We expect to grow further through further investment, so there's no reason to think this is going to be any great revolution.'[3]

But it would be. Even at this early stage the private equity buyout plan carried the Macquarie signature of being funded by a massive amount of debt, which would be saddled onto the airline. Dixon was confident the debt would not affect the day-to-day running of Qantas and emphatically rejected statements by financial analysts Moody's that the debt would see it downgraded to junk status.

Meanwhile, the chairman, Jackson, was cheesed off that journalists should see fit to question the role of James Packer in the deal. Packer held a seat on the Qantas board and was also the biggest single shareholder in Macquarie Bank. Did that mean he had absented himself from takeover discussions at the Qantas board table because of his interest? 'I think that's absolutely an absurd suggestion . . . of course I did not ask James to remove himself from the decision-making process,' Jackson expostulated. 'I don't believe that James had any conflict of interest, and I find it offensive that you might even suggest that.'[4]

After all, Jackson should know what a decent chap he was – she held a position on an advisory board of Packer's Consolidated Press Holdings and was invited to his wedding to Erica Baxter in the South of France. But if Jackson and Packer were close, which they were, Dixon also got on well enough with him to take a seat on the board of Packer's Publishing and Broadcasting Limited. All friends together. It was just unfortunate that the big hug at the end of the press conference had shown the world how friendly the chairman and the CEO were, and raised the question of exactly who was guarding the interests of the shareholders and who was looking after the staff.

The deal had been put together by the brightest brains from the big end of town. Ten years after Project Suzie, Nicholas

Moore was once again heading the charge for Macquarie Bank. The original partners from Project Suzie, David Bonderman's Texas Pacific Group, were joined by David Coe's Allco Group, who had assured Qantas shareholders they were not the barbarians at the gate, and the Canadian Onex Group. Macquarie was taking less than 15 per cent of the final equity in the company but was in line to make hundreds of millions of dollars in fees when the deal went through. They were not alone. The Qantas executives stood to make $91 million once the deal was signed. Dixon would walk out of his office on the last day of the old Qantas with an $8 million cash payout and walk back into the same office the next day as part of the new Qantas to be greeted with a golden hello. And what a welcome. For sitting back in his old chair he would get a performance fee of up to $60 million.

Thirty-six Qantas managers were looking at cash bonuses of up to 200 per cent of their salaries and a stake in the new company of up to 4.5 per cent. Dixon would be paid the 30,000 performance-related shares he had been given by the board in October at the new price, even though he had not had time to make the targets. A tidy $1.7 million towards his $8 million. Not that he really needed the money. According to the Qantas annual report for the year before the bid, Dixon took home $5.3 million. In fact, Dixon did not want the money. He announced that he would be giving his share to charity – medical research and Indigenous health and education. It was a decision that astonished his old mate, advertising guru John Singleton: 'I said to him, "Mate, you will become a charity." Jesus Christ.'[5]

Dixon, the man who made bumper profits partly through

tough wage restraints on Qantas workers, said: 'I wouldn't say I am embarrassed by money, but I think I've got enough. Look, I'm not going to say I don't like having money and being comfortable. But how much do I need? And that was a lot of money and I would have had the greatest thrill in the world being able to give it away. I didn't want the money. I really didn't.'[6] But even though he was giving his share away, he conceded that the huge amount of money on offer 'without doubt' clouded the Qantas executives' judgement: 'If I had my time again, I'd say [to the bidding consortium], "Yeah, this is such a good offer it should be considered, but you'd have to make that offer under no circumstances with the management being offered part of it." I think people saw us compromised.'[7]

Another executive standing to make a lot of money was Chief Financial Officer Peter Gregg, who already earned $3.7 million a year. He was in line to trouser a bonus of $5 million if the deal to put 100 per cent of Qantas into private hands went through. Gregg was a fishing buddy of Mark Carnegie, from airline advisor Carnegie Wylie, who also stood to pocket a large part of the $96 million success fee if the bid went through. Gregg was most put out to be asked about his relationship with Carnegie at the 2007 Qantas Annual General Meeting. He told shareholder activist Stephen Mayne:

I like to fish and I regularly fish when I can get the opportunity. Yes, I did go fishing with Mark Carnegie a number of months after the deal collapsed, but I also do a lot of other things with Mark Carnegie like aiding him in some of the charities he is involved with for Indigenous children and for children in overseas depressed countries, so I make no apologies of going fishing, but I do reject any insinuation that I did something that was illegal or under cover in this process. I don't think you have any right to make that suggestion.[8]

The APA bid had to get through a number of hurdles. The Foreign Investment Review Board had to give it the green light to ensure it did not breach the 49 per cent foreign ownership specified in the Qantas Sale Act. An independent review of the Qantas business conducted by investment bank Grant Samuel endorsed the directors' decision to sell, saying any offer over $5.18 a share was 'fair value'.[9] And Prime Minister John Howard weighed in to say that although there were 'understandable concerns' about the sale, it would bring about a 'savage reaction' from business if the government interfered. 'I understand the view that [Qantas] is an icon but the personal views of the prime minister, the treasurer or senior ministers shouldn't be allowed in a free enterprise economy to influence who owns companies provided the law is observed and the rules are obeyed,' he said, effectively conceding that there was a great deal of public disquiet about the sale. 'You can't determine the ownership of companies and affect the right of people to deal with their property, namely their shares, according to the popularity of a particular takeover. You just can't operate that way,' he said. [10]

Treasurer Peter Costello had warned that companies such as Qantas should ignore excessive debt so that they could ride out any 'external shocks' that might hit the economy. But once he received the Foreign Investment Review Board recommendations he removed any government objection to the deal. After being given the assurance that the new owners would not cull regional services, he said: 'The Government is not recommending this bid. The Government will allow shareholders to make their decision.'[11] Australian Competition and Consumer Commission chairman Graeme Samuel also said his organisation had been through the deal with 'more than a fine tooth comb' and found nothing to stop it going ahead.[12] The Commission had considered whether Macquarie's interests in Sydney airport and a new holding in Qantas would lead it to favour the airline but found that there was no incentive for it to do so.

The unions were not happy. A Senate inquiry was looking into whether the Qantas sale would not restrict new owners from sidestepping controls and sending maintenance overseas. It was a golden chance for the Australian Licensed Aircraft Engineers' Association to raise concerns about poor standards in Singapore and the Philippines, where some maintenance work was conducted.

Of even greater concern was the Australian Workers' Union fear that the consortium intended to raid the Qantas superannuation fund. A spokesman for Airline Partners Australia said: 'It has never been an issue in this takeover proposal. Each time the issue has been raised, Airline Partners has been clear that the superannuation fund will not be touched.'[13] The Qantas pilots' union, the Australian and International Pilots' Association, complained to the Takeovers Panel that the APA bid exaggerated the Texas Pacific Group's experience in running airlines. It said the Texas group had only had investments in Ryanair and American

West for 18 months. The Takeovers Panel agreed and the consortium had to quickly send out a supplementary bidders' statement to Qantas shareholders.

Those shareholders seemed to be getting restless. Nowhere near enough of them were pledging their shares to the new consortium. To help things along, APA offered brokers $750 cash for every Qantas client they got to accept the deal. It extended the acceptance period from 3 to 20 April. But the big hedge funds were not convinced. UBS Global Asset Management, which controlled six per cent of Qantas, was doubtful. Balanced Equity Management, which controlled four per cent of Qantas, sent the airline a binding fax saying it would not accept the bid because the sharemarket value had gone up since the offer was first made. Tasmanian Liberal Senator John Watson said: 'I just say good luck to [Balanced Equity] – they're doing a good job. Everyone seems to want to get rid of Qantas except a few thoughtful people.'[14]

One person who was not being too thoughtful at the time was chairman Margaret Jackson. In hospital with her arm elevated and in a sling, she decided to speak to the media to help things along. 'I would be devastated if [the bid] didn't go through as this is an outstanding opportunity for share-holders,' she said.[15] Warming to her theme, she warned that 40 per cent of Qantas shares were held by hedge funds that would dump them if the deal did not go through. She said the airline would be 'destabilised' as the market scrambled to find the $5 billion of equity dumped by the funds. 'If anyone thinks this will happen without affecting the share price then they have a mental problem with how the market works.'[16]

Whoops. Nobody, particularly shareholders, it seems, likes to be condescendingly told they have a mental problem for not doing what the chairman thinks is best for them. 'They weren't the best sentences I have uttered in my life, but my concern for shareholders was genuine,' she said when the dust had settled, more than a year later.[17] Appalled suits in the financial sector believed she had gone too far. They argued it was not her job to be spruiking enthusiastically on behalf of the bidder. 'I don't think I was a lobbyist or barracker for APA,' she said. 'I recommended the bid, as did the board, because we thought it was good at the time for shareholders.'[18]

The problem with the deal, which was viewed with deep suspicion by the Australian public and gained little political support, was the fact that it saddled the airline with a massive debt. The executives would walk out with bucketloads of cash and the airline would be left to keep operating while struggling under a giant burden of borrowed money. The global financial crisis two years later would destroy companies taken over in this way. The APA bid was to be 75 to 80 per cent funded by borrowed cash. Government MPs, including Nationals leader John Anderson, raised serious concerns about these astronomical debt levels, fearing any downturn in global aviation could lead Qantas to collapse, just as Ansett had done in 2001.

In order to pay off some of that debt, the consortium intended to strip $4.5 billion from the Qantas balance sheet in the first year of operation. That meant selling off key parts of the business, such as the Frequent Flyer Program, which had 4.6 million members. The real extent of the asset-stripping did not become clear until April, five months after the deal was first endorsed by the board and management of Qantas. Independent Senator Barnaby Joyce fumed: 'This could be implied by some to be misleading. They are not playing with their money. They are playing with everybody else's money and they are playing with our economy. This deal had hairs on it from the start. It's getting hairier by the moment.'[19] Federal Liberal MP Bruce Baird voiced his concern and said: 'Perhaps in the light of these new aspects of the bid further review should be carried out on it.'[20] In an eerie premonition of global government rescue packages two years later, Australian Shareholders Association Executive Director Stuart Wilson warned that Australian taxpayers would be the ones left bailing out Qantas if the economy nose-dived 'whilst the private equity players get their money back and more'.[21]

None of the speculation was affecting the airline, where it was business as usual. Management called for voluntary redundancies from 50 maintenance crew, 150 long-haul cabin crew, an undisclosed number of short-haul cabin crew and also announced its fourth profit upgrade in a bumper year that saw 86.6 per cent of passenger seats filled on international routes. It anticipated a 40 per cent jump in profit on the previous year, to $672 million.

Meanwhile, the deal was dragging on. Qantas publicly urged the consortium to get on with it. Shareholders dithered, hanging on for a better offer in the light of the revised profit forecast and an improved share price. Airline Partners Australia restructured its deal. At first it aimed to get at least 90 per cent and then compulsorily buy up the stragglers. As hedge funds held out, the consortium said it would buy at least 70 per cent and then have the others on the board as minority shareholders. The deal closed on Friday 4 May 2007 – but if more than 50 per cent of shareholders pledged their shares then they would automatically get a two-week extension. At the time that was seen as a given. The real battle would be to find at least another 30 per cent. Then it all went pear-shaped.

On the evening of Friday 4 May, Geoff Dixon and CFO Peter Gregg were having a couple of drinks in the lobby lounge of the Sofitel Wentworth in Sydney. It was just before 7 pm, the deadline for the crack squad from Macquarie Bank to deliver the 50 per cent of shareholders needed to trigger the two-week extension. It was a time for quiet celebration for the two men as they contemplated a future in which a cashed-up Qantas would, they believed, be free of shareholder constraints. They would also be personally rich. Wealthy enough for Dixon to start his own private charity. The deal, unpopular as it was with the public, staff, unions, politicians and many of the suits in the big end of town, was in the safest of hands. Macquarie Bank was the best in the business at this kind of thing. So when Geoff Dixon's mobile phone rang just before 7 pm, it was not with the news he was expecting.

The Macquarie team had been struggling to get the numbers. They were relying on Heyman Investment Associates in America, the Qantas shares owned by the Connecticut-based billionaire Heyman family, to get them over the line. As the day wore on they had placed increasingly frantic calls to Heyman's chief investment officer, Jim Hoffman, to come forward with the shares. But, according to the *Sydney*

Morning Herald, 'Hoffman had had enough of Macquarie Bank and what he believed was its arrogant approach to the takeover. He simply did not believe the bid would fail without his acceptance.'[22] Hoffman, like many American investors, believed Macquarie Bank had the numbers and was trying to get the 70 per cent it needed to completely seal the deal in one go. The investors thought they would get more money for their shares later if Macquarie only just squeaked over the line at 50 per cent. Two hours before the bid closed Macquarie was advised to put out a bulletin, a legal document, showing exactly how many shares it controlled. It would have been the proof Hoffman needed to know that the investment bank was not bluffing. For some reason the bankers did not take the advice and Hoffman hung on to his shares. Instead, just before 7 pm, the bankers were calling Geoff Dixon on his mobile phone and saying they were preparing to put out a statement. They only had 46 per cent acceptances for the bid.

'This is one of the great fuck-ups of the world,' one senior executive involved in the deal later told the *Sydney Morning Herald*.[23] Several Australian investors contacted by the newspaper immediately after the deal had gone through said they had not even been contacted by Macquarie to sell their shares in the final days of the bid.

Dixon and Gregg shook their heads in disbelief, made some calls, finished their drinks and went home. At 8.55 pm the Airline Partners Australia consortium put out a statement: 'It appears that acceptances have not reached the 50 per cent level required to extend the offer. If this is confirmed, APA's offer for Qantas Airways Ltd will not proceed. APA wishes

Qantas every success.'[24] The Macquarie Bank team, including lawyers from Mallesons Stephen Jaques, started drinking at The Senate beneath Macquarie Bank's slick Martin Place offices in Sydney's CBD. Then the unthinkable happened: word came in that Hoffman had called with an acceptance of half of billionaire Heyman's shares – enough to take the deal to 50.6 per cent.

But hadn't the full-time whistle already been blown? The team rushed back to start looking at the figures. At midnight the consortium put in an appeal to the Takeovers Panel to include the late acceptance by Heyman.

The Qantas board held an emergency meeting on Saturday morning. At the same time the Heyman spokesman, Hoffman, read a statement to a reporter from the *Sydney Morning Herald* from his office in New York. 'While we have consistently indicated to advisors that this has always been a close call for us, we are hopeful that our tender will facilitate the successful completion of the transaction.'[25] They all held their breath.

At 3 pm on Sunday the Takeovers Panel rejected the appeal, saying Heyman should 'have been well aware of the closing time and date for the offer'.[26] The consortium sought a review of that decision 30 minutes later but were trumped by Qantas which, at 8.30 pm on Sunday night, put out a statement saying the deal was dead.

Monday morning ushered in a new week and a new take on the old deal. The consortium said it was considering a number of alternatives and the possibility of a fresh $5.45 a share offer. Its lawyers were looking at clause 7.3 of the bid terms, which said that anyone who accepted with part of their shares was deemed to have accepted with all of them, which would have meant the APA had more than the 50 per cent it needed on Friday night. Senator Barnaby Joyce was damning. 'If they are relying on that clause, they should have been open about that prior to the acceptance deadline. Just like someone who got 49 out of 100 in an exam, they failed. To try and rely on this other thing now is just sneaky.'[27] Qantas called for a halt in trading on its shares and raised the question of the clause, suggesting the bid may have succeeded after all. But feeling against the 'Gordon Gecko type characters' behind the bid was hardening.

Very little had been seen of the consortium members since the announcement months before, leaving a sense of something mysterious and sinister about the Texan buyers behind it all. Treasurer Peter Costello said: 'This is a message from the shareholders that a majority of the shareholders did not want to accept that offer as it was put within the time limit. If anyone wants to start a new bid, the whole thing starts again. Everything starts again.'[28] APA certainly did not want to go through the whole thing again. Australian Shareholders Association deputy chairman Stephen Matthews said: 'Given what's happened and what's planned with regard to the [proposed debt] gearing of Qantas, their revelation that they are only interested in financially engineering the balance sheet rather than running an airline, I wonder if [Foreign Investment Review Board] approval might take longer this time around.'[29]

APA had had enough. On Tuesday morning it threw in the towel. A statement said: 'APA believes that Qantas shareholders need more certainty and, accordingly, it has determined that its bid should be treated as having lapsed on 4 May 2007.'[30] The deal really was dead and an awful lot of money had been wasted.

Time would show that Qantas had had a very lucky escape. News of the collapse of the deal was greeted with howls of outrage and calls for the resignation of the woman seen as its biggest advocate, Qantas chairman Margaret Jackson. Six months before, she had the complete support of the board; informal soundings now indicated that many board members felt she should go. She decided to jump rather than wait to be pushed and announced she would step down at the next AGM. Jackson's friend James Packer decided to step down too, partly, it was said, to shield her from the appearance of singly taking the blame. Former Qantas CEO James Strong indicated that he would like the job, even though it would require the company to change its board charter, before former Rio Tinto boss Leigh Clifford finally stepped in to fill her shoes.

Just before her retirement after 16 years on the Qantas board, seven of which she was chairman, Jackson said reflectively:

> If I go back over the APA bid, there's probably very little else the board could have done. I think we did the right thing in putting it to the shareholders. The share price had been stuck between $3 and $4 for five years. Along came APA and they saw more value than the market

did. They made some mistakes in their bid and I'm sure we did as well. The shareholders voted and we moved on. I think we unleashed more value in implementing a lot of things quickly when the bid failed. I think the bid failed because of the underlying strength of the economy and the impact on our results, probably the delay in the consortium's time horizon and the fact they said it was final and the move in the share price.[31]

The board asked the management team to stay on with Dixon at its head. It was a difficult time, with Tiger Airways due to add some stiff competition. The management team had to get over the fact that they were not about to personally pocket a major windfall. Dixon said: 'I think lesser companies and a lesser management team could have imploded. There could have been real problems. They could have taken their eye off the job, but they didn't.'[32] Giving them all bumper pay rises certainly helped them come to terms with it. Coming in with a $1.03 billion pre-tax profit and the promise of $1.3 billion in the next year also helped keep the 141,000 shareholders happy. And the team pushed ahead with cost-cutting and building Jetstar. It was going to be okay.

Reflecting back on the deal he so heartily endorsed, Dixon said: 'It didn't happen and I'm very pleased now it didn't happen and we can get on with our lives.'[33]

He is not alone. The global financial crisis has taken its toll on the backers of deals like this. Macquarie Bank has cut its executive salaries, Allco has gone into administration, Texas Pacific Group is reeling from bad investments and the major lenders to the deal have been the biggest losers in the economic downturn: Morgan Stanley, Greenwich Capital Markets, Citigroup and Royal Bank of Scotland. With the wisdom of hindsight and knowledge of the global financial crisis, it is easy to see that the players in the botched debt-funded takeover were the men – and woman – who so nearly killed Qantas.

QF13

AIRLINE FOR
SCANDAL

On 24 January 2007 English actor Ralph Fiennes, the star of *The English Patient*, among other highly regarded films, was sitting in seat 2K on the right-hand side of the business-class section of Qantas flight QF123 from Sydney to Mumbai. It was to be a memorable flight. Fiennes was one of only 12 business-class passengers – there was no first-class cabin – for the overnight flight to India. He made himself comfortable, declined dinner from the rather attractive blonde flight attendant and sipped his way through a couple of glasses of shiraz. The flight attendant, Lisa Robertson, certainly noticed the star. As she served him she blurted out: 'I love your films. I hope you don't mind me saying this. It's a little unprofessional of me.' 'Not at all. You're gorgeous,'

Fiennes allegedly replied. 'There was an instant chemistry between us,' Robertson told Australian magazine *Woman's Day* in a paid interview a month after the flight.[1]

After a couple of hours the cabin lights were dimmed for passengers to sleep or watch movies. As 38-year-old Robertson walked through the cabin, she briefly sat next to the 46-year-old actor to talk before her break. According to Robertson, Fiennes asked if he could join her on the crew jump seats when she took her break, and she agreed. Once there the two chatted for about an hour before engaging in passionate physical foreplay. After ten minutes or so they locked themselves in the cabin toilet where, Robertson says, they had sex. Unfortunately for the flight attendant, a male staff member saw Fiennes and Robertson leaving the toilet separately and told the cabin manager, who sent her to work in the economy section for the remainder of the flight, advising Robertson that she intended to report her once they had returned to Sydney. That did not stop Robertson from later joining Fiennes in his Mumbai hotel suite.

Back in Sydney, Robertson was suspended without pay. At a meeting between Robertson, the Flight Attendants' Association, Qantas and airline services contractor Morris Alexander Management, the company accused her of breaching Qantas corporate and cabin-crew policies. The first breach was allowing Fiennes to sit in the jump seat; the second being in the toilet with him. Initially Robertson filed a statement that downplayed the incident:

While conversing with Mr Fiennes during my break, I expressed a need to go to the toilet. I went to the nearby toilet and entered it, he followed me and entered the same toilet. I explained to him that this was inappropriate and asked him to leave. Mr Fiennes became amorous towards me and, after a short period of time, I convinced him to leave the toilet, which he did. I left the toilet a short time later. At no time did any crew member come to my assistance. At no time were any other customers aware of this incident. At no time did I put the Qantas name or reputation in jeopardy. [2]

At the time of the hearing Robertson was correct in saying she had not put the Qantas name or reputation in jeopardy. But, on suspension without pay, she was struggling for money. In desperation she took her story to the *Sunday Telegraph* in Sydney, which put it on the front page. The Qantas hostie and the Hollywood star's mile-high-club fling in a toilet at 35,000 feet dominated headlines around the world. A Qantas spokesman stiffly told the newspaper: 'All we can do is confirm that a flight attendant was stood down following an onboard incident.'[3] Although initially Fiennes remained silent, a week later his personal publicist, Sara Keene, came out fighting, claiming that Robertson had instigated the sexual encounter. It was all too much for Qantas, which sacked Robertson on Monday morning.

Having been suspended by Qantas, Robertson was so short of cash she turned to prostitution, working, she confessed to the *Sunday Telegraph*, one night a week at The Gateway Club under the name of Skye. But that was not the first time she had earned money as a prostitute. While subcontracted to work for Qantas by agency Jetconnect in New

Zealand, she had taken another job at a brothel called The Pelican Club. Working under the name Kendall, she supplemented her $NZ29,000 hostess pay with $NZ600 a night from prostitution. When she moved to Sydney with Qantas she took her night-time activity to the high-class Stiletto brothel in Camperdown, which is owned by racing identity Eddie Hayson.

Before joining Qantas, Robertson had worked for the New South Wales police as an undercover policewoman. As a young police officer she had seen a fellow graduate accidentally shot by a colleague. It led to a lifelong battle with mental illness. Her 14 years with the police service exacerbated her depression and led to suicidal tendencies. 'There came a period of time that I decided to take my own life. I took 200 pills and drank a couple of bottles of Dom Perignon – so I did it in style. My boyfriend at the time called me and I was incoherent. I remember cutting my arm and I remember my choice that night to die and I went to sleep dressed in the clothes I wanted to be buried in. I left notes to my mum and dad, my brothers and my dog and my parrot, who are now both deceased. I was quite sure that my decision was the right one,' Robertson told the *Sunday Telegraph*.[4] She woke up in hospital the next day having had her stomach pumped.

Robertson sold the tawdry tale of her tryst with Fiennes to Fleet Street, women's magazines and television, including Channel 9's *60 Minutes*. But her position as a bankrupt, after losing an expensive negligence battle with the police force, meant she was not allowed to keep the money. In fact, she had her home raided by the tax office.

It is safe to assume Qantas hated the mile-high publicity,

especially as the incident spawned a host of anecdotes about mid-air sex, providing journalists with an excuse to bring up high jinks such as Kylie Minogue's romp with the late INXS frontman Michael Hutchence while then Australian Prime Minister Bob Hawke sat a few rows in front. More importantly, the embarrassing scandal for Qantas left several difficult questions unanswered, not least of which was whether Robertson's managers should have known about the perilous financial and mental state of one of their employees, who in the course of her duties was responsible for the lives of hundreds of passengers should an emergency occur.

In a statement in response to questions about Lisa Robertson, the airline said previous employment and medical checks were carried out on all applicants, which included a 'check for relevant pre-existing mental illnesses which could impact on a person's ability to perform the role of a flight attendant.' It was still using the agency Maurice Alexander Management, which employed Lisa Robertson, and was happy that cabin crew were paid competitive salaries.

A big company like Qantas is always going to have its fair share of scandals, what the press office might call public relations issues. That is why Qantas hired David Epstein, Australian Prime Minister Kevin Rudd's former chief of staff, to be the new head of corporate affairs, reporting directly to the CEO. His first job as spin-doctor-in-chief in November 2008 was to hose down outrage at his appointment. The Coalition's Special Minister of State, Michael Ronaldson, said the appointment was in direct contravention of the new Labor government's lobbyist code designed to prevent political advisors from cashing in on insider knowledge when they joined the corporate world. 'Kevin Rudd's former right-hand man is taking a lobbyist job on the very issues he has inside information on,' said Mr Ronaldson.[5]

Epstein denied there was any hypocrisy over a potential breach of the lobbyists' code. 'I've not had any substantive involvement in issues touching Qantas, and it was only on that basis that I accepted their approach for the role,' he said. 'There was no involvement with Qantas. The prime minister was not involved and was not aware of any discussions I had with Qantas.' And Qantas CEO Geoff Dixon was quick to point out the undeniable benefits to the company: 'Mr Epstein comes to Qantas with a strong background in government, media relations and public affairs, most recently as chief of staff and principal adviser to the Prime Minister Kevin Rudd.'[6] Exactly.

Mr Epstein was quick to find his corporate feet. On Monday 30 March 2009 he took an exasperated tone that implied a close affiliation with passengers when ground crew walked off the job, plunging the domestic and international terminals into chaos. The Transport Workers' Union was angry that jobs were being outsourced and feared that a quarter of private contract employees would not have security clearance before they started work at the airport. Mr Epstein dismissed their claim. But then he found himself having to defend the company decision to dock workers' pay by four hours which, in turn, caused the industrial action to last longer than the union planned. Mr Epstein was unapologetic: 'There were no grounds for the action and they've chosen to do it and there are consequences for that sort of thing,' he said. 'The law is quite simple: if people walk off in unauthorised industrial action, they don't get paid for four hours. We make no apologies whatsoever for taking a hard line on unauthorised industrial action.'[7] That turned into a legal stoush, with the airline seeking an injunction in the Federal Court to stop similar actions in the future.

Even before the PR department got its new, well-connected chief, it had plenty to deal with. Another long-haul hostie appeared in the papers reported as having a form of mental illness. Naomi Williams, the 35-year-old daughter of surf legend Nat Young, appeared in Manly Local Court in April 2007 accused of theft. She had been spotted by a security officer in Target in Warringah Mall on Sydney's northern beaches stuffing Stella McCartney designer wear into her handbag. Her solicitor, Arthur Carney, told the court: 'There are extenuating circumstances. She had just gotten off a long-haul flight from London the night before. Her kids woke her up very early the next morning. She wasn't thinking. Not only that, the hostess was on medication for post-natal depression and suffered from bipolar disease, which could have triggered the behaviour.'[8] She was given a 12-month good behaviour bond for the crime, which was her first offence.

That incident followed the very public unfair dismissal case of Qantas steward Philip Woodward-Brown. After 32 years of loyal service the steward was stopped at Narita airport in Japan and found to have 16 individually wrapped macadamia nut chocolates, three biscuits, one satchel of sugar, one coffee stirrer and two Qantas pens in his pockets. For this grievous calumny he was given the sack – part of the airline's zero-tolerance-to-theft policy. The Australian Industrial Relations Commission found that Mr Woodward-Brown regarded these items as waste that were to be thrown away at the end of the flight and gave him his job back. The loyal 57-year-old steward had been searched as part of a 'behavioural performance review' by the airline, which handled the matter publicly in its customary fashion by refusing to comment.[9] The Australian media, meanwhile, had a field day, dubbing the case Chocgate.

In August 1996 the airline faced another scandal because of the behaviour of one of its staff. Steward John Travers Robertson would often knock on the door of female colleagues during overnight stops across the world to discuss problems he was having with his girlfriend. He would make the girls cups of strikingly sweet hot chocolate. It was laced with a stupefying drug – probably the date-rape drug Rohypnol. When the groggy stewardesses passed out, he would strip them and take photographs. The Qantas steward was finally caught after giving his knockout chocolate to a stewardess at the Hilton Hotel in Cairns on 6 April 1994. They had been out to dinner with the rest of the cabin crew on the stopover when he knocked on her door for a chat and a hot chocolate. She noticed it took an unusually long time to make the drink and seemed sweeter than normal when she drank it. The stewardess, who was fully clothed at the time, started to feel groggy and then blacked out. She woke up after an abnormally long sleep of more than 12 hours wearing only her panties and feeling quite sick. She reported the incident. A police raid on Robertson's Gold Coast home found photographic negatives of two naked and clearly unconscious Qantas hosties, one of whom had been placed in a 'demeaning and indecent' position on the bed.[10] When called in, the shocked women had absolutely no recollection of the photographs being taken.

In fact Qantas staff had been troubled by rumours about female flight attendants being drugged and taken advantage of at stopovers across the globe. In total, 14 would report suffering similar symptoms of grogginess having shared a hot chocolate with John Robertson. Four would come forward to tell of incidents in Los Angeles, Pretoria and Harare in 1992 and in London in 1994. At Robertson's trial in Southport District Court in Queensland in 1996, the stewardess who was attacked in London described how the last thing she remembered was him touching her breasts before she slipped into unconsciousness. She was so badly affected by the drug that she had to fly back to Australia as a passenger two days later.

Crown prosecutor Craig Chowdhury said that the attacks amounted to indecent assault: 'It's an evil, wicked thing to do to render someone so unconscious they can't defend themselves,' he said. 'It's a tragedy how this accused abused the trust of these women.'[11] The jury agreed and found the 35-year-old steward guilty. The emotional stewardesses hugged each other at the back of the court while Robertson sat in the dock shaking his head. Judge Robert Hall said Robertson had abused the women's trust so he could 'gain some sort of voyeuristic thrill' and sentenced him to six years in jail, which was reduced to four on appeal. Judge Hall said Robertson had shown not 'the slightest trace of remorse' and did not recommend early parole.[12]

The court case was embarrassing to Qantas and once again raised the question of exactly how much care the company was offering its staff. But, of course, in a large company there are always bound to be some bad apples. And staff are not the only potential risk of embarrassment to a busy and successful airline. By the very nature of its business, Qantas can also become embroiled in the scandals of its paying customers. On a quiet Sunday afternoon in March 2009, an unfortunate chain of events put the airline back onto the front page of the nation's newspapers and at the top of television news bulletins.

On Sunday 22 March the president of the Hells Angels Guildford chapter, Derek Wainohu, boarded Qantas flight QF430 in Melbourne to return to Sydney. He had been in Victoria to assure his Hells Angels counterparts there that the bikie gang war troubles in Sydney would soon be over and the push for membership for the Free Australia political party could go ahead. With him was fellow Hells Angel Peter Zervas and his 29-year-old brother Anthony Zervas. Unfortunately, six heavily tattooed members of rival gang the Comancheros happened to be on the same plane. They had been in Melbourne for the premiere of the boxing movie *Two Fists, One Heart*. It was a terrible coincidence. According to the Sydney *Daily Telegraph*: 'Wainohu did what any quick-thinking gangster would do. He texted ahead for back up.'[13]

To make matters worse the two groups were seated together, one behind the other. Other passengers said the groups became increasingly agitated as the flight wore on, exchanging threats mid-flight and frantically texting on their mobile phones. By the time the plane landed in

Sydney at 1.30 pm, the cavalry had arrived with knives and knuckle-dusters. Four Comancheros passed through the metal detectors to meet the plane at the gate, leaving two in the arrivals hall with the weapons. The Hells Angels had arrived in force too, and were in the arrivals hall while the two groups of bikies pushed and shoved each other as they attempted to disembark from the Qantas plane.

As the Hells Angels trio emerged from the airbridge to be met by the Comancheros at Gate 5, Wainohu and Comanchero president Mick Hawi told their members to pull it in. Then, according to the *Daily Telegraph*, 'a Hells Angel smiled'. Police say a Comanchero snarled: 'What the fuck are you laughing at?'[14] One of the bikies shouted: 'Come on, boys, let's go, let's go.' And a mass brawl erupted as two armed federal police officers waited for back-up to try to tackle the brawl that erupted inside the security barrier then moved towards the terminal doors 'like one big rolling ball of mayhem'.[15]

'When the two groups saw each other it exploded. The larger group charged at the others, screaming and swearing, and the brawl was on,' one witness told the *Sydney Morning Herald*:

Initially they were punching and kicking, using kick-boxing, but within about five seconds the brawl had moved towards the sliding doors near the entrance next to the road where the taxis drop off. As they surged past check-in counters at least five of them grabbed the steel bollards that are used to corral people waiting to check in their bags and began swinging . . .

They were swinging the bollards like they were cricket bats, using the bases to hit. Passengers ducked for cover. One fellow being attacked dropped to the ground and some of the others just laid into him, hitting him with the bollard and kicking him too. A security guy was screaming, 'Don't let them get away'.[16]

One witness told the newspaper, 'I heard his head crack',[17] while another onlooker said of the attack on the downed bikie:

One lady who looked about 40 was waiting to check in with her husband when the brawl swept past. They hit him [the bikie] when he was down, they kicked him when he was down, a big bloke who called him 'brother' tried to pull them off him and they ran off when they saw the blood spurting from his head. The lady got people to help roll him over and started to work on him. She just jumped straight in and tried to help. They weren't even out the doors and she was working on him trying to get his heart going by doing cardiac massage.

Another woman, a trainee nurse, tried to help, and there was a doctor who ran across and worked with the woman, one trying to stop the bleeding and the other working on his heart. She said, 'He's clearly got a fractured skull.' He was dead before the ambulance got there.[18]

Kneeling beside the dying bikie was a 'big guy' holding his hand and saying: 'Hang on, Tone, hang on, Tone, c'mon,

Tone, hang on.'[19] But Qantas passenger Anthony Zervas, who was not even believed to have been a bikie, was dead. Four bikies were arrested as they fled the airport in a taxi and a spate of shootings followed the attack as the gang war spilled onto Sydney's streets.

Witnesses to the incredible brawl in what is supposed to be one of the securest environments in the country were still struggling to come to terms with what they had seen. 'I couldn't believe it,' said one. 'I stood there stunned, turned around and there was this little girl of about five clinging to her mother's hand, and her face was just white. She had seen it all, the guys swinging these heavy bollards at each other and then this massive pool of blood and a guy being worked on furiously by some onlookers.'[20] But if the little girl had seen it all, unfortunately the CCTV footage had not, and the brawl turned into a public relations problem for Qantas.

In the aftermath a witch-hunt sought to assign blame for the breach of security. Newspapers reported that Big W has better security than the airport and that vital video evidence could have been lost in the fragmented system. A New South Wales police source told the *Sydney Morning Herald*: 'There are four, five different CCTV systems covering the sky bridge to the check-in area to the car park. The systems aren't in any standardised format and they're not recorded at a central point so [police investigators] have to try and get them into a format that can be used for evidentiary purposes. It's possible that it has never been tested in this way before, but you would think there would be some kind of co-ordination between the different systems.'[21]

Terminal 3, where the brawl occurred, is run by Qantas,

which is responsible for video coverage inside the terminal. It conceded that a security camera just metres from where the bikie died could not move quickly enough to record the incident. A Qantas spokesman told the *Sydney Morning Herald*: 'The camera located immediately above the group is a fixed camera that covers the wider check-in area. A moveable camera which can be clearly seen some metres further along was trained on the location of the attack as soon as a number of duress alarms were activated by staff.'[22]

Sydney airport is owned by the Sydney Airport Corporation, which is owned by Macquarie Airports, which in turn is managed by the Macquarie Group. It is responsible for security outside the terminal in the car parks and roads. In the year before the brawl, Sydney airport charged airlines $73 million for security. The airlines pass that charge on to passengers, the same ones who watched the brawl unfold. Despite this, the Airport Corporation was quick to point to Qantas as being responsible for security inside the terminal as part of the airline's 99-year lease to run Terminal 3. But the airline told the *Sydney Morning Herald* that its role was to provide security screening, baggage checks and the like. So, while Qantas accepted it had a responsibility to stop terrorists, it placed the job of dealing with crime, such as bikie murders inside the terminal, squarely at the feet of the Australian federal police.

Public sentiment following this was best summed up in an email reprinted in David Penberthy's column in the *Daily Telegraph* three days after the event: 'When I'm at the departure area of Qantas domestic tomorrow taking off my belt, removing my shoes, assuring 22 people at the X-ray and metal-detecting machines that I have indeed nothing left in my pockets and that, no, I do not have a laptop in my back-pack and that, yes, I am well aware my nail scissors pose a real danger to world peace, should I bother them with the news that 15 hoodlums are bashing someone to death 20 m to my left? Yours, perplexed, Sydney.'[23]

These are just a few of the scandals that have beset Qan-tas in more recent times. As with all good companies, of course, the best scandals are the ones that the lawyers say cannot be written about.

QF14

EXPLOSION

TARA KYNNERSLEY HAD the world at her feet the day she flew home to Melbourne on QF30 from London via Hong Kong to celebrate her 31st birthday with family and friends. It was July 2008 and she had big news for them, following her four-week European vacation with her boyfriend, Brent. He had proposed to her on the clifftops at Positano overlooking the Mediterranean on Italy's romantic Amalfi Coast. Now, 55 minutes into the flight from Hong Kong and with the plane comfortably cruising at 29,000 feet, she was dreamily leafing through a bridal magazine as the crew began the cabin service. Brent was returning home on a different flight.

Maths researcher Jason Jeffers was on his way home to Melbourne after collecting his PhD from Cambridge

University. He was sitting in a window seat and had just been served breakfast. 'There was a "bang", but not an explosion bang – more like something falling over or a thud. And suddenly, after the bang, you could see the curtains swirling away and there was a sudden rush of wind and a loss of pressure in the cabin. And then the masks fell down from the ceiling,' he said.[1]

Eighteen-year-old Rachael Angley was sitting in seat 48C next to her 15-year-old brother, Ben Wallace, en route from their home in England to visit family and friends in Adelaide. She had been catching up on missed episodes of *The Chaser* and was just drifting off to sleep. She also heard the bang. 'Instantly a cold gust of wind whistled in. I panicked as the plane dipped to one side and wind gushed around the cabin. I knew this shouldn't be happening mid flight. As the plane shook with the change in air pressure I thought I was a goner. Air masks immediately sprung down in front of all of us. I looked around and I see . . . my fellow passengers frantically fitting the masks. Three young children were sitting around me. Their mums and dads held the masks forcefully against the struggling and crying toddlers,' she said.[2]

Newly engaged Tara Kynnersley said: 'It was a sudden plunge, then the plane plateaued. I didn't hear the noise . . . but I thought that was it. We watch a lot of air-crash investigation shows. There was a bit of a panic because of the oxygen masks not working . . . I spoke to a woman whose kids' masks were not working and the hosties were sitting with them, patting her on the back.'[3] Suddenly, on the brink of a new life, Tara thought she was going to die. Somehow she found the inner strength to accept it. 'I just thought,

"I'm really happy with life. I have a beautiful fiancé, family, friends – I have a wonderful life". And I thought, "I'm on a plane, there's nothing I can really do about it".⁴

As papers and detritus howled through the depressurised cabin, a rumour quickly passed among the passengers that perhaps a door had popped out. Rachael Angley said: 'I thought there must be a hole in the plane of some sort and wondered what if people got sucked out like some kind of horror film. I feared we would suffocate or the plane would crack in half and we would fall to our death. It sounds a bit clichéd but I thought; "I'm too young to die".' In the seat next to her, brother Ben was having no such qualms. Once he had secured his oxygen mask he calmly put his headset back on and tuned in to the in-flight music. 'Once Ben and I both had our masks on and felt confident with them, I looked around – there were aisles and aisles of pale faces. We started to descend as if we were coming in for a steep, quick landing as the captain guided the plane down to a safe level where cabin air pressure was restored,' she said.⁵

The calming voice of veteran Qantas pilot Captain John Bartels came over the intercom. Rachael Angley said the pilot reassured passengers and crew. Another passenger recalled him saying: 'There's a large hole in the side of the plane. I don't know how it got there.'⁶ In a statement released later, he described the crucial moments after his Boeing 747-400 series jet suddenly depressurised over the South China Sea on Friday 25 July 2008 with 365 passengers and crew on board. 'As soon as we realised there was decompression, I immediately pulled out my memory checklist. There were three of us in the cockpit and we all worked together and focused on doing what we had to do to get the aircraft down safely, which is exactly what we are trained to do. I have no doubt every Qantas captain in the same situation would have had the same result. Throughout it all, the cabin crew did a tremendous job of looking after our passengers.'[7]

In fact, they didn't. Air Transport Safety Bureau investigators interviewed all the passengers and crew after the incident and were told that some of the junior cabin crew had frozen when the cabin lost pressure. The preliminary ATSB report said: 'Several cabin crew members had become very distressed during the depressurisation and were initially unable to carry out emergency tasks. Senior cabin crew reported that those staff were withdrawn from duty for a period, after which they were able to resume duties and assist passengers.'[8]

That was not the only problem. 'The oxygen masks were fucked,' said passenger David Saunders from St Kilda in Victoria. 'The elastic was so old that it had deteriorated. I couldn't get it around my head. In fact, there was one area where the masks didn't drop down at all.'[9] Other passengers reported that people's faces appeared to be going blue in the five and a half minutes it took to get to the safer lower altitude. Some of the passengers were wearing the masks but had not pulled them in order to activate the flow of oxygen. The ATSB report confirmed that there were some isolated problems, although 476 oxygen masks had successfully deployed. The forward crew rest and customer support manager masks had not dropped down, the air hose on the mask of seat 4K was not attached, and the centre overhead passenger service unit in row 53 containing the lights, air vents, seatbelt signs and crew call button was dangling down. As the plane depressurised, the cabin crew had grabbed their nearest available mask. Some sat with passengers and one even used the mask in a toilet.

Rachael Angley said: 'Ben and I fly internationally at least twice a year and have become slack when listening to the safety instructions at the beginning of the flight. At that instant I wished I had listened harder this time.'[10] It would have been no use tuning in to the normal audio track on the safety video – it was not working. Instead, the cabin services manager had to recite the familiar safety briefing over the cabin's public address system.

On the flight deck the first officer had been flying the plane when he heard a 'loud bang or cracking sound' and felt a jolt to the airframe.[11] The automatic pilot disengaged and the first officer took manual control of the aircraft. Multiple warning lights flashed around the cockpit, including ones warning about the cabin altitude and the status of the right-hand door second from the front of the plane. The second officer rushed forward from the crew rest area and all three flight crew pulled on their emergency oxygen masks before running through the 'cabin altitude non-normal' checklist. Twenty seconds after the first bang, the captain reduced the thrust on the four Rolls-Royce jet engines and extended the speed brakes to slow the jet down. The first officer began the immediate descent of the aircraft from 29,000 feet to 10,000 feet, where it would be possible to breathe without oxygen, and the captain made the international call for urgent assistance, MAYDAY, on the radio to the air traffic controllers in Manila 475 miles away.

What their myriad flashing warning lights could not tell

them was exactly what had happened. The three members of the flight crew in the stricken jet's cockpit knew they were in trouble. But it would only be on subsequent investigation that all 19 crew and 346 passengers on flight QF30 would realise just how close they came to becoming the first victims of a fatal Qantas jet crash. The Longreach plane had a gaping hole in its fuselage in front of the wing, underneath the economy cabin right-hand door. The entire right wing forward leading edge-to-fuselage fairing had been ripped away, leaving a hole two metres long and one and a half metres wide. The cause, according to the preliminary ATSB report, appeared 'to remain unique in world wide experience'.[12]

One of the seven emergency oxygen bottles bolted into the side wall of the forward cargo hold had exploded. The explosion had ripped the giant hole in the fuselage and sent a large part of the green oxygen cylinder, with the valve still attached, shooting up through the cabin floor like an airborne torpedo. After punching through the floor, the cylinder struck the R2 door frame and handle, knocking the handle up into the one-o-clock position, and knocking off the valve from the top of the bottle. The handle was moved 120 degrees from the closed position, shearing the handle as part of the safety mechanism to prevent the door being opened in flight. The impact with the door handle turned the speeding cylinder upside down as it continued to shoot upwards. Still rotating, the cylinder smashed into the overhead storage bin above the door, crushing the locker, before falling to the floor and being sucked back out through the holes in the floor and side of the plane. At least that's what the experts at the ATSB believed, because the vital evidence, the oxygen cylinder, was nowhere to be seen and was 'presumably lying at the bottom of the South China Sea'.[13]

When the cylinder ruptured the metal hull of the aircraft, its two pressure relief valves vented air from the aircraft, forcing open the two circular blowout doors on the left side of the jet and easing pressure on the damaged door. Fortunately, none of the wreckage had gone into the spinning blades of the closest Rolls-Royce jet engine. Parts of the missing leading edge fairing panel were found on the number three engine pylon and a cut was found on the engine intake. The engine was later replaced as a precaution.

The Qantas jet was lucky. In 1989 a United Airlines Boeing 747 on its way to Australia suffered a catastrophic door failure. The fuselage of that plane was ripped open and nine passengers were sucked out of the jet by the sudden change in cabin pressure. The plane eventually landed safely.

Although one of the passenger oxygen bottles was missing, there was still enough air in the remaining bottles for 65 minutes. The flight deck was supplied by its own separate emergency oxygen supply. Once the plane had levelled out at 10,000 feet the use of oxygen was no longer necessary, but Captain Bartels faced another problem. The exploding oxygen cylinder had also cut through electrical and mechanical systems needed to fly the plane. On the flight deck the crew were assessing just how much of their equipment was still operational. A total of 85 wires had been damaged by the cylinder. Almost half of these affected the oxygen system itself, stopping the crew from resetting the passenger oxygen supply or even from turning it on or off.

More importantly, the first officer's aileron control cables running along the right side of the aircraft had been cut, meaning it was impossible for him to fly the aircraft. Modern aircraft duplicate many systems as a safety back-up. Cables controlling those ailerons also run from the captain's controls down the left side of the aircraft. Captain Bartels could still fly the jet, without the usual first officer back-up, from his controls. The jet was also displaying still more system failure messages including those for all three instrument landing systems, the left flight management computer, the left very high frequency omni-directional radio-range navigation instrument and the aircraft's anti-skid braking system. Captain Bartels, a former navy flyer, was back to basics.

The plane was diverted to Manila's Ninoy Aquino international airport for an emergency landing. The flight crew began dumping fuel and received vectoring assistance from Manila air traffic control. Captain Bartels used visual aids to conduct a smooth touchdown on runway 06, using full reverse thrust and minimal braking. The passengers broke into a round of spontaneous applause.

International Federation of Airline Pilots technical director Richard Woodward said that Qantas pilots were trained to land without the use of landing systems. 'It's practised regularly in the flight simulator and in my experience this pilot's pretty good at assessing constant glide paths and the angles down to landing without any aids on the runway, even though it's the requirement of transport aeroplanes to have some. Given the conditions, the captain did a very good job.'[14] Even Captain Bartels' wife joined in the praise. 'I am very proud of him. I always have been. He's a good operator and I've got faith in him as a pilot, for sure,' she told journalists once he had landed. 'He's been flying for 23 years with Qantas and [of that time] he's had 16 years in command. But there are many like him in Qantas who would have done the same job.'[15]

Once a ground engineer had given the plane a quick look-over, it was towed to the airbridge to disembark the passengers. No one was injured, but several reported feeling faint, light-headed and shaky. 'It was unclear as to whether those symptoms were associated with hypoxic effects, or the anxiety brought upon by the situation,' said the ATSB report.[16] Manila airport operations officer Ding Lima told local radio: 'Upon disembarkation, there were some passengers who vomited. You can see in their faces they were really scared.'[17] Others broke down in tears.

Passenger Sarah Lucas said: 'When we landed there were a lot of people who rushed up to see the [right] side of the plane so I knew there was something on that side and then we walked round to have a look.' It was only then, when looking at the gaping hole in the fuselage, that many passengers fully realised just how lucky they were to be back on the ground. 'I didn't realise how bad it was until we got down,' said Ms Lucas.[18] Teenager Rachael Angley said: 'Once we'd seen the outside of the plane and could see the hole and the bags hanging out it hit me that I might have lost my bag. Then I realised I had survived and knew that was so much more important. One woman who was on the plane with her three children broke down in tears. I was really impressed with the way Qantas's staff cared for Ben and me during the flight.'[19]

Back in Australia, Qantas CEO Geoff Dixon said he was

'horrified' when he learned about the explosion on QF30. 'This was an absolutely serious incident; we do not downplay this. Obviously the aircraft was traumatised. I suspect there were many things on the aircraft that may well have been damaged,' he said at a press conference the following day. 'I would like to praise the work done by the pilots, cabin crew and the passengers in what must have been a very frightening situation, but we are incredibly proud of how our people reacted to this,' he continued, before being questioned about the airline's safety standards. 'I don't think we have falling safety standards, we have one of the highest standards of safety and operations of anywhere in the world,' he said. At that stage it was still unclear what had happened. 'Our team has not had access to the aircraft as yet. We cannot speculate at this stage the cause of the accident but we can say that we've had a preliminary look at the records of the aircraft involved. It did a D check in Sydney, which is the major check for aircraft, in 2004. Subsequently it did a C check at Avalon in 2006 and another C check in 2008. They were routine checks and nothing untoward was found.'[20]

However, 'aviation sources' were already informing newspapers that the routine corrosion checks mentioned by Dixon had in fact revealed that the 17-year-old Boeing jet was a 'rust bucket'. [21] The Melbourne *Age* reported a plane spotters' website claim that the jet, VH-OJK, named *The City of Newcastle*, had been sent in for 'serious corrosion issues' in February.[22] The jet was 17 years old at the time of the incident, old by international 747 standards, where the average age is 15. Qantas had also just given the old jet an internal refit to modernise the interior for passengers.

The ATSB probe into the incident naturally focused on the damaged oxygen bottle. Months before the explosion on QF30, US authorities had ordered that all US-registered Boeing 747-400 series aircraft undergo a thorough check of the oxygen cylinders. It came after a report showed that many oxygen cylinders had not been properly heat treated. They needed to be replaced. The US Federal Aviation Administration directive said: 'We are issuing this to prevent failure of the oxygen cylinder support under the most critical flight load conditions, which could cause the oxygen cylinder to come loose and leak oxygen. Leakage of oxygen could result in oxygen being unavailable for the flight crew or could result in a fire hazard in the vicinity of the leakage.'[23] Australian authorities had already told Qantas to check its 747-400 oxygen bottles. The ATSB preliminary report said that the number four oxygen cylinder had 'sustained a failure that allowed a sudden and complete release of the pressurised contents'.[24] As the damaged cylinder was missing, other cylinders from the same 1996 batch as the QF30 one were located and subjected to a series of destructive and non-destructive tests. One was found to have 'multiple linear indications . . . radiating outward from the cylinder neck'.[25] The largest of these crack-like features was 12 mm long.

Just three days before the oxygen bottle exploded, the crew of VH-OJK noted in the technical log on a flight from Los Angeles to Sydney that the passenger oxygen needed to be refilled. But when maintenance staff on the ground checked the oxygen, they found that the servicing display panel and the cylinders themselves were within serviceable limits. The separate crew oxygen system had also had problems in the month before the explosion. The oxygen indicators on the flight deck recorded fluctuations in the crew oxygen levels. Each time the levels had to be checked manually and were found to be okay. Special approval was obtained from the Civil Aviation Safety Authority to keep flying the plane with this defect in the crew oxygen levels.

The ATSB investigation into the incident was hampered because vital information on one of the plane's two black box flight recorders was taped over. The information cockpit voice recorder (CVR) monitoring system records the total audio environment in the cockpit. It runs on a continuous two-hour loop. Unfortunately, it kept recording as the aircraft was towed to the gate at Manila airport and wiped out the crucial time when the oxygen bottle exploded. Instead, investigators had to rely on the flight data recorder (FDR) black box system, which runs on a 25-hour continuous loop, and the non-crash protected quick access recorder (QAR) system, which is used by Qantas engineers to monitor maintenance issues. It was in sleep mode when the oxygen bottle exploded, but began recording four seconds later.

The incident came in the middle of a terrible year for Qantas in terms of its public image. The company did little to help itself by alienating some passengers on flight QF30 such as John Westcott, a London-based commercial aircraft captain with 20 years' experience. He praised the crew on the flight but was scathing about Qantas's follow-up care for him. 'They are concerned about two things: their bottom line and damage control,' he said.[26] Unsurprisingly, it had been his first explosive decompression. 'Your lungs suddenly empty of air. It is like someone sitting on your sternum with a hand over your mouth,' he said, adding that he would be taking leave from his flying job when he got back to England.[27] Despite the experience, no one from Qantas had contacted him to offer counselling or discuss how the emergency was handled. Instead, he was called by a 'customer care executive', who offered him a refund and a travel voucher. He had thought the five extra staff rostered on for the replacement aircraft for the homeward journey might be trained counsellors but, when he spoke to one, he found she was the marketing manager from Singapore.

At the time of the explosion, Qantas was also involved in a bitter pay dispute with its 1500 licensed engineers, which had resulted in many flights being cancelled or delayed. A senior Qantas pilot was quick to add his voice to the concern of the unions after the QF30 explosion. 'This could well be the direct result of Qantas having stand-in engineers, or from outsourcing maintenance to Malaysia,' he told the *Herald Sun* in Melbourne the day after the incident. 'It has been talked about a lot here and we have been told to be extra vigilant when you walk around aircraft. With Qantas outsourcing to Malaysia [it] is certainly worrying a lot of us pilots. There have been aircraft with dodgy staples to secure wiring,' he said.[28]

The union was upset that 15 to 20 per cent of Qantas engineering was done offshore – as it had been for the last 50 years. It said that overseas standards were inferior and an increasing number of incidents seemed to be confirming its point. A few months before the oxygen cylinder explosion, a Qantas 747 had been forced to make an emergency landing at Bangkok after losing all the power from its generators. It was able to land on battery power because the failure happened near the airport. The cause of that incident was identified as a leaking drip tray in the galley that had corroded the generator directly underneath, leading to its failure. In March passengers on a 747-400 landing at Los Angeles were told to adopt the brace position as the jumbo landed and blew three tyres.

Qantas knew there was a problem with its offshore maintenance. An internal audit report into maintenance carried out on Qantas jets in Singapore in August 2006 was damning of the work done there. Qantas sent its jets to Singapore for the major D-Check overhauls, the enormous service where the aircraft is completely stripped and checked out. The surveillance audit was carried out over three separate visits to the Singapore Airlines Engineering Company heavy maintenance facility in August and September 2006. 'This audit has served to clearly demonstrate that previously highlighted quality issues have not been effectively addressed,' read the report's executive summary. 'The general quality trend appears to be heading in a negative direction with numerous quality deficiencies considered to be of a serious nature.' The report went on to list a catalogue of problems, including unapproved repairs to floor panels that 'were found to be just bogged up with filler'.[29] The Australian auditors found poor lighting for work on complex electronic parts, the maintenance area cluttered with bits of plane stacked all over the workshop, tool boxes with odd screws lying around, discarded metal swarf in electric wiring looms, inadequate records and many, many more problems. 'Qantas management must consider whether the risks of continued usage of this supplier are acceptable to Qantas and, with close scrutiny, if quality improvement will be demonstrated with future checks,' said the report.[30]

Qantas had been in dispute with its engineers for most of the last decade – even before the dreadful 1997 decision to sack 53 engineering apprentices, including the apprentice of the year, at the end of their four-year training. Most of them did not find work back in the aviation industry and the union felt the fresh talent needed for the future in Australia was lost. So the airline's management should not have been surprised when the engineering union contradicted it consistently in the media.

Fewer than three weeks after the QF30 incident, Qantas's fleet of six Boeing 737-400 jets were grounded for what the airline described as an 'irregularity with paperwork'.[31] However, Steve Purvinas from the Australian Licensed Aircraft Engineers' Association (ALAEA) said the real reason was because support clips that should have been riveted to the bulkhead to ensure the cabin remained pressurised were missing. Qantas had failed to act on an airworthiness directive from the US Federal Aviation Administration, Boeing and Australia's Civil Aviation Safety Authority that had been issued five years earlier, in 2003. Qantas was told to do the work 'to prevent fatigue cracking on critical areas of the forward pressure bulkhead, which could result in rapid decompression of the aircraft fuselage'.[32] Purvinas said: 'It's interesting, Qantas often say that something may not be a safety issue but I wonder at what point in time things do become a safety issue – is it when someone's dead?'[33]

The airline dismissed the union claims as misleading and wheeled out head of engineering David Cox to repeat his oft-said lines that the union was scaremongering, and that there were not more maintenance issues but simply more media attention on those incidents. That debate was pushed along when the engine of a Qantas 747-300 series jet switched to idle as the plane came in to land in Auckland on the same day as he made those comments. The passengers waiting to fly back to Melbourne had to spend another night in New Zealand while the fuel-flow regulator was fixed.

Two weeks after that, at the start of September, the Civil Aviation Safety Authority finally acted. It had been criti-cised in a Senate inquiry into CASA for being too close to Qantas. Senator Kerry O'Brien was a member of the inquiry and said: 'CASA should be issuing Qantas with a "please explain" about the matters which have come to public atten-tion recently. It is nothing less than their job to inquire into public concerns about Qantas.' For good measure he added: 'It is not good enough for the regulator to respond after the event. One would hope they had been applying the same level of scrutiny or something approaching it, in the lead up to these events.'[34]

Now the aviation watchdog wanted to be seen to be cut-ting the cosy ties. CASA warned of 'emerging problems' within Qantas maintenance operations and announced two intensive audits of its operations.[35] Some Qantas Air-ways maintenance procedures were not only failing to meet CASA's standards, said the watchdog, they were even failing to meet the airline's own internal standards.

CASA Deputy Chief Executive Officer of operations Mick Quinn said: 'CASA has looked carefully at the Qantas maintenance systems and performance and uncovered signs of emerging problems. The review found maintenance performance within Qantas is showing some adverse trends and is now below the airline's own benchmarks.'[36] A full maintenance audit would be conducted on each of the airline's major aircraft types – the Boeing 747, 737 and 767 jets. Qantas refused to respond, instead saying it would work closely with CASA and adding that the review confirmed its position that there had been no increase in the number of incidents over the last two years. Two months ahead of his own departure from the airline, CEO Geoff Dixon instead pointed the finger of blame at the union:

> As we have publicly acknowledged, certain [key performance indicators] and despatch reliability have been significantly impacted by the industrial action between Qantas and the ALAEA over past months. These issues are not about safety or compliance and we are working to bring our network performance back to the standards which have earned us a reputation as one of the best and most reliable airlines in the world. These difficulties, while improving, will continue for a few weeks yet as our policy of safety before schedule is sacrosanct.[37]

Two thousand and eight had been a tough year for Qantas. In addition to all these incidents, the fuel bill was up by

$1 billion, profits were expected to be down by 46 per cent to $750 million, and the share price had dropped by 53 per cent from $5.44 at the start of 2008 to $2.53 by the end. Surely things couldn't get any worse. Could they?

QF15

TURBULENT TIMES

On the flight deck of QF72 from Singapore to Perth on 7 October 2008 everything was normal. The weather was fine and crew noted there had been no turbulence for the entire flight. On board the modern Airbus A330 were 303 passengers, nine cabin crew and three flight crew. Just five years old, the French-built jet was one of the most modern aeroplanes in the Qantas fleet, featuring the latest fly-by-wire computer controls. Even when flown manually, the movements from the pilot were filtered through the on-board computers, which could override the pilot's instructions if he went outside prescribed safe limits.

At 12.39 pm local time the experienced captain was at the controls, the first officer had just gone back to the galley on a scheduled rest break, and the second officer had moved over to sit in the right control seat. The autopilot and autothrust systems were engaged and the plane was cruising uneventfully at 37,000 feet to the west of Learmouth in Western Australia. In the main cabin, just over three hours into the flight, the meal service had finished and passengers were making their way to and from the toilets. Some noticed the plane climb slightly.

In the cockpit the autopilot had disengaged. The electronic centralised aircraft monitor warned AUTO FLT AP OFF (meaning the autopilot was off) and the master caution chimes sounded. The captain took manual control of the plane and unsuccessfully attempted to engage autopilot 2 and then autopilot 1. The plane climbed 200 feet and then returned to the normal cruising altitude. The pilot and second officer cleared the AUTO FLT warning message and then received one saying the navigation system was faulty. Other alarms were sounding, and the airspeed and altitude indicators on the captain's primary flight display were fluctuating. The second officer got onto the cabin interphone to call the first officer back to the flight deck. Abruptly the plane pitched nose-down, at an angle of 8.4 degrees and, with a g-force of -0.80 g, the plane dropped 650 feet.

Back in the passenger cabin it was chaos. Ben Cave from Perth was not wearing his seatbelt and was slammed into the cabin roof. He feared for his life 'and saw a bit of a flash before me. I hit the ceiling but I was OK.'[1] Andrea Hutchins from Singapore said that as the plane dropped, some of the passengers were pinned to the ceiling and others were suspended in midair. 'The plane was dropping quite quickly so they actually stayed in the air and then they came crashing down,' she said. 'The people who were wearing seatbelts, like myself, were OK. The people who were standing were the ones who got hurt the most.'[2] Englishman Henry Bishop, on his first trip to Australia with wife Doreen, said: 'Unfortunately some people who were walking back to the seats were the ones who copped it, as it were, when the overhead [lockers] came down on them.'[3]

One of those returning to his seat from the bathroom was 69-year-old Yip How Wong. 'All of a sudden there was a big bang boom and I found myself up in the ceiling for a second or two and then I fell. [Passengers] were screaming because all of a sudden there was a drop. I couldn't get up,' he said.[4] Sitting in the middle row with his seatbelt on, 22-year-old Tim Ellett said: 'I could see five or six people stuck to the roof. They didn't have their seatbelts on. One woman was stuck in one of the panels, which got knocked out.' The woman sitting next to him was injured. 'She just flew up in the air and busted her leg,' he said.[5]

Meanwhile, in the cockpit the captain was frantically pulling back on the joystick to arrest the sudden plunge, while the second officer activated the fasten seatbelts sign and made a public announcement for people to return to their seats and buckle up. The control panels were flashing with warnings. After clearing the navigation fault they were faced with a PRIM 3 FAULT warning, which meant the flight control primary computer was not working. They turned it off for five seconds and then turned it on again. A few seconds later the aircraft suddenly pitched down once more, this time dropping 400 feet before the captain's pressure on the joystick arrested the descent and the plane returned to the normal cruising altitude. The first officer scrambled back to the flight deck and the three flight officers discussed what to do. 'They were not confident that further pitch-down events would not occur,' said the ATSB preliminary report into the incident.[6]

The crew decided to land the plane as soon as possible and made an emergency priority broadcast (PAN) to air traffic control for permission to land at Learmouth, over 1000 kilometres north of Perth. Meanwhile, the cockpit was filled with warning chimes as fault messages scrolled wildly over the main screen. The crew could not stop the flickering messages or the regular warnings that the plane was about to stall. The captain could not trust the information being displayed so he switched to the standby flight instruments, trimmed the plane manually because the automatic elevator trim was not working, and disconnected the autothrust to enable him to fly the plane manually.

Later, a close friend of the captain, who had previously been a Mirage fighter pilot, said: 'It would have been tense, no two ways about it. But I know the captain – he would have been very calm.'[7] Michael Glynn, fellow A330 pilot and then acting president of the Australian and International Pilots' Association, added: 'I believe the situations he was faced with have not been seen before. But that's one of the things we are trained to prepare for – when things crop up that you've not seen or thought up before and you have to . . . get the aircraft to ground safely.'[8] Captain Glynn said the QF72 captain's calmness in trying to solve the problem of what was happening to the plane would have been vital. 'Sometimes the best thing to do as a pilot in that situation is to sit back and get a sense of what's going on, instead of leaping in and trying to fix it without understanding what's going on.'

But at the heart of the problem was the plane itself. 'The thing to remember about Airbus is the flight control computer is always flying the plane – even when you're controlling it by hand, you're controlling it through the flight control computer.'[9] And the flight control computer was not making any sense at all.

The crew contacted the operator's maintenance watch unit by satphone to seek assistance. The technicians confirmed the faults by datalink but could offer no cure other than to turn off the faulty computer, which the crew did. The fluctuating warning messages just kept on flashing. In the meantime, the cabin crew advised the flight crew that there were extensive injuries, including a broken leg. The crew radioed a MAYDAY and told the air traffic controllers they had several injuries on board. On the ground at Learmouth, emergency services prepared to meet the disaster-stricken plane.

As the jet approached Learmouth, the flight crew found they could not enter the GPS coordinates for the landing into the flight management computer. The captain brought it in on a straight visual approach to runway 36 and the plane landed without further incident. The passengers applauded delightedly when the wheels touched the tarmac.

Worst hurt were those at the middle and rear of the plane. Eighteen passengers had been standing or walking in the aisles when the aircraft suddenly dropped; all were injured and two thirds of them had to go to hospital. Four had serious multiple injuries, including cuts and spinal damage. Two passengers who were in the toilets at the time suffered multiple injuries. An infant suffered minor head injuries and a flight attendant standing in the rear galley was badly hurt.

Sixty-one passengers were seated without their seatbelts fastened and 91 per cent of them were hurt, mostly suffering head and neck injuries from slamming into the overhead lockers, and bruising to the back and legs when crashing back down. A third of the passengers who had their seatbelts on were also injured. More alarmingly, four passengers who had their seatbelts loosely fastened said the seatbelts had not restrained them. Accident investigators worked out that the belts could release if the buckle slipped off the passenger's hip and dropped under the armrest. When the plane dropped suddenly, the latch of the buckle released itself on the armrest. This prompted official warnings to always have the seatbelt properly adjusted.

The Australian Transport Safety Bureau investigation into the incident uncovered a fault with one of the jet's three air data inertial reference units (ADIRUs). Just before the autopilot disconnected, ADIRU 1 started sending incorrect data spikes to other parts of the aircraft's operating systems. A check of the A330's main computer traced the error messages, and tests of the components identified by the ADIRU found there was nothing wrong with them. The problem was compounded when the jet's flight control computers did not filter out the data spikes about the angle of attack – the method of measuring the aircraft's movement through the atmosphere. According to the ATSB preliminary report: 'On the A330, angle of attack data was processed differently to other parameters and, in a very specific situation, the flight control computers could generate an undesired pitch-down elevator command.'[10] The three ADIRU units from the A330 were sent to manufacturer Northrop Grumman in Los Angeles for testing.

ATSB checks found that the same Qantas jet, VH-QPA, had suffered a fault with ADIRU 1 during a flight from Hong Kong to Perth on 12 December 2006. The crew reported similar fault messages but the plane did not pitch down suddenly as it did two years later. Then, on 27 December 2008, another Qantas Airbus flying from Perth to Singapore had its autopilot automatically disconnected after it had reached its 36,000 feet cruising altitude. The crew was deluged with warning messages similar to those experienced on the flight deck of QF72 two months earlier. They decided to turn around and made a safe, overweight landing back at Perth airport without incident. Airbus identified a similar fault on another airline flight from Sydney to Saigon, which seemed to rule out the cause being electromagnetic transmissions from the Harold E. Holt Naval Communication Station near Learmouth. The ADIRU from the second Qantas flight joined the ones from the first incident for testing. The need for that testing to be done quickly was underscored by the crash of an Air New Zealand Airbus in November 2008. The A320 was on a maintenance flight when it crashed into the Mediterranean in good weather and with no emergency call, killing all seven aboard. It was not known what caused the crash.

Faulty ADIRUs had also caused problems in the past. Boeing 777 aircraft flew for six years before a fault in the ADIRU software was discovered when a Malaysian Airlines jet suddenly pitched up in a 3000-feet climb climb. The pilots raced to override the false information being sent by the ADIRU to the aircraft's operating systems before the plane stalled. They succeeded and a bug was found in the computer software.

Qantas dealt with the passengers from the QF72 accident in its customary fashion. Not everyone in hospital was happy to receive their money back and a one-way ticket to London. A Qantas spokesman said: 'We will be talking to our customers directly about any other needs according to their individual circumstances and in particular in association with any injuries sustained as a result of this incident.'[11] At least ten of the most seriously injured were preparing compensation claims with the law firms Carter Capner and Slater & Gordon. One woman who was badly injured during the flight told the *Sydney Morning Herald* that a Qantas representative had entered her hospital room unannounced, asked her how she was injured and then asked her to sign a draft copy of her answers. 'It is not right for Qantas to try to get a "statement" from me without telling me that they are from Qantas in the first place. It is as if they are trying to cross-examine me,' said the woman, who declined to be named.[12] Qantas denied the 28 October visit ever took place. But the injured passenger's family obtained closed-circuit television footage of a woman visiting her on that day. They alleged it was an attempt by the airline to get evidence before a compensation claim was lodged. The woman's daughter said the visitor 'told my mum that she has come because of the Qantas accident and asked my mum to sign that piece of paper which she has drafted. When my mum heard that she is from

Qantas she told her that she doesn't want to talk any more. This is very scary and stressful for us.'[13]

Fellow passengers Sam and Rani Samaratunga were not happy with the airline's offer of compensation, which included $300 for out-of-pocket expenses, and engaged Melbourne lawyer Roger Singh to press their claim for as much as $100,000. 'This is the worst experience we've had. During the process we saw our own deaths,' said Mr Samaratunga, 68, who claimed he hurt his neck when he smashed into the overhead locker.[14] His 62-year-old wife suffered spinal, neck and head injuries as well as losing several teeth. They held a press conference to explain that they wanted the airline to pay for ongoing medical care in Sri Lanka and to cover the cost of care for Mrs Samaratunga's 87-year-old mother, for whom she was the sole carer. Mr Singh said: 'Claims for compensation in my mind need to be substantial in this case. With the number of people on board the plane, I think some 303 people, we could be talking about claims which are going to be in the multi-million dollar mark.'[15]

The QF72 incident came in the month before Qantas CEO Geoff Dixon's contract was due to end. He would stand down at the Annual General Meeting in November 2008. It had been a tough year, with the QF30 exploding oxygen bottle incident bringing a raft of bad publicity that was amplified by the QF72 nose-dive. It raised questions about exactly what shape Dixon was leaving the airline in. A survey by Labor pollsters UMR Research published in the *Australian*

in December showed that passengers were worried about the airline's safety standards. Six out of ten Australians believed safety standards had dropped in the last two years, but two-thirds still believed Qantas was safe to fly.

Qantas argued back that the Qantas Group's rate of turn-backs – 98 for 350,000 flights – compared favourably to other airlines. But that group figure included Jetstar which, at five years old, had a very new fleet. The Qantas planes were all getting on a bit and were due for replacement in a $30 billion capital expenditure program that included the giant new Airbus A380s and Boeing 787 Dreamliners. However, at the end of 2008 it was still flying mostly 747s, a plane that first rolled off the production line over 30 years earlier when Holden was still making Monaros and John Travolta was more famous for his role in *Saturday Night Fever* than for flying around the world as a Qantas ambassador.

Dixon's legacy, apart from low staff morale, was a feeling that engineering and maintenance standards were slipping. Union representatives were happy to express their concerns anonymously to the *Australian Financial Review*. 'Qantas engineers are under-trained and under-resourced and are getting more work than they can cope with. At the turn of the decade, Qantas was getting about 1,000 [engineering] apprentices a year, now it's about 180,' said one.[16] Another told how the Australian Licensed Aircraft Engineers' Association had written to the Civil Aviation Safety Authority about other incidents. These included one in which a Boeing 747 was green-lit to fly by an operations manager, despite his engineering team saying it should not be sent into the air because of an oil leak in its landing gear. 'Anything could happen with these aircraft, you just don't know which is going to cause an aircraft to be lost,' a source said.[17]

The anonymous sources also told how a foreman in Sydney had been demoted for not getting aircraft out on time, even though he felt the aircraft were not fit to fly. Steve Purvinas, the Association's federal secretary, repeated a story to the *Australian Financial Review* from a Cairns-based duty manager who said that the airline used to be 95 per cent about engineering ability and five per cent about the company. 'Now it's the other way round,' he said. 'Qantas used to promote and encourage the best engineers but now it's about the most time spent playing golf with the boss.'[18]

The boss, Geoff Dixon, reflecting back on his time at the airline, told the *Australian Financial Review*: 'To me it is the end of a very, very terrific job, but you move on. All I've done is my job really. What I would say is that the company is in a very strong position. The industry is absolutely going through a crisis but Qantas is well placed to see it through. I don't think you can expect anything more than that.'[19] Dixon bowed out at the AGM in November, with 40 per cent of the company's shareholders angrily voting against his $12 million golden parachute. The feeling across the floor was that huge executive pay packets were a 'slap in the face' to the airline's 35,000 workers whose pay Dixon had tried to cap at just three per cent.[20] It was definitely time for a change.

The search for Dixon's replacement had just begun when the straight-shooting former Rio Tinto boss Leigh Clifford took over the chairman's job from Margaret Jackson. Clifford was keen to make a break with the boys' club style of management and the team responsible for the embarrassing and botched private equity bid the year before. Executive recruitment firm Heidrick and Struggles had been hired to manage the process, which had come down to three internal candidates. CFO Peter Gregg, 53, made no secret of the fact that he was keen for the job. He had been appointed by Dixon and worked hand in glove with him, taking responsibility for being the architect of the airline's strong financial position. John Borghetti, 52, a 35-year Qantas veteran and stalwart of Dixon's executive team, was the outside chance. The favourite was Alan Joyce, the 42-year-old chief executive of Jetstar, who had built up an airline and made it profitable in just a few years.

Only Joyce was invited to make a presentation to the board, having being told he was the favoured candidate. On the day of his presentation the other two candidates, unaware of what was happening on the other side of the city, were meeting to discuss the delivery of the new Airbus A380. Clifford later argued to the *Australian Financial Review* that the process had been exhaustive and that getting all three to present their views for the future would have led the other candidates 'up the garden path'. He explained: 'You don't want to put people in a situation where it's one shot. Good boards are not going to make their judgements like that.'[21]

Clifford clearly wanted to make a break with the past. Joyce's running of Jetstar was very different to Dixon's running of Qantas. Dixon was from the tough old school and liked people to see things his way. Joyce was younger and happier to listen to people's views. He was not a macho man. Perhaps the first step to ending the public's view of the company as arrogant was to put a completely different face at the top.

A new era for Qantas was being born. Both Gregg and Borghetti would be gone from the airline within a year, together with a raft of redundant senior managers. Once his appointment became public, Joyce quickly noticed the difference. 'At Jetstar, people would criticise you behind your back. At Qantas, they are willing to say it directly to your face,' he joked.[22]

But his smile was about to become a lot more strained. After the terrible year Qantas had suffered, few people would have argued that Dixon had quit before the going got tough. But he had. Alan Joyce was about to reap the whirlwind.

QF16

ANNUS HORRIBILIS

AT THE END of 2008 Qantas finally had something to brag about. New state-of-the-art planes. The Airbus A380 super-jumbos cost over $330 million each, carry 450 passengers, boast six self-serve bars and, from the ergonomically designed chairs, give passengers laptop power to connect to email, and the choice of 100 movies, 350 television options and 30 PC-style games. Australian celebrity chef and Qantas catering coordinator Neil Perry said delightedly: 'It's got a toaster.'[1] The arrival of the first double decker A380 even reunited John Travolta and Olivia Newton-John when it was unveiled in Los Angeles. So it seems a bit of a shame that they don't always work.

It was bad enough when the plane's 80-metre wingspan

proved too big for Los Angeles airport, bringing all ground traffic to a standstill when it was moved around the runways. But in March 2009 all three of the new Qantas A380s were grounded. Two of them had fungus growing on the probes in the fuel tanks, which led to false fuel readings in the cockpit. Often caused by water in the fuel tank and treated with biocides, the fungus grounded the two jets while engineers cleaned the probes. The third was grounded in London by a ground steering problem and fuel leak.

Qantas executive general manager of operations Lyell Strambi, one of Alan Joyce's old mates and part of the new guard at Qantas, was fielded to deal with questions about the stranded jets. 'It's just unfortunate with only three aircraft in the fleet that we just happened to have three problems in the one day. It looks really bad and we disappoint the customers, which is really the problem here,' he said.[2] What? Looks bad, disappoint the customers. Where was that old Qantas arrogance?

Maybe it had been beaten out of them. New MD Alan Joyce faced a true annus horribilis in 2009. He had taken over just as deal-maker Geoff Dixon's last great play was coming to fruition. On the surface it seemed the perfect antidote to the coming tough times – a merger with another airline to make it a truly global player. British Airways had sold its shares in Qantas four years earlier to bale itself out of debt, but it was still the natural choice for a partner. The airlines had a shared history on the Kangaroo Route and were founding partners in the OneWorld Alliance (the alliance between ten airlines that had formed to allow passengers to travel the globe on one ticket). New chairman Leigh Clifford saw the opportunity in Dixon's vision and began talks with British Airways chairman Martin Broughton and BA's Irish CEO Willie Walsh. When Dixon stepped out of his office and into a four-month consultancy role before retirement, he had paved the way for Alan Joyce to see the deal through. The talks were bound to be friendly. The two Irish CEOs had worked together at Aer Lingus and are even related. Joyce once let slip that his mother is the second cousin of Walsh's wife. However, it would need more than the love of a good Irish family to get this deal over the line.

The advantages were obvious. Strategically, Qantas would have first-class access to one of the world's great aviation hubs, Heathrow airport, and the two airlines would be able to deploy Jetstar into Europe. The problem was the merger ratio – British Airways wanted it to be a 50:50 split and Qantas didn't. Even after Prime Minister Kevin Rudd's Labor government agreed to ease the foreign ownership restrictions, the Qantas Sale Act insisted the flying kangaroo be 51 per cent Australian owned. The deal was worth over $8 billion and Qantas was by far the sexier suitor. British Airways carried a $3.7 billion pension liability that was only going to get bigger and had a much weaker balance sheet, thanks to the struggling British economy and cut-throat competition in Europe. Qantas was coming into the deal on the back of record profits and wanted the merger ratio skewed in its favour. The Brits swallowed their pride and said the head office could be in Australia and an Aussie, Leigh Clifford, could be the first joint chairman.

To complicate matters, other balls were in play. BA had already been in talks with Iberia about a possible merger. The

Spaniards were not too happy when it came out that the Brits had gone behind their back and snuggled up with their old Aussie mates. Qantas had also sounded out partners in Asia, including Malaysian Airlines and Cathay in Hong Kong. However, when news of the Qantas and British Airways talks emerged in December 2008, that partnership seemed the best option. On the surface, historically and culturally, the two airlines had a great deal in common, including language and highly skilled, highly unionised workforces.

But the merger was just too hard. The 51 per cent Australian ownership condition was a deal breaker. 'Despite the potential longer-term benefits for Qantas and BA, the airlines have not been able to come to an agreement,' Qantas said in a statement at the end of 2008.[3] Alan Joyce was going to have to face his annus horribilis alone.

Two thousand and nine started badly and then got worse. The problem with a global financial crisis is that nobody wants to travel. IATA predicted the global aviation market would lose $6.7 billion in 2009. Qantas was not immune. In February the number of passengers flying on Qantas planes dropped by 8.4 per cent. At Easter there were 10 per cent fewer domestic travellers and 17 per cent fewer international travellers. Qantas services to Los Angeles, London, Hong Kong and South Africa were cut back as Sydney airport reflected the global market with an 8.7 per cent drop in international passenger numbers in March – the fifth drop in consecutive months.

The opening up of the trans-Pacific route between Australia and America, one of the last truly profitable routes in the world, was further bad news for Qantas. Domestic rival

Virgin Blue unveiled V Australia flights to Los Angeles, while Delta's Boeing 777s added almost 20,000 more seats a month to the route. Before Delta decided to fly the route it was putting 200 of its passengers a day on Qantas jets under a code-share deal (when two airlines use one plane and two flight numbers on a route to save money). Obviously they would now be flying Delta. 'If you're the incumbent carrier this is a disaster – if you're the non-incumbent carrier this is an opportunity,' said Delta's network planning chief, Glen Hauenstein.[4] Qantas was not helped by Delta and Virgin agreeing to allow passengers to use a single ticket to travel on either network, giving passengers extensive links to domestic networks in Australia and the US.

The stiff competition sparked a loss-making fare war, with Qantas offering return economy tickets to New York for as little as $1,100 including taxes. Business-class travel was particularly badly hit on all routes and still the competition kept coming, with Abu Dhabi-based carrier Etihad increasing flights to Australia.

Qantas responded swiftly to the plunging market. It stopped spending. Orders for four new Airbus A380 superjumbos and 12 new Boeing 737-800s were put on ice and talks began on delaying delivery of 15 long-awaited Boeing 787 Dreamliners. Twenty of Qantas's existing fleet, including Boeing 747-300, 747-400 and 767-300 jets, were parked in the desert at Tuscon in Arizona to await an upturn in the economy. 'We are not exiting from any of our routes. What we are doing is scaling back our existing networks,' Joyce said in April.[5] He also announced that the airline would probably make a $180 million loss for the first six months of the year, which in turn pushed the share price down as low as $1.74. 'Is today my toughest day? It's been four months of tough days,' said Joyce.[6]

The falling share market also hit the Qantas super fund. The collapse in value meant it was almost $300 million short of the money it needed to meet its obligations. More than 13,000 current and former Qantas employees had guaranteed fixed payouts on retirement, no matter what happened to the fund. The airline was faced with the possibility of having to meet the shortfall, threatening to put another massive burden on the already beleaguered bottom line.

Joyce responded by swinging the axe. Qantas had already laid off 1,500 workers at the end of 2008 and shelved plans to hire another 1,200. In March Joyce saved $24 million a year by slashing 20 per cent of the senior management team – axing 90 management roles. One of the first ten to go was head of engineering David Cox, who himself had overseen the cutting in operation costs that had saved $500 million and led to the ongoing battle with the unions on maintenance issues. Another 68 managers were tapped on the shoulder and told to leave and 12 others were offered different, lower paid positions. Another $2.69 million was saved when Dixon's old commercial chief, John Borghetti, quit after 36 years with the company. However, two people had to be appointed to fill his shoes: Rob Gurney took over the commercial side and Lesley Grant became the executive manager of Customer, Product and Marketing. The old Dixon segmented style of management was being dumped and a new 'flatter' model brought in, together with a management pay freeze.

Joyce was leading from the front. Mahogany row had been

a pretty cushy place for a while so Joyce had plenty of fat to trim. Three weeks later he announced another 1,750 jobs would be axed, 500 of those in more junior management. 'It's certainly the toughest period I have seen and I have been in the industry for 20 years,' he said.[7] And you know things are bad when the unions start agreeing with the management. ACTU secretary Jeff Lawrence came out to say the airline needed to be 'saved' from foreign government-backed airlines. 'We are also concerned about the unfair competition Qantas faces from airlines which are owned or propped up by overseas governments,' he said.[8]

The fear stemmed from a Green Paper in which the government said it was committed to liberalisation. However, it also said that commitment had to be balanced against the national interest. Many stakeholders had their say. A White Paper with recommendations for the government to consider on the future of the Australian aviation industry was due out at the end of the annus horribilis. Watching it keenly would be the 35,000 Qantas employees who have a strong link with the airline's past as well as a stake in its future.

Qantas is full of staff who remember the good old days. They were the good old days because it was a nationalised industry full of fat. Taxpayer-funded fat. A system that was ripe for abuse. A pilot recalled: 'My neighbour needed some parts for his barbecue. Because of the high temperatures involved, these four rings needed to be made of a special metal and the quotes were coming in at hundreds of dollars each. I told him not to worry. On my next flight I asked a purser who owed me a favour to slip me a bottle of Scotch. I took that down to the engineering department and by the

end of the day my neighbour had four new parts for his barbecue.'⁹ This is the kind of abuse that is cited as the reason
for changing the way things worked. The question is, have
things changed for the better? Instead of a pilot's neighbour
getting a few parts for his barbecue, it is the fat cats at the
very top who are pocketing huge amounts of money. But
even that is not the real issue.

Qantas is full of staff who remember the good old days
when the emphasis was on safety, not profit. All that fat,
including readily available materials, meant broken parts
were fixed fast. In fact, things were fixed before they were
broken. If the manual said a part needed to be replaced after
so many hours' flying time – and aircraft manufacturers
build in big margins for safety – it would be. Even if it was
not broken. Qantas built its enviable jet safety record on a
superb, well-trained and well-funded engineering department that maintained planes to an impeccable standard.

Qantas is full of staff who reminisce about the good old
days because the future does not look so bright. They are
worried about what will happen tomorrow – not just to
their jobs, but to the people who have trusted them with
their lives. A huge number of 'minor' aircraft malfunctions
have occurred within the Qantas fleet just in the last two
years. These are maintenance-related issues. Qantas argues
that this is normal for any airline and has been highlighted
because of media attention. That media attention has been
intense because Qantas planes have suffered from major
mid-air incidents such as the exploding oxygen bottle that
resulted in the emergency landing in Manila. Qantas has
been lucky. What if that oxygen bottle had exploded on one

of the Qantas charters that fly over the Antarctic? There are no handy landing strips there. The point was underscored in September 2009 when the same plane developed a fuel leak on a flight from Singapore to Sydney. The crew shut down one of the jet's four engines and the plane, with 290 passengers on board, was diverted to Perth. It took engineers two and a half hours to check the engine and declare the plane safe.

Qantas management does not like the attention on these 'minor' maintenance issues. In the Dixon era, it seemed to fail to realise the harm its cost-cutting ways were doing to the public perception of the airline and to staff morale. With such a big workforce it is not hard to find people who work for Qantas in Australia. But it is very difficult to find one who is happy. And passengers, faced with yet another flight on an ageing or poorly maintained plane with a broken entertainment system, wonder what else has not been fixed properly.

Qantas founder Hudson Fysh wrote a pamphlet called 'Ethics and Other Things', which he distributed to senior staff in 1938. It was updated in 1948 and reproduced as a booklet and distributed to a select Qantas circle in 1955. It set out the airline founder's personal views on loyalty, staff, diplomacy and, above all, service. It would have made interesting reading for the Qantas board and management team that was considering the $11 billion private equity buyout. 'It may be maintained that duty towards our shareholders comes before our duty to the public. I maintain that duty to the public comes first, in that, if we are unable to provide that "worthy service", it is doubtful if we should be in business,' wrote Fysh.[10]

Sir Hudson Fysh's only son, John, now 83 and living on the Central Coast, spent 30 years working for Qantas after leaving the air force as a 'half-trained' pilot. He went into the administrative side of the business because poor eyesight ruled him out of commercial flying. 'My father always thought of Qantas as a noble endeavour. After he left it became more bureaucratic and then, with the amalgamation of TAA and once the blue tails came in, it became much more of a business.'

Fysh said the decision to try to sell the airline to APA as part of a leveraged buyout was the nadir.

The recent years of executives rewarding themselves with large salaries, and looking to sell Qantas off, was a long way from my father's beliefs. They did it just to make money, that's all. Any question of noble endeavour was laughable. I thought [the buyout] was wrong in principle and was absolutely delighted when it failed. If people noticed the ground shaking in Dural at the time, it was my father turning in his grave. Many, many people were relieved when it didn't go through. Not for emotional reasons, but because the national carrier was in danger.

Fysh added that he was relieved the airline was back in the hands of a chief executive with kerosene in his nostrils. 'I have seen tough economic times, where there is over-capacity in the market, and it requires a bit of managing through. Alan Joyce may be the man to do it.'[11]

Hudson Fysh also had some notes on character, which may

have been forgotten by some of his successors. 'According to his character, so does a man react under the imposition of the various conditions. Real character is often brought out under the stress of great pressure. The manner in which an individual accepts success or praise provides an index to character. An exaggerated sense of importance or overbearing manner are signs of weakness, and the test of a man is how he "stands corn"' – how he meets the approval of those around him.[12] The test of standing corn is currently being applied, with an economic blowtorch, to Alan Joyce's financial testicles.

The one bright star in the Qantas firmament is Jetstar, the airline Joyce built. He was unpopular because he did it by cutting costs; today it is starting to look like he saved jobs. But even he admits that it is not possible to apply the Jetstar formula of success to all Qantas routes. 'Qantas international routes to LA and London need the combination of premium and leisure traffic. They will never be Jetstar routes. Where the problems are, Jetstar is not the solution,' he said in 2009.[13] In a year that saw over 30 airlines go to the wall, Qantas remained one of the better contenders for survival, largely because of the performance of Jetstar. Qantas, together with Singapore Airlines, remained one of only four carriers in the world to have an investment-grade credit rating.

But being the best swimmer on a sinking ship is no guarantee of survival. 'We have to be prepared for it to get worse, but also better. There is a lot of volatility and if you get ten economists in they'll tell you ten different things and that makes it hard for us to forecast and to predict. We've been very good throughout our history of adapting to the changing environment,' said Joyce.[14]

He backed that up in June 2009, telling the *Australian*'s aviation writer, Steve Creedy, that the airline was in 'preservation mode'.[15] All plans to float the Frequent Flyer, pilot training, engineering and freight arms of the airline as separate businesses were put on hold. He said that deferring the delivery of new aircraft promised a $1 billion cash boost to swell the $3 billion reserves sitting in the bank. On top of that, Qantas was coping with the 20 to 30 per cent drop in premium-class passengers by simply reallocating first-class seats as business, and some of the business-class seats as premium-economy. 'So, by taking first class off the selling [configuration] we saved a cabin crew member,' he said, very practically.[16] Of course the redundancies were also saving money, as was getting the staff to take all their holidays. 'We have a large number of pilots and cabin crew now on long-service leave and leave without pay, and we're working through the airport staff on the same arrangements,' he said.[17]

At least Joyce was not asking his staff to work for a month for free, as partner British Airways was doing. BA Chief Executive Willie Walsh led the charge by forgoing his bonus and working for nothing for the month of July – of course, he could afford to after receiving a 5 per cent pay rise that pumped his basic salary up to $1.5 million. The staff was not happy. Given the British airline's parlous financial state, Joyce was probably hugging himself in relief that the partnership deal had fallen through.

However, he still had practical problems to contend with. Later, in June 2009, Jetstar came under attack in parliament when government MP Paul Gibson lambasted the airline for blaming the cancellation of half-empty flights on mechanical problems. Mr Gibson, furious after six friends travelling to Sydney for a State of Origin match almost missed the game, told parliament: 'If Jetstar has to cancel so many flights because of mechanical problems, one has got to ask the question, should they be in the air in the first place?'[18] Jetstar quickly issued a statement saying that flights that could not be filled were sometimes cancelled for scheduling reasons, but never for maintenance problems.

Earlier that month, a Qantas Airbus A330 with 203 people on board had to make an emergency landing in Guam. The plane was four hours into its flight from Osaka, in Japan, to the Gold Coast when the pilot noticed a small flame near the window and smoke in the cockpit. The electrical fault in a window heating element was quickly dealt with by a pilot, who used a fire extinguisher to put out the blaze. Nerves were on edge because, just the week before, an Air France Airbus 330 had crashed into the Atlantic en route from Brazil to Paris, killing all 228 people on board. The worst that the Jetstar Guam incident provoked was a minor delay for the passengers while another plane was sent to pick them up, and a slanging match between the unions and Qantas management about overseas maintenance. Qantas operations chief Lyell Strambi was quick to tell the engineering union that the electrical component had not been part of the service undertaken on the nearly new plane in Manila the year before. 'There has been no requirement to touch this component since the aircraft was delivered, there is no history of it being an issue with our A330 fleet and there have been no directives from Airbus covering this component,' he said.[19]

That incident was followed a few days later by another A330 hitting turbulence over Borneo on its way to Perth, sending 13 passengers, including three children, to hospital. Qantas corporate affairs manager David Epstein was immediately on to Fairfax Radio to calm nerves and assure travellers it was simply turbulence and not a computer glitch. 'About four hours out of Hong Kong while it was flying over Borneo, it hit some very severe turbulence which the captain unfortunately didn't get a lot of notice about and, as a result, six passengers and one crew member sustained minor injuries,' he said, giving the initial injury figures, which were later upgraded.[20] Veteran Captain Brett Flack said there had been no time to warn passengers, many of whom were sleeping, to buckle up. One of the 206 passengers on board, who only gave his name as John, said there had been a loud bang and dramatic drop in altitude. 'I was sitting at the exit door and I had this lady, [who] was waiting at the restroom and she flew up and hit the ceiling and came crashing down to the floor. It was just a matter of a few seconds but it was really sudden and things went flying. She was on the floor and she was just traumatised.'[21] Passenger Chris Rose described the turbulence: 'It was total free-fall. No question, it's the worst I've ever been in. There was lightning everywhere . . . obviously we were right in the middle of a storm or thunder but it was pretty severe.'[22] Investigators pointed out there was no specific issue with Airbus aircraft, but said they would be looking at the characteristics of that incident in relation to earlier ones.

The Qantas corporate affairs team was quick to respond to those incidents, perhaps finally acknowledging that one of Australia's premier brands was still being dragged into the mud and that simply treating the travelling public with disdain would no longer put bums on seats. Meanwhile, the Qantas image continued to take a battering elsewhere. The flagship A380's frequent delays earned it the nicknames A3-Lately and A180, because faults meant that no sooner had the aircraft been wheeled out of the hanger than it had to be turned around and put back in again. The actor Russell Crowe apparently complained about the peace and quiet of first class being shattered by people banging up and down the stairs. A piece in the *Sydney Morning Herald* by columnist Miranda Devine articulated the fears of many passengers that the new generation of planes allowed the computers to override the pilots rather than the other way round. Couple that with the swine-flu pandemic, which was stopping people from travelling anyway, and Alan Joyce's annus horribilis was not looking likely to improve.

The annus horribilis continued in August 2009, when the company posted its smallest profit since privatisation in 1995. Unveiling his first full year of results since taking the top job, Joyce said: 'This is the toughest period that aviation has seen; certainly the toughest years in my 20 or so years in aviation.'[23] But in an industry that was pushing a loss of $US9 billion globally, any kind of profit was considered a good result. Qantas had made an annual net profit of $123 million, down from $1.4 billion the year before, which included the second-ever second-half-year loss since listing as a public company. Bright lights included Jetstar and the Frequent Flyer Program, which Geoff Dixon had wanted to get rid of.

To cope with the ongoing crisis, Joyce announced 1.5

billion dollars' worth of cost-cutting, called Q Future. At least $100 million of the savings would come from information technology changes. And the rest? A Qantas insider worried: 'You can only cut costs on maintenance and engineering for so long before planes start dropping into the sea. It's a very fine line.'[24]

But Joyce was hopeful the market was stabilising and quoted the Qantas revenue forecaster who had seen a financial swallow in the market. 'Whether it makes the spring or the summer is probably too early to say,' he said.[25]

The Australian Licensed Aircraft Engineers Association was also putting pressure on the airline. Federal Secretary Steve Purvinas told the *Sun-Herald* about a string of maintenance problems. In one case a Qantas Boeing 747 was allowed to fly for at least a month before Australian engineers discovered that all four of its engines had been mounted incorrectly during servicing in Hong Kong. In another, a Boeing 767 that landed in Cairns after flying through severe turbulence was allowed to fly again after 10 mandatory checks were deferred to the plane's next scheduled service. Mr Purvinas was scathing about Qantas. But the new management came out fighting. Qantas operations chief Lyell Strambi offered full and detailed explanations of each of the union's points. The incorrect engine mounting was down to a couple of missing washers and the Cairns checks were in line with the level of turbulence the plane had endured. Then he blasted the union: 'This is another example of the ALAEA's leadership distorting the facts as part of an ill-defined industrial agenda.' Not content with that, he made the attack personal: 'Steve Purvinas knows the truth behind each of the issues he is raising. He knows we have responded to each of them in detail and he knows that we meet all of our CASA obligations, which we take extremely seriously.'[26]

Mr Purvinas had also excoriated the airline's close relationship with aircraft watchdog CASA. But while that may have been true in the past, the watchdog was keen to show it was on top of Qantas now. CASA Deputy Chief Executive Officer Operations Mick Quinn had just been to the Senate to tell the Estimates Committee about the recent audit of the flying kangaroo. Things had been bad, he said. The airline's technical 15 – the ability to dispatch any aircraft in the fleet reliably within 15 minutes – had been below their own targets and struggling to reach the world average. That, together with a raft of other technical issues CASA identified, had been dramatically improved.

He also said CASA had conducted a tail audit of three aircraft, a 747, 767 and 737. This meant going back over all the documentation and checking that every airworthiness directive issued for each aircraft had been correctly applied over its life. In the case of the 767 and 737, the watchdog had to issue 13 requests for corrective action. The 747 had not been finished at that time, but Qantas later confirmed there was just one area that was still under discussion with CASA.

So clearly things had not been great in the past either. But Mr Quinn was upbeat. He had met with senior Qantas executives to discuss the internal organisation of the airline, particularly in relation to how CASA could regulate its internal workings. Mr Quinn had clearly been concerned the global financial downturn and enforced redundancies would affect the airline's commitment to put an improved internal structure in place. He was pretty happy to report:

> The new chief executive, Mr Joyce, has put in place a model which largely resembles what is a legacy airline model, significantly less complex than the previous model which was a segmented business model. That organisation aligns much better from a regulatory point of view. There is a lot of transparency, a lot of clarity, for us to identify how the organisation works in terms of day-to-day compliance with the regulations, and, also, it streamlines the processes in which their business runs on a day-to-day basis, particularly in the areas of maintenance, continuing airworthiness moni-toring, flight operations and flight training.[27]

Of course, the other way of reading that is to say the frag-mented business model Geoff Dixon had employed had been opaque, hard to regulate and had prevented the business from flowing smoothly, leading to problems with mainte-nance and flight operations. Qantas may be in trouble, with demand for air travel falling globally but, at least according to CASA's Mick Quinn, it was in better shape than it had been 12 months ago.

It could be said that if Qantas were an aeroplane rather than an airline, today it would be screaming towards earth in a steep dive with smoke pouring from at least two of the engines. The passengers, who look awfully like shareholders, with their strained white faces, would be hanging on for dear life and praying for a happy outcome. The crew, Qantas staff one and all, would be buckling up their seatbelts for a bumpy ride and providing the professional expertise for which they have become known. The plane's owners, fat cats in suits and looking rather like Qantas board members, would have taken the only golden parachutes and bailed out, already calculating the insurance payout on the plane and its occupants when it finally crashed. (Naturally, they would not even think that it was their profit-seeking cost-cutting that caused the engines to fail in the first place.)

And that leaves the pilot battling at the controls, the only one who can pull off the miracle and help the plane survive its terrifying dive. Straining at the joystick, face set, he looks a lot like Alan Joyce.

ABBREVIATIONS

ACCC   Australian Competition and Consumer Commission
ADIRU   air data inertial reference unit
AGM   annual general meeting
ALAEA   Australian Licensed Aircraft Engineers' Association
APA   Airline Partners Australia
APU   auxiliary power unit
ASIC   Australian Securities and Investment Commission
ASIR   Air Safety Incident Report
ATSB   Air Transport Safety Bureau
BA   British Airways
BCPA   British Commonwealth Pacific Airlines
BOAC   British Overseas Airways Corporation
CASA   Civil Aviation Safety Authority
CVR   cockpit voice recorder

FDR	flight data recorder
IATA	International Air Transport Association
PAN	emergency priority broadcast
QAR	quick access recorder
QEA	Qantas Empire Airways
RAAF	Royal Australian Air Force
RAF	Royal Air Force
TAA	Trans-Australia Airlines
TEAL	Tasman Empire Airways
TOA	Trans Oceanic Airways
TWU	Transport Workers' Union

NOTES

QF1
Cut-price touchdown

1   Information about the events described in this chapter in relation to QF1's landing in Bangkok, and the dialogue between air crew personnel, comes from the Australian Transport Safety Bureau Report, number 199904538, 'Boeing 747-438, VH-OJH Bangkok, Thailand', published on 23 September 1999.

2   Darren Goodsir and Joseph Kerr with Stathi Paxinos, 'Welcome to Bangkok', *Age*, 26 April 2001.

3   Robert Wainwright and Joseph Kerr, 'Qantas Denies Crash Error', *Sydney Morning Herald*, 25 September 1999.

4 Goodsir and Kerr with Paxinos, 'Welcome to Bangkok', *Sydney Morning Herald*.

5 Ibid.

6 Bruce Cheeseman and Ben Sandilands, 'An Accident Waiting to Happen', *Australian Financial Review*, 3 November 1999.

7 Goodsir and Kerr with Paxinos, 'Welcome to Bangkok', *Sydney Morning Herald*.

8 Sophie Tedmanson, 'Woman Fears Death Every Time She Flies', *Australian*, 26 April 2001.

9 ATSB report, 'Boeing 747-438, VH-OJH Bangkok, Thailand', p. 68.

10 Ibid.

11 Ibid.

12 ATSB report, p. 67.

13 Goodsir and Kerr with Paxinos, 'Welcome to Bangkok', *Sydney Morning Herald*.

14 Ibid.

15 ATSB report, p. 59.

16 ibid.

17 Tedmanson, 'Woman Fears Death Every Time She Flies', *Australian*.

18 Wainwright and Kerr, 'Qantas Denies Crash Error', *Sydney Morning Herald*.

19 Cheeseman and Sandilands, 'An Accident Waiting to Happen', *Australian Financial Review*.

20 ATSB report, executive summary, p. vi.

21 ATSB report, p. 37.

22 Ibid.

23 ATSB report, p. 154.

24 Ibid.

25 ATSB report, executive summary, p. viii.

26 Ibid.

27 ATSB report, p. 97.

28 Tedmanson, 'Woman Fears Death Every Time She Flies', *Australian*.

QF2
Early emergency

1 Sir Hudson Fysh, *Qantas Rising*, Angus & Robertson, Sydney, 1965, p. 101.

2 Ibid., p. 102.

3 Macarthur Job, *Air Crash, volume 1, 1921–39*, Aerospace Publications, ACT, 1991, p. 20.

4 John Gunn, *The Defeat of Distance, Qantas 1919–1939*, University of Queensland Press, Brisbane, 1985, p. 16. Gunn had access to Fergus McMaster's papers, including a narrative of the founding years of Qantas. He refers to these collectively as the McMaster Papers. Reference to those papers is drawn from Gunn's extensive research.

5 Gunn, *The Defeat of Distance*, from McMaster's papers, p. 21.

6 Ibid., p. 30.

7 Ibid.

8 Ibid., p. 31.

9 Fysh, *Qantas Rising*, p. 197.

10 Ibid.

11 *Sydney Morning Herald*, 21 April 1934.

QF3
Cover-up

1 Sir Hudson Fysh, *Qantas at War*, Angus & Robertson, Sydney, 1968, p. 3.
2 Ibid., p. 4.
3 Ibid., p. 7.
4 Job, *Air Crash*, p. 73.
5 Ibid., p. 74.
6 Ibid., p. 78.
7 Ibid., p. 90.
8 Ibid., p. 78.
9 Ibid., p. 79.
10 Fysh, *Qantas at War*, p. 39.
11 Job, *Air Crash*, p. 85.
12 Ibid., pp. 86–7.
13 Ibid.
14 Ibid.
15 Ibid.
16 Ibid.
17 Ibid.
18 Ibid.
19 Ibid.

QF4
Qantas at war

1 John Gunn, *Challenging Horizons*, University of Queensland Press, Brisbane, 1987, p. 51.
2 Fysh, *Qantas at War*, p. 135.
3 Ibid., pp. 139–40.

4 Ibid., p. 136.

5 Ibid., p. 71.

6 Ibid., p. 69.

7 Ibid., p. 156.

8 Ibid., p. 130.

9 Ibid.

10 Gunn, *Challenging Horizons*, p. 56.

11 Brain's diary is quoted in Neil Cadigan, *A Man among Mavericks*, ABC Books, Sydney, 2008, p. 148.

12 Ibid.

13 Fysh, *Qantas at War*, p. 155.

14 Ibid., p. 67.

15 Gunn, *Challenging Horizons*, p. 104.

16 John Stackhouse, *The Dawn of Aviation*, Focus Publishing, Sydney, 1995, p. 93.

17 Fysh, *Qantas at War*, p. 185.

18 Ibid., p. 186

19 Ibid., p.181.

QF5
The big lie

1 Macarthur Job, 'Misadventure at Mauritius', *Flight Safety Australia*, January–February 2000, p. 49.

2 Ibid.

3 Ibid.

4 Ibid.

5 Ibid.

6 Fysh, *Qantas at War*, p. 203.

7 Ibid.

8 Hudson Fysh, *Wings to the World*, Angus & Robertson, Sydney, 1970, p. 17.

9 Ibid., p. 18.

10 Fysh, *Qantas at War*, p. 209.

11 Fysh, *Wings to the World*, p. 28.

12 Ibid., p. 30.

13 Stackhouse, *The Dawn of Aviation*.

14 Fysh, *Wings to the World*, p. 71.

15 Ibid., p. 71.

16 Gunn, *Challenging Horizons*, p. 259.

17 Fysh, *Wings to the World*, p. 72.

18 Laura Cochrane, 'Qantas Won't Send Airplanes to Malaysia for Maintenance Checks', Bloomberg, 9 August 2008.

19 Letter from Macarthur Job to Laura Cochrane, 9 August 2008, in reference to article quoted on Bloomberg.

20 Ibid.

21 Interview with author, 4 September 2009.

QF6
Extortion

1 Basil Sweeney and Gavin Souter, 'The Real Mr Brown', *Sydney Morning Herald*, 31 January 1972.

2 Ibid.

3 *Sydney Morning Herald*, 28 January 1972.

4 Ibid.

5 Ibid.

6 Basil Sweeney and Gavin Souter, 'Prelude to Extortion', *Sydney Morning Herald*, 29 January 1972.

7 Basil Sweeney, 'Mr Brown Link to Murder Mystery', *Sun-Herald*, 18 September 1994.

8 Hudson Fysh, *Wings to the World*, p. 113.

9 Stackhouse, *The Dawn of Aviation*, p. 123.

10 Ibid., p. 63.

11 Ibid.

12 Fysh, *Wings to the World*, p. 169.

13 Ibid.

14 Ibid.

15 Ibid., p. 170.

16 John Gunn, *Contested Skies, Trans-Australian Airlines, Australian Airlines, 1946–1992*, University of Queensland Press, 1999, p. 443.

17 Ibid., p. 445.

18 Ibid.

19 Ibid., p. 448.

QF7
Project Suzie

1 Gunn, *Contested Skies*, p. 458.

2 As reported by Gunn in *Contested Skies*, p. 489.

3 *Sydney Morning Herald*, 21 March 1992.

4 Gunn, *Contested Skies*, p. 493.

5 Michelle Grattan, *Age*, 3 June 1992.

6 As reported by Gunn in *Contested Skies*, p. 496.

7 Ian Verrender, 'Why Qantas Must Not Fly Away', *Sydney Morning Herald*, 21 November 1992.

8 Eric Ellis, 'Rocky Ride for the World's Favourite Airline', *Sydney Morning Herald*, 23 January 1993.

9   Keith Gosman, 'Qantas's Future Gloomy', *Sun-Herald*, 7 February 1993.
10 Ian Thomas, 'Anatomy of a Merger', *Australian Financial Review*, 27 August 1993.
11 Conversation with author.
12 Jennifer Hewett, 'He's Strong But Can He Make a Boomer of the Flying Kangaroo?' *Australian Financial Review*, 18 March 1994.
13 Ian Thomas, 'Old Guard from Australian takes Qantas under its Wing', *Australian Financial Review*, 29 December 1993.
14 Sally Jackson, 'Foreign Stake "Manageable"', *Australian*, 25 August 1995.
15 Ibid.
16 Kate Askew and Scott Rochfort, 'If You Knew Suzie...' *Sydney Morning Herald*, 26 May 2007.
17 Ibid.
18 Ibid.
19 Ibid.

QF8
Angel and demon

1   *The 7.30 Report*, ABC Television, 24 April 2000.
2   Ibid.
3   Ibid.
4   Ibid.
5   Ibid.
6   Ibid.
7   Vesna Poljak, 'Qantas Weathers the Storm', *Australian Financial Review*, 22 August 2008.

8   Katrina Nicholas, 'Cleared for Take-off', *Australian Financial Review Magazine*, 30 March 2007.

9   Ibid.

10 Jamie Walker, 'Captain Kangaroo', *Australian Financial Review Magazine*, 6 July 2002.

11 Claire Harvey, 'Taking Flight for a Higher Calling,' *Sunday Telegraph*, 16 November 2008.

12 Ibid.

13 Ibid.

14 Ibid.

15 Ibid.

16 Tom Ballantyne, 'Phoenix Rising', *Sydney Morning Herald*, 18 June 1994.

17 Walker, 'Captain Kangaroo', *Australian Financial Review Magazine*.

18 Ibid.

19 Alan Deans and Ian Thomas, 'Frequent Flyer', *Australian Financial Review*, 9 August 1986.

20 Walker, 'Captain Kangaroo', *Australian Financial Review Magazine*.

21 Matthew Benns, 'The Brand Man', *Sun-Herald*, 31 May 2009.

22 Ibid.

23 Peter Mitchell, 'Travolta to Continue Links to Qantas', *Age*, 16 April 2004.

24 Ibid.

25 Ibid.

26 Nicholas, 'Cleared for Take-off', *Australian Financial Review Magazine*.

27 Ibid.

28 Ibid.

29 Walker, 'Captain Kangaroo', *Australian*.

30 Ibid.

31 Ibid.

QF9
Toxic air

1   Interview with author.

2   Matthew Benns, 'Air Sickness', *Sun-Herald*, 21 October 2007.

3   Interview with author, 4 September 2009.

4   Benns, 'Air Sickness', *Sun-Herald*.

5   CASA regulations, CAAP, 51-1(0).

6   Benns, 'Air Sickness', *Sun-Herald*.

7   Interview with author, 4 September 2009.

8   Ibid.

9   Ibid.

10 Benns, 'Air Sickness', *Sun-Herald*.

11 Ibid.

12 *The Age*, 13 October 2000.

13 Benns, 'Air Sickness', *Sun-Herald*.

14 Matthew Benns, 'Plane Fumes Inquiry Call', *Sun-Herald*, 28 October 2007.

15 Ibid.

16 Matthew Benns, 'The Plane Truth about Toxic Fumes', *Sun-Herald*, 6 January 2008.

17 Ibid.

QF10
Jetstar

1 'Passengers Tell of Mid-air Scare', *Herald Sun*, 19 July 2004.
2 Ibid.
3 Jane Boyle, 'Virgin Cites Predatory Qantas, *Australian Financial Review*, 24 January 2001.
4 Ibid.
5 *The 7.30 Report*, ABC Television, 1 May 2001.
6 *AM*, ABC Radio National, 18 November 2003.
7 Ibid.
8 Glenda Korporaal, 'The Dubliner', *Australian*, 17 October 2008.
9 Ibid.
10 Ibid.
11 Ibid.
12 Ibid.
13 Ibid.
14 Richard Webb, 'O'Leary's Cost-cutting Ways Helped Jetstar off the Ground', *Sunday Age*, 10 July 2005.
15 Ibid.
16 Ibid.
17 Ibid.
18 Scott Rochfort, 'Qantas Soars to Great Hypes', *Sydney Morning Herald*, 11 May 2004.
19 Ibid.
20 Scott Rochfort, 'Jetstar Mishap Blamed on Poor Training', *Age*, 23 June 2004.
21 Ibid.
22 Steve Creedy, 'Jetstar Accused on Safety of Staff', *Australian*, 19 July 2004.

23 Ibid.

24 Jamie Freed, 'Jetstar Yet to Show True Colours', *Sydney Morning Herald*, 25 May 2004.

25 Scott Rochfort, 'Jetstar Plan for New Planes Runs into a Spot of Trouble', *Sydney Morning Herald*, 28 June 2004.

26 Ibid.

27 'Jetstar Gets OK for Pilot Safety Inspections', *Age*, 4 May 2004.

28 Conversation with author.

29 Scott Rochfort, 'Jetstar to Put Pilots on AWAs', *Sydney Morning Herald*, 14 May 2007.

30 Ibid.

31 Ibid.

32 Damon Kitney and Mark Skulley, 'Jetstar Set for Tiger with Tough Pay Deal', *Australian Financial Review*, 28 December 2007.

33 Interview with author, 4 September 2009.

QF11
Freight cartel

1 Geoffrey and Flossie Arend, 'Facing Air Cargo Price Fix Jail Time; Qantas Freight's Bruce McCaffrey Is Undefeated', *Air Cargo News*, 12 January 2009.

2 Ibid.

3 Ibid.

4 Matt O'Sullivan, 'Qantas Counts Cost of Freight Cartel', *Sydney Morning Herald*, 15 December 2008.

5 Ibid.

6 Ibid.

7   Arend, 'Facing Air Cargo Price Fix Jail Time', *Air Cargo News*.

8   Geoffrey Arend, 'Price Fix Probe Continues', *Air Cargo News*, 26 January 2009.

9   Reported in Matthew Drummond, 'Staff Vulnerable in Qantas Cartel Case', *Australian Financial Review*, 17 January 2008.

10 'Former Qantas Boss Gets Jail Term', *Illawarra Mercury*, 30 July 2008.

11 Peter Mitchell, 'Qantas Executive Faces Prospect of Eight Months' Jail in US', *Age*, 29 July 2008.

12 'Sick Qantas Exec Jailed for Price Scam', *Age*, 29 July 2008.

13 Stefanie Balogh, 'US Family Furious with Qantas; Our Brother a Scapegoat', *Herald Sun*, 25 July 2008.

14 'Executives Unscathed', *Adelaide Advertiser*, 30 July 2008.

15 Arend, 'Facing Air Cargo Price Fix Jail Time', *Air Cargo News*.

16 O'Sullivan, 'Qantas Counts Cost of Freight Cartel', *Sydney Morning Herald*.

17 Matt O'Sullivan, 'Qantas Facing Cartel Action in NZ', *Sydney Morning Herald*, 16 December 2008.

18 'Steve Creedy, 'Fines Bolster Class Action against Qantas', *Australian*, 6 August 2007.

19 Ibid.

20 Australian Competition and Consumer Commission, media release, 28 October 2008.

21 Frank Zumbo, 'We Pay Millions for Corporate Fix,' *Herald Sun*, 16 September 2008.

QF12
Mental

1 *Four Corners*, ABC Television, 28 May 2007.

2 Ibid.

3 Ibid.

4 Kate Askew and Scott Rochfort, 'If You Knew Suzie', *Sydney Morning Herald*, 26 May 2007.

5 Harvey, 'Taking Flight for a Higher Calling', *Sunday Telegraph*.

6 Ibid.

7 Ibid.

8 Stephen Mayne, 'Geoff Dixon Replaced by Younger Qantas Model, *Crikey*, 28 July 2008.

9 Jesse Hogan, 'Qantas Bidders Clear Another Hurdle', *Age*, 13 February 2007.

10 David Crowe and Laura Tingle, 'PM Backs $11bn Qantas Sale', *Australian Financial Review*, 26 February 2007.

11 Scott Rochfort, 'Qantas Shareholders, It's Your Call', *Sydney Morning Herald*, 7 March 2007.

12 Steve Creedy, 'Qantas Bid Has ACCC Approval', *Australian*, 2 March 2007.

13 Mark Skulley, 'Qantas Super Fears Fuel Unease', *Australian Financial Review*, 21 March 2007.

14 James Hall with David Crowe, '$11bn Qantas Bid in Crisis', *Australian Financial Review*, 24 March 2007.

15 Glenda Korporaal, 'Rejection Would Be Devastating: Jackson', *Australian*, 21 March 2007.

16 Skulley, 'Qantas Super Fears Fuel Unease', *Australian Financial Review*.

17 Helen Dalley, 'On Board the Qantas Bid', *Australian*, 7 July 2007.

18 Ibid.

19 Scott Rochfort and Jacqueline Maley, 'MPs Angry Over APA Debt Plan for Qantas, *Age*, 14 April 2007.

20 Ibid.

21 Ibid.

22 Kate Askew, 'How MacBank Tanked on the Numbers', *Sydney Morning Herald*, 7 May 2007.

23 Ibid.

24 Alan Kohler, 'Risk-averse APA Failed To Recognise the Risk in an Early Concession on Qantas', *Age*, 12 May 2007.

25 Askew, 'How MacBank Tanked on the Numbers', *Sydney Morning Herald*.

26 Scott Rochfort and Lisa Murray, 'The Qantas Flying Circus', *Sydney Morning Herald*, 8 May 2007.

27 Ibid.

28 Ibid.

29 Ibid.

30 'Qantas Bid Group Declares Offer Lapsed', Reuters, 7 May 2007.

31 Damon Kitney, 'Jackson Goes Out with a Flight', *Australian Financial Review*, 10 November 2007.

32 Harvey, 'Taking Flight for a Higher Calling', *Sunday Telegraph*.

33 Ibid.

QF13
Airline for scandal

1 'Aussie Air Hostess Tells "My Wild Fling with Ralph Fiennes"', *Woman's Day*, 26 February 2007.

2 Marnie O'Neill, 'Hostess Denies Sex in Toilet with Actor', *Sunday Telegraph*, 11 February 2007.

3 Ibid.

4 Marnie O'Neill, '"I Confess": Ralph Fiennes' Mile-high Hostie was an Escort', *Sunday Telegraph*, 18 March 2007.

5 Jacob Saulwick, 'New Qantas Recruit Tests PM's Code for Lobbyists', *Sydney Morning Herald*, 12 November 2008.

6 Steve Lewis, 'Libs Lash Jobs to PM Adviser', *Illawarra Mercury*, 12 November 2008.

7 *Australian*, March 30 2009.

8 Angela Kamper, 'I Had Very Bad Jet Lag', *Daily Telegraph*, 5 April 2007.

9 *National Nine News*, 27 July 2007.

10 Phil Bartsch, 'Qantas Sex Fiend Jailed for Six Years', *Daily Telegraph*, 2 August 1996.

11 Ibid.

12 Ibid.

13 Paul Kent and Kara Lawrence, 'The Clash of Blood Enemies: a City Under Siege', *Daily Telegraph*, 25 March 2009.

14 Ibid.

15 Dylan Welch, Rick Feneley, Bellinda Kontominas and Arjun Ramachandran, 'Come on, Boys, Let's Go, Let's Go: Battle Cry that Led to a Brutal Death', *Sydney Morning Herald*, 29 March 2009.

16 Matthew Moore, 'Terrified Onlookers Ducked for Cover', *Sydney Morning Herald*, 23 March 2009.

17 Ibid.

18 Ibid.

19 Ibid.

20 Ibid.
21 Paul Bibby and Yuko Narushima, 'Vital Video Evidence May Have Been Lost', *Sydney Morning Herald*, 23 March 2009.
22 Paul Bibby, 'Silent Witness That Saw Nothing', *Sydney Morning Herald*, 28 March 2009.
23 David Penberthy, 'Security is Now a Joke', *Daily Telegraph*, 25 March 2009.

QF14
Explosion

1 Clay Lucas, Mex Cooper and Bridie Smith, 'It Was Absolutely Terrifying', *Age*, 26 July 2008.
2 'Lucky Escape as the Plane Shook, I Thought I was a Goner', *Sunday Mail*, 27 July 2008.
3 Michael Bachelard and Mark Russell, 'Relief as QF30 Passengers Fly in to Melbourne', *The Sunday Age*, 27 July 2008.
4 Ibid.
5 Ibid.
6 Jonathan Dart, Mex Cooper and Matthew Burgess, 'There's a Large Hole in the Plane, Says Pilot', *Sydney Morning Herald*, 26 July 2008.
7 'Lucky Escape as the Plane Shook', *Sunday Mail*.
8 Aviation Occurrence Investigation, ATSB Transport Safety report, AO-2008-053 Interim Factual, 'Depressurisation 475 km north-west of Manila, Philippines', 25 July 2008, Boeing Company 747-438, VH-OJK'.
9 Jonathan Dart, Matt O'Sullivan and Dan Oakes, 'US

Warning on Oxygen Tank Risk', *Sydney Morning Herald*, 28 July 2008.

10 'Lucky Escape as the Plane Shook', *Sunday Mail*.

11 Aviation Occurrence Investigation, ATSB Transport Safety report, AO-2008-053 Preliminary, 'Depressurisation 475 km north-west of Manila, Philippines, 25 July 2008, Boeing Company 747-438, VH-OJK'.

12 Ibid.

13 ATSB Transport Safety report, AO-2008-053 Interim Factual.

14 Steve Creedy, 'Qantas Jet Blast "Turned Door Handle"', *Australian*, 30 July 2008.

15 Steve Drill and Andrew Chesterton, 'I'm So Proud of My Hero Husband', *Sunday Telegraph*, 27 July 2008.

16 ATSB Transport Safety report, AO-2008-053 Interim Factual.

17 Dart, Cooper and Burgess, 'There's a Large Hole in the Plane, Says Pilot', *Sydney Morning Herald*.

18 Ibid.

19 'Lucky Escape as the Plane Shook', *Sunday Mail*.

20 Matthew Benns and Louise Hall, 'Pilot Relies on Skill to Land Crippled Jumbo', *Sun-Herald*, 27 July 2008.

21 Ian McPhedran and Kate Sikora, 'Rust Bucket: Stricken Qantas Jet's History of Corrosion', *Daily Telegraph*, 26 July 2008.

22 Clay Lucas, Mex Cooper and Bridie Smith with Jonathan Dart, 'It Was Absolutely Terrifying', *Age*, 26 July 2008.

23 Dart, O'Sullivan and Oakes, 'US Warning on Oxygen Tank Risk', *Sydney Morning Herald*.

24 ATSB Transport Safety report, AO-2008-053 Preliminary.

25 Ibid.

26 Geoff Strong, 'Lack of Counselling Brings Airline a Rap', *Age*, 29 July 2008.

27 Ibid.

28 'Pilot: Outsourcing Work is to Blame', *Herald Sun*, 26 July 2008.

29 Qantas, 'Quality System Compliance Internal Audit Report', 10 August 2006.

30 Ibid.

31 Evelyn Yamine, 'Six 737s Sidelined over "Paperwork" checks', *Daily Telegraph*, 13 August 2008.

32 Mathew Murphy and Dewi Cooke, 'Another Mishap as Qantas Accused of Safety Negligence', *Age*, 14 August 2008.

33 Ibid.

34 Matthew Benns, 'Aviation Watchdog "Too close" to Qantas', *Sun-Herald*, 10 August 2008.

35 Mathew Murphy, 'Aviation Reporter Qantas Rebuked over Maintenance Problems', *Age*, 2 September 2008.

36 Vesna Poljak, 'Qantas Told to Improve Maintenance', *Australian Financial Review*, 2 September 2008.

37 Ibid.

QF15
Turbulent times

1   AAP, 'On-Board Horror as Flight Flails, *Newcastle Herald*, 9 October 2008.

2   AAP, 'Passengers Tell of Horror,' *Age*, 9 October 2008.

3   Ibid.

4   Michelle Cazzulino and Alison Rehn, 'Inside Hell Flight QF72', *Daily Telegraph*, 9 October 2008.

5   Ibid.

6   ATSB Transport Safety report, Aviation Occurrence Investigation AO-2008-070 Interim Factual, 'In-flight Upset 154 km West of Learmonth, WA', October 2008 VH-QPA Airbus A330-303.

7   Arjun Ramachandran, 'Ex-fighter Pilot Saved QF72', *Sydney Morning Herald*, 16 October 2008.

8   Ibid.

9   Ibid.

10 ATSB Transport Safety report, Aviation Occurrence Investigation AO-2008-070 Interim Factual.

11 Andrea Hayward and Simon Jenkins, 'A Free Trip to London: Qantas Pays for Nosedive', *Daily Telegraph*, 10 June 2008.

12 Paul Bibby, 'Qantas Tried to Trick Me: Passenger', *Sydney Morning Herald*, 8 November 2008.

13 Ibid.

14 Kelly Ryan, 'Tourists Thought They'd Die', *Herald Sun*, 7 November 2008.

15 Reko Rennie, 'Qantas Couple's "Terrifying ordeal"', *Sydney Morning Herald*, 6 November 2008.

16 Katrina Nicholas, 'Qantas: a Reputation to Lose', *Australian Financial Review*, 2 August 2008.

17 Ibid.

18 Ibid.

19 Katrina Nicholas, 'A Long-haul Pilot Finally Coming in to Land', *Australian Financial Review*, 29 July 2008.

20 Matt O'Sullivan, 'Shareholders Vent Anger at Qantas AGM', *Sydney Morning Herald*, 29 November 2008.

21 Damon Kitney, Katrina Nicholas and Vesna Poljak with Andrew Cornell, 'Joyce Promotion to Top Job Breaks up Qantas Club', *Australian Financial Review*, 18 August 2008.

22 Damon Kitney, 'Joyce Puts Qantas on New Flight Path', *Australian Financial Review*, 28 November 2008.

QF16
Annus horribilis

1 Charles Miranda, 'A Welcome Toast for the Flying Roo', *Daily Telegraph*, 22 September 2008.

2 Steve Creedy, 'Aviation Writer, Fuel Bugs Infect Qantas A380s', *Australian*, 6 March 2009.

3 Vesna Poljak and Michael Smith, 'Qantas Scraps $8bn British Airways Deal', *Australian Financial Review*, 19 September 2008.

4 Matt O'Sullivan, 'We'll be a Disaster for Qantas: Delta', *Sydney Morning Herald*, 23 April 2009.

5 Andrew Carswell, 'Qantas Slashes Staff and Services', *Daily Telegraph*, 15 April 2009.

6 Ibid.

7 Matt O'Sullivan, 'Qantas Flies into Growing Turbulence', *Sydney Morning Herald*, 15 April 2009.

8 Ben Schneiders with Mathew Murphy, 'Save Qantas from Unfair Practices, Unions Urge', *Sydney Morning Herald*, 20 April 2009.

9 Conversation with author.

10 Fysh, *Wings to the World*, p. 197.

11 Interview with author.

12 Fysh, *Wings to the World*, p. 197.

13 Andrew Carswell, 'Navigating Downturn a Tricky Manoeuvre', *Daily Telegraph*, 18 April 2009.

14 Ibid.

15 Steve Creedy, 'Qantas to Jettison its Float Plans', *Australian*, 12 June 2009.

16 Ibid.

17 Ibid.

18 Gemma Jones, 'MP Slams Jetstar on Delays', *Daily Telegraph*, 26 June 2009.

19 Qantas media release, Sydney, 11 June 2009.

20 David Prestipino, 'Qantas Passenger Hits Roof in Mid-air Turbulence Drama', *Age*, 22 June 2009.

21 Ibid.

22 Joseph Sapienza, 'Qantas Jet Went into "Total Free-fall" ', *Sydney Morning Herald*, 22 June 2009.

23 Michael Smith, 'Qantas to Jettison $1.5bn in Costs', *Australian Financial Review*, 20 August 2009.

24 Conversation with author.

25 Michael Evans, 'Easy Line to Swallow', *Sydney Morning Herald*, 20 August 2009.

26 Qantas's response to questions from author, 4 July 2009.

27 Senate Estimates Committee, *Hansard*, 28 May 2009, Rural Regional Affairs and Transport, p. 68.

BIBLIOGRAPHY

E. A. Crome, *Qantas Aeriana*, Francis J. Field Ltd, Sutton Coldfield, England, 1955.

Sir Hudson Fysh, *Qantas at War*, Angus & Robertson, Sydney, 1968.

Sir Hudson Fysh, *Qantas Rising*, Angus & Robertston, Sydney, 1965.

Sir Hudson Fysh, *Wings to the World*, Angus & Robertson, Sydney, 1970.

John Gunn, *Challenging Horizons*, University of Queensland Press, Brisbane, 1987.

John Gunn, *Contested Skies, Trans-Australian Airlines, Australian Airlines, 1946–1992*, University of Queensland Press, Brisbane, 1999.

John Gunn, *The Defeat of Distance*, University of Queensland Press, Brisbane, 1985.

John Gunn, *High Corridors*, University of Queensland Press, Brisbane, 1988.

Timothy Hall, *Flying High*, Methuen of Australia, Brisbane, 1979.

Macarthur Job, *Air Crash*, Aerospace Publications, ACT, 1991.

Anthony Sampson, *Empires of the Sky*, Hodder & Stoughton, London, 1984.

Archie J. Smith, *East–West Eagles*, Robert Brown and Associates, Cairns, 1989.

John Stackhouse, *From the Dawn of Aviation*, Focus Publishing, Sydney, 1995.

Chronicle of Australia, Penguin Books, Melbourne, 1993.

ACKNOWLEDGEMENTS

THIS BOOK COULD not have been written without the help, support and wisdom of a special group of people. First and foremost must come publisher Alison Urquhart, a woman of vision who also understands the way writers work and the way publishing meetings need to be conducted. Alison is part of a wonderful team at Random House, headed up by Nikki Christer. Special thanks have to go to the sales and marketing experts at Random, who threw their weight behind this book. Any mistakes are totally my responsibility; the vast majority were picked up by the eagle eyes of two thorough and tireless editors, Catherine Hill and Jo Jarrah.

Research, particularly for the early years, was brilliantly and enthusiastically assisted by Manuel Mitternacht.

Air-crash investigator Macarthur Job was very generous in sharing his extensive knowledge and allowing me permission to quote from his excellent book, *Air Crash*. Research for stories that I have written on Qantas for the *Sun-Herald* has always been greatly assisted by the diligent, thorough and professional library staff at Fairfax. Helen Bayliss has been particularly supportive of my more outlandish requests. My immediate bosses at the *Sun-Herald*, editor Simon Dulhunty, deputy editor Liz Hannan and chief of staff Chad Watson have also been incredibly supportive. Lawyer Richard Coleman gave up his own time to read the manuscript and offer advice and Richard Potter also brought his extensive legal knowledge to bear on the book.

Australia has many excellent journalists in all mediums, whose work and unsparing scrutiny of Qantas over the years, and particularly recently, has greatly helped in assembling the relevant facts for this book. They have my continued admiration. Of course, my personal thanks also need to go to my colleagues, family and friends, who tolerated without complaint the long absences and tired surliness that goes with a project of this kind. Most importantly, though, my thanks and respect go to the many people within Qantas who spoke to me about the concerns they have for the airline they all care so deeply about. For obvious reasons, they cannot be named here. I hope this book does justice to the faith they placed in me.

INDEX

293